THE LAST WILD ISLAND
SAVING TETEPARE

JOHN READ

"This is a journey to one of the last wild specks of land left on Earth by an author every bit as readable as Tim Flannery - a page turner that will leave readers dazzled that such an island still exists."

JAMES WOODFORD
AUTHOR, JOURNALIST, EDITOR WWW.REALDIRT.COM.AU

Published in Australia by
Page Digital Publishing Group,
3 Park Road, Kensington Park SA 5068
pagepublishingaustralia@gmail.com
www.pagepublishing.com.au

Copyright © John Read 2011

All rights reserved. No part of this publication may be reproduced, stored in a retrieval system or transmitted in any for by any means without the prior permission of the copyright owner.

National Library of Australia
Cataloguing-in-Publication data:

Read, John L. The Last Wild Island: Saving Tetepare

ISBN 9780980760033

1. Solomon Islands - logging - environmental - travel

Enquiries regarding this book can be directed to pagepublishingaustralia@gmail.com. Enquiries regarding Dr John Read and his work, or the Tetepare Descendants Association can be directed to www.ecologicalhorizons.com or ecological@active8.net.au.

Text photos by J. Read, K. Moseby, Christophe Rouziou, Steve Trutwin, Matthew Suka and Tim Jarvis.
Maps by J. Fewster – Exploris Mapping
Cover photo by Christophe Rouziou

*For Mary Bea,
who demonstrated that 'little' women can stand up
to 'big' men to make a difference.*

Contents

Glossary		vi
1	HONEYMOON IN PARADISE	1
	Mission #1	12
	Whoaboys and Log Ponds	22
	Marovo Wonderland	34
	Solomon Time	47
2	THE LAST WILD ISLAND	62
	Tetepare tug-of-war	73
	Innocence Lost	78
	Lokuru Connection	90
	TDA is Born	113
	More than a Name	127
	Reality Check	138
	Operation Suicide	151
	Olisogo's Curse	170
3	MARY'S DREAM	184
	The Black-and-White Pig	184
	Development at Last	201
	Meeting Vena	213
	Tetepare's Big Five	221
	New Life	231
	The Roller-Coaster Continues	247
Acknowledgements		259
References		262

GLOSSARY

Pijin was derived from the Cantonese word for business and originally blended elements of Cantonese, Portuguese and English. Pijin is a phonetic language and readers can usually decipher the meaning by sounding the word. This glossary is not exhaustive of Pijin words used in text but should provide enough examples to render all Pijin text readable.

bagarap	(bugger-up) broken
beleran	(bellyrun) diarrhoea
bifo	before
iufala	you (fella)
iumi	you and I
iutufala	you two people
karae	(cry) sound, call
kasim	catch, go
kolosap	close(up)
laek	like
lavalava	sarong
lelebet	little bit
maet	might

manis	months
nau	now
nomoa	(no more) only
olketa	everyone, all
olsem	same
plen	plane
taem	time
tok ples	(talk place) local language
tufala	two people
sanbis	(sand) beach
save	(savvy) know, understand
semsem	same
stap	(stop) here
tingting	think
vaka	white person
waetfala	(white-fella) expatriate
waka	work
wantok	(one talk) relative

1
Honeymoon in Paradise

'You there?' I yelled with added urgency.
Still no answer.

The spider web on my face had freaked me out. Realising the others had not broken its titanium silk confirmed my fears. The scratchy arachnid pinned to my cheek was barely a distraction.

The last time I glimpsed Katherine's white bucket hat through the inky gloom was about five minutes earlier. Too dark to discern tracks, spider webs or even the telltale cut leaves left by the guide's trail slashing, I was lost. Compounding my predicament, the dense mangroves suffocated the breeze and perspiration streamed down my brow, stinging my eyes. I had no idea whether the village was five minutes or five hours away. The only sound audible was the sucking squelch of my feet as I sludged through the stinky mud.

Stopping, I screamed 'Katherine!' and shocked myself with the edge of panic in my voice.

The thud of my racing pulse beat loudly in my ears as I strained to hear a reply.

Nothing.

My right foot, gashed earlier by a broken mussel shell buried in the ooze, was burning with the sting of salty mud. Stumbling through the gnarly mangroves on my outstep, I couldn't keep up the pace and had lost my sense of direction. Katherine would be single-mindedly pursuing our mute local guide and would assume that I was right behind her. Focused on getting out of the mosquito-infested swamp as fast as she could, she would be cursing the spiders and crocs and probably me too. I had to find her. My bride of one week was alone and scared in a dark mangrove swamp with a complete stranger.

I inhaled aggressively and let rip, 'KATHERINE!'

'Hurry up!' snapped the distant reply, obviously annoyed that I was slowing her down.

Running forward with renewed conviction through unseen branches that raked across my chest and arms, I followed her calls. The relief of our impending reunion masked the searing pain in my foot. Katherine was about to get a big sweaty hug, in keeping with our vow made barely a week earlier to demonstrate more affection and compassion. Yet before I had even reached her she ushered the sinewy guide forward and set off again purposefully, walking exactly two paces behind. Her typically glowing strawberry blonde hair was trussed into an untidy plait that lurched aggressively from side to side as she stomped off.

'Remember Lilian's brother!' she panted, still looking directly ahead.

As the only female in the village who volunteered any Pijin, Lilian had struck up a conversation with Katherine the previous day. When asked how many brothers and sisters she had, Lilian nonchalantly replied that she used to have eight but a crocodile ate one. Her brother had been taken from the very river that we were now stumbling alongside.

'We're walking way too fast for crocs,' I muttered lamely, hoping in vain that she would slow down so I could keep up. I was meant to be the protector; the one in control. Instead I was dragging the chain, increasing our risks and discomfort.

'It's not only the crocs' Katherine lamented tersely. 'I'm getting monstered by mossies . . . We'll probably get malaria now . . . What the hell are we doing here?'

Our tropical honeymoon, first tentatively scripted months earlier from our Australian desert home, was rapidly derailing. Attracting only a handful of tourists a year, the alluringly nicknamed 'Happy Isles' promised neither beachside resorts nor fancy cuisine. Instead, coral reefs, rainforests and the world's largest skink were Solomon Islands' key attractions. The real lure for us was a passing guide book reference to a backwater island that was set to become 'the next big battleground between the loggers and advocates of low-impact eco-tourism'. This key battle within the international campaign to save the last of Solomon Islands' lowland rainforests and reefs from unscrupulous international loggers offered us the adventure we craved. From the moment we read that sentence, any images of a cocktail-sipping beach honeymoon were banished. I couldn't imagine another place in the world where a couple of unshackled young ecologists could make such a difference. Katherine too had been lured by the intrigue and excitement. She loved unplanned travel and revelled in fighting for a cause. Any notion of satisfaction with conventional marital bliss back home in Australia was smashed like a clear-felled rainforest.

Our naive desire for a rewarding and bonding honeymoon saving rainforests had somehow led us to this ordeal. Katherine trudged on, doggedly following the guide and ignoring my small talk. Eventually she snapped.

'You're always pushing it too far! Why didn't you ask them to leave earlier when I said so? If you want to spend all night getting eaten alive that's your problem but its not fair dragging me along too. You call this a holiday!'

I started to protest but she spun around seething 'We shouldn't be in bloody Choiseul anyway, we should . . .'

She cut short her diatribe mid-sentence. Through the gloom I saw her emotions switch from anger to horror, then amusement as she stared at me.

'Get that thing off your face,' she implored me smirking. Instinctively I wiped my face with my forearm, like I used to when

Mum complained that I'd left half my dinner behind. The big spider that I had completely forgotten about squirmed valiantly but was still ensconced in its web that shrouded my head like a hairnet. I clawed it out and flung it to the ground, then raked the rest of the web out of my hair.

'And the other side,' she said, barely able to keep a straight face. My right forearm smeared a sizeable dollop of mud from under my eye. I playfully tucked in my shirt and pretended to brush the mud off my shorts. Then I got my hug, no doubt to the bemusement of the guide who looked on perplexed.

•

After deciding to visit the Solomons, we noticed the distinctive archipelago just above the weather reader's head on our evening news. Nearly one thousand islands spilled out into the Pacific Ocean from New Guinea towards Fiji. They were so close to Australia that the Qantas flight to Honiara was shorter than our domestic flight from Adelaide to Brisbane.

Our first awesome views of the precipitous island of Guadalcanal lived up to our expectations of luscious tropical wilderness. Jagged mountains displaying every shade and texture of dark green were not interrupted by a single village, or road, or garden until the cabin crew had been instructed to cross-check the doors in preparation for landing. The first sign of habitation was blue twists of smoke rising through a patchwork of gardens and coconut plantations. Moments before touchdown, the small town of Honiara came into view, squeezed between the mountains and the ink blue seas of the aptly named Ironbottom Sound. I wondered which of the rusting hulks offshore were the renowned World War II wrecks or the results of more recent shipping calamities.

Honiara had sprung up around the US Henderson airfield in the frantic last couple of years of World War II and quickly replaced the small township of Tulagi as the British protectorate's capital. Despite the added importance of housing the independent

National Government since 1978, Honiara remained little more than a country town. Simmering ethnic tensions had escalated a few months earlier in 1999 and we were advised to spend as little time as necessary in the troubled town. This news barely concerned us because our main destination was Tetepare Island, the logging battleground in the Western Province.

Stifling heat and humidity surged inside the plane's cabin once the doors were opened. But that was where the similarities with typical equatorial tourist destinations ended. We sweated across the baking tarmac and completed our immigration formalities, very slowly, in an un-air-conditioned terminal. None of the handful of taxi drivers lounging around the broken footpath seemed particularly interested in driving us anywhere, let alone the few hundred metres to the domestic terminal. So, like most backpackers embarking on a new trip, we strode out into the midday sun. A hundred metres later we realised our mistake. The heat and humidity immediately stripped the gloss from our exotic South Seas adventure. Sweat trickled into our eyes, blinding us and we stumbled into deep muddy puddles concealed among unkempt grass.

The domestic terminal was a filthy concrete-floored shed. Two uniformed officials behind the counter seemed to have little knowledge, or interest, in whether we were booked on the connecting domestic flight. There were no other passengers or flight crew to be seen. Katherine and I perched apprehensively on the broken plastic chairs, red faced, drenched in sweat and wondering what we had let ourselves in for. Eventually a trickle of locals checked in.

'Is the Gizo plane on time?' I enquired of a middle-aged woman dressed like a missionary in a pressed smock with a Peter Pan collar and uncomfortable leather shoes. 'Solomon time,' she quipped, without any sign of surprise or concern.

About half an hour after our listed departure time a Twin Otter, resplendent in the national colours of green, blue and yellow, taxied up to the far side of the shed. '*Plen blo iumi,*' our missionary friend reassured us. This was our first experience with Solomon Islands Pijin and Katherine proudly whispered the literal translation to me: 'This plane belongs to you and me.'

Sure enough, ten minutes later one of the two uniformed men announced, 'Gizo, Gizo' to no-one in particular. Fellow passengers wandered off across the tarmac. Without boarding passes or a security check, we followed their lead into the eighteen-seater winged sauna.

Before we left for the Solomon Islands I had found the address of the national office of the Worldwide Fund for Nature, or WWF, in a town that sounded like a Muppet character. We had seen the valuable work that WWF had performed in other countries. Contact by phone or email proved fruitless but we decided to visit anyway, hoping that meeting the staff would enable us to take part in the battle for Tetepare. WWF were based at Gizo, the provincial capital of the Western Province. Somewhat confusingly, Gizo, the town, was situated on the island of Ghizo.

The small town of Honiara disappeared before we had reached cruising altitude and was replaced by a twinkling sea that I dissected in search of dugongs or whales or lost sailors. Once my view had been obscured by billowing afternoon storm-clouds, I scanned the cabin. The missionary must have detected my gaze. Even before she looked up from her book, her easy smile was calming and contagious. I envied the solace her brown eyes conveyed, the demeanor of a confident soul satisfied in the pursuit of an unambiguous mission. Self-fulfilment is an under-rated emotion, an essential ingredient of a content and driven personality. What did she see through the hazel portals to my psyche during that instant before I averted my gaze? A sparkle of adventure and excitement maybe, but definitely not the assured-ness and satisfaction that accompanies single-mindedly striving for a goal. Sitting next to my soul mate and lover, I wondered whether we too would find our mission and our contentment on this adventure.

Just over an hour, one hundred islands and one thousand clouds after take-off, our plane descended to only metres above the turquoise sea. There was no airstrip, let alone any land below us. A small forested atoll whizzed past on the left, and a split second before we seemed destined for a disturbing watery encounter, a patch of cleared grass appeared. Our Twin Otter touched down surprisingly smoothly on the airstrip littered with lumps of crushed coral and tussocks of grass. We pulled up alongside an open concrete shed with a peeling sign that proclaimed 'Welcome to Nusa Tupe'. Flat land on Ghizo is at a premium and as a result Gizo's airstrip occupies the nearby elongated atoll of Nusa Tupe. I watched through the window as two men rolled a fuel drum past a still-spinning propeller to refuel the plane. Following the lead of our missionary friend, we grabbed our bags from under the wing of the rapidly reloading plane and lugged them to a rocky jetty.

Our shirts that had temporarily dried during the flight were again drenched with sweat from our brief walk in the thick tropical air. Katherine and I looked around for a ride to the main island. This was nothing like our travels in Africa or South-East Asia, where we had been besieged by taxi, rickshaw or becak operators thrusting their services upon us. We had wanted to visit a remote tourism backwater, but now we felt a bit lost. Eventually a friendly islander approached us. Patson introduced himself with English that was far more comprehensible than our rudimentary grasp of Solomon Pijin. For only eight Solomon dollars Patson offered to transfer us to Gizo in his canoe. Instinctively, like all tourists, we made the conversion to about four Australian dollars for the ten-minute journey. Patson also knew the best beaches and snorkelling reefs and claimed to provide cheaper canoe rides than either of the two dive operators in town.

We stared in amazement at the strange settlement that we approached in Patson's fibreglass canoe. Despite being the Solomon Islands' second largest town, Gizo was a ramshackle coastal version of a John Wayne movie set. Closer inspection revealed shops with pockmarked rusted iron walls that had been strafed by Japanese bullets in the war that put the islands on the international map for our parents' generation.

Leaving the milling masses at the waterfront, we sweated up the hill behind the town, the contents of our water bottles being sucked from our bodies by the intense afternoon sun. Following the sketch map in our Lonely Planet guide we eventually located the WWF headquarters, its identity only revealed by a rusted forty-four gallon drum rubbish bin emblazoned with a panda. After drying ourselves as best we could, we entered the building. A local woman, preoccupied with cleaning her impressive fingernails, peered at us apprehensively over a bare desk. In my best Pijin I explained: '*Mitufala Australian biologists laek help lo Tetepare or volunteer lo WWF.*'

After a long embarrassed silence, the woman politely informed us that Tetepare was very difficult to visit and WWF did not have any volunteering opportunities. We were surprised and disappointed. When we hesitated to leave, a shy young man sitting at an equally uncluttered desk eventually suggested, '*Sapos iutufala kam bak next tomoro, wanfala waetfala staff maet stap.*' We gathered that an expat, or *waetfela*, might be around if we returned the day after tomorrow.

Deflated that our offer of assistance had been rebuffed, our mood soon changed on our way back down the hill as we surveyed the views. Gizo once earned the title of the most beautiful town in the Pacific. The mango-lined avenue provided glimpses of a collage of postcard views. Rippling surf breaks to the south gave way to uncountable islands to the east and a mighty conical volcano to the north. Waiting for a couple of days would allow us to explore this paradise.

A haphazard waterfront market occupied most of Gizo's foreshore. Fisherfolk paddled from adjacent villages or islands in their dugout canoes with the day's catch of iridescent fish that seemed more appropriate for an aquarium than a food stall. Next to the brilliant reef fish were phenomenal-sized tuna and kingfish that had been caught on handlines. These monsters, weighing in excess of twenty kilos, must have led their catchers on a mighty wild tow as they attempted to drag them back to their little canoes. The fishermen typically had long straight hair, in contrast to most of the islanders who were the more typical fuzzy-wuzzy Melanesians. These fishermen were of Gilbertese origin and had been resettled in the Solomons in the past couple of generations when their Micronesian islands, now named Kiribati, became overcrowded. Along with their renowned fishing skills, the Gilbertese brought their rhythmic and seductive Micronesian dancing to the Solomons. Whole families from toddlers to grandparents dressed up and danced all night at village celebrations and for the few dive tours that visited.

Vendors from Simbo, a rough two-hour canoe ride away, sold eggs from wild megapodes. These bantam-like birds laid their rich eggs in the warm volcanic soils near their village. Gardeners from other islands converged on the market and arranged small piles of betel nut, bananas, coconuts, cassava or potatoes on banana leaves or old plastic sheets. Elongated purple and white eggplants and cherry-tomato-sized capsicums added flavour and colour to the market. Depending on the time of day, their produce was typically either doused in mud or sprinkled with dust from the adjacent main street. No-one seemed concerned about the dust or mud, as long as the fishmongers lazily swished flies from their catch with a wet coconut frond.

Next to the market, stores were emblazoned with freshly painted signs spelling out 'Mok Yu Wah', 'Mrs Ng Chai Store', 'Chan Corporation' or 'Leung Hong'. Each store sold the same ad hoc collection of goods. Tinned Taiyo tuna, packet noodles, cheap Asian watches, kerosene lanterns, buckets, gaudy material, 'ladies' bras and rubber thongs, or 'slippers', could be purchased at all of these stores. A classic that had Katherine and me grinning for hours was the handwritten advertisement for *hanger-chiefs*, presumably marketed for those really sticky sneezes!

Even more incomprehensible was that tinned fish and noodles were peddled not only by the general stores, but also the hardware store, electrical shop and even the post office. Despite this ridiculous duplication, none of the stores stocked fresh milk, orange juice or red meat. A few of the upmarket shops boasted a fridge out the back stocked with Coke, Sprite or pineapple Fanta cans from faraway places like South Africa, Malaysia or New Zealand. The cans from New Guinea were particularly eye-catching with a heavily bearded black-skinned Father Christmas enjoying a Coke cloaked in his thickest Arctic red.

Uncharacteristically blank-faced locals handed our money to grim Chinese shopkeepers behind the till, many of whom clearly neither trusted their staff nor were keen to teach them the intricacies of calculating change. Like the sellers at the market, none of the dozen or so stores made any effort to advertise their sales or to undercut competitors. However, the Wing Sun store became a favourite of every expatriate in town when they received a shipment of Mars Bars and Crunchies. Weeks later work stopped for several hours when news rapidly spread that cheese had temporarily appeared in the Wing Sun fridge.

Tailors and post offices selling tinned tuna were not the only surprises that confronted us in Gizo. Policemen sauntering their beat in 'slippers' were seemingly not interested in the prisoners that checked themselves into and out of the jail on the outskirts of town. Several generations of barbed and razor wire draped around the bent rusty poles that roughly marked the area within which the prisoners were supposed to remain. Families hovered outside the hospital that serviced most of the Western Province, preparing dinner for their sick relations.

The pace of the town was incredibly slow. Even when deliberately slowing to a saunter, we raced past the locals who had perfected a more relaxed way of passing time. Many sat or stood under the shady shore-side casuarina trees telling stories or watching the world go by at a tropical pace. Youths ambled with their little fingers linked in camaraderie, stooped old folks contentedly gazed nowhere in particular as if the local scene had not changed enough for several decades to captivate their attention. Everywhere the distinctive blood orange colour of betelnut spittle stained the road and pavement.

School children sported unbelievably crisp white shirts, although many did not wear shoes. Something about one little girl caught my eye but as I stared, she averted her little brown eyes. I backed off then surreptitiously sidled closer, using the same technique I use when closing in to photograph a nervous animal without the challenging 'walk-right-up' approach. Suddenly it dawned on me that her maroon T-shirt was emblazoned with the white Linden tree and the faded but clearly distinguishable words 'Linden Park Primary School'. This girl wore a shirt that had probably been 'popped in the mission bin' at the shopping centre near my former suburban Adelaide primary school.

Despite our inability to conform with its pace, something quaint about the town made us feel like locals within days of arriving. In a country that barely required five-digit telephone numbers and four-digit car plates, we soon recognised many of the people on the beachfront esplanade where all the action took place. In half an hour at the market we invariably bumped into the local member of parliament, the bank and hotel managers, the waitress at a restaurant bearing the name of J.F. Kennedy's sunken PT109 boat and one of the handful of pilots on the national register.

Eventually we met with Phil Shearman, the *waetfala*, at the WWF office. Unfortunately he was unfamiliar with Tetepare and did not know how we could assist with the 'battle' there, which dampened our enthusiasm. Instead Phil lamented that he was not able to conduct a logging audit on another island before he left the country. Landholders from the far north-western island of Choiseul had been waiting for nearly two years to lodge an environmental and cultural damages claim against an international logging company. Their case would soon be thrown out of court if no evidence of damages and unpaid royalties was forthcoming.

'Do you know anything about logging?' asked the lanky Australian, his accent noticeably thinned by the singing overtone of Pijin.

Katherine and I glanced at each other sheepishly. We lived in the Australian desert. Neither of us had ever witnessed logging first-hand, nor seen a recently logged rainforest.

'We used a chainsaw to build stockyards on our farm. Does that count?' I joked, as I thought back to Dad's puny yellow Makita that was no match for a rainforest giant.

Sensing that my joke had fallen short, Katherine sensibly explained that we were ecologists with experience in assessing environmental impacts.

Although we were rank novices in the business of logging, Phil felt our experience would enable us to come up with a 'moderately back-upable statement that the land has been trashed'. When we pushed him further he conceded that no-one else could help the villagers. Phil urged us to walk back down the hill to the Public Solicitor's Office, near the basketball court, to find out if we could help.

This project sounded like depressing work, not the adventure holiday we were yearning for. However, we conceded that helping out WWF might open opportunities for us to become involved with the Tetepare battle, if indeed such a showdown with loggers was actually occurring. Furthermore, a visit to Choiseul would introduce us to the environmental and social consequences of Solomon-style logging, which could be invaluable for our Tetepare quest.

MISSION #1

A loose congregation of locals lounged under trees around Gizo's bright-green Public Solicitor's Office. We were not sure if they constituted a queue but after waiting by the steps of the small stilted building for a while we tentatively peeped through the open door. At an immaculate desk sat a well-groomed Scotsman, who enthusiastically beckoned us in like old friends. Steve Watt was clearly a dedicated and committed young lawyer frustrated by the lack of technical support for many of his cases. He had served as the Public Solicitor for the Western Province group of islands and the large backwater island of Choiseul for several years.

A North Korean company had allegedly illegally logged the forests owned by several of Steve's clients from Choiseul. We learned that most of the land in the Solomons was owned by family or tribal groups, whose permission was required to take a coconut, erect a hut or clear-fell the forest. Steve could not present the cases to court unless independent assessors could prove that this unauthorised logging had taken place.

'Why don't the timber control officers assess these claims?' I enquired, exposing my naivety for the second time in as many hours.

Steve sighed, 'Corruption, bribery, politicians.' The landowners were not only fighting the loggers but their own government as well.

'How would we know if the loggers entered illegally or not and whose land is whose?' questioned Katherine.

'Don't worry about that,' Steve replied in his cheery Scottish manner. 'Benae will show you everything you need to know. All you have to do is document what he tells you in a professional manner.'

Sensing our next question, Steve stood up and summoned an elfin old man from under the trees. Chief Benae Bangakujuku had made the six-hour canoe ride from his village on several occasions to prompt the Public Solicitor into action. Each time Steve had disappointed him with the unfortunate news that no-one was available to help and Benae returned to his village empty handed.

Benae shyly looked at his feet as he shuffled into Steve's office yet again, presumably resigned to more bad news. We got the gist of Steve's Pijin explanation that we *tufala* from Australia would help him with his claim. The old man beamed an irregular-toothed smile in my direction as if he had just met his Saviour. In thirty seconds, we had been elevated from rank novices to reliable experts who could guarantee his compensation. Benae whispered something to us in muffled yet machine-gun Pijin. Steve replied on our behalf. Apparently we would try to arrange a plane flight for Choiseul tomorrow. As an aside, Steve suggested that while we were assessing the claim we might like to conduct an environmental audit of the logging operation. Again anticipating our question, Steve handed us the Solomon Islands Code of Practice for Timber Harvesting and the Standard Logging Agreement.

Back on the verandah of Phoebe's Resthouse, which overlooked the panorama of turquoise-rimmed islands and surf breaks that we had marvelled at on our walk down the hill, I skimmed through the legal jargon. I was pleasantly surprised to read that the fledgling nation's logging laws had been designed to sustainably manage the forest resource, rather than the slapdash rape and pillage that Steve had suggested was more typical. Logging companies were obliged to avoid working near cultural sites and riverbanks and to preserve rare tree species or those used for canoes, ceremonies, food or medicine. Mature trees of harvestable species should remain as seed stocks after logging, and roads and bridges required rehabilitation.

However, as we read on our inexperience became apparent. 'What's a log pond, a skid track, a *whoaboy*?' we asked each other rhetorically. 'How do we distinguish a protected *Artocarpus* tree from a harvestable *Pometia* or *Vitex*?' Equally concerning was our ignorance of what constituted unacceptable log waste, a significant cultural *tabu* site or insufficient rehabilitation. Katherine remained upbeat. 'It can't be that hard,' she declared confidently. 'Benae will help us to nail the bastards.'

I wasn't so sure. Back home I had sometimes been frustrated by ill-informed assessments of environmental impacts that had been prepared to justify preconceptions. My limited understanding of tropical ecology was that trees grew big and fast and that forests evolved with natural cyclones and landslides. Logging, by the rules that we had just read, could well be an environmentally appropriate method for the Solomons to earn hard currency. The loggers we were auditing may have operated largely within the rules on permitted land and Benae may have harboured a retrospective gripe over his share of the loot. Producing an emotive and damning report on a logging operation and a society that we did not understand didn't appeal to me.

The following morning we were informed by the staff at Solomons Airlines, located across the road from Steve Watt's office, that we and Benae might be able to get a flight to Choiseul within an hour or so. However, they could not be certain. Sometimes an influential politician or a *wantok* of the pilot called the planes out on a different route. Other flights were turned back or delayed due to bad weather or repairs. With only four planes operating in the country, SolAir found it difficult to make up time, often throwing flight schedules into disarray and providing credence to their unauthorised catch-cry, 'Time to spare . . . fly Sol Air!'

We threw freshly washed clothes into a backpack, found Benae down at the market and arranged for Patson to ferry us across to the airport. Just after draping our damp clothes on the airport fence a tropical deluge drenched them within seconds. '*Bigfala ren*,' Benae announced knowingly, about five seconds too late. Through the rumbling thunder we could make out the drone of a plane, which flew over twice but did not land. Then surprisingly, because the torrential downpour had not subsided in the slightest, the same plane that we had flown in from Honiara a few days earlier splashed down.

Benae confidently strode over to the plane. 'They can't possibly take off in this rain!' Katherine stated, voicing my opinion but not my prediction. Just in case, we stuffed our now saturated clothes into our bulging backpack, becoming drenched in the process. The pilot looked unfazed by his aquatic landing and his impending challenging take-off. If he was cool, I was cool, but

Katherine wasn't. Fingernails clawed into my knee as she uttered the barely audible prophesy, 'We are going to die' as the leaking little plane shuddered its way through lake-sized puddles. The pilot searched intently for the runway, his vision comparable to looking through a shower screen with the tap on full.

Locals had clapped enthusiastically when we touched down at Henderson Airport in Honiara on the international flight from Brisbane. At the time I considered it a quaint and enthusiastic act of appreciation from people who had rarely flown, but now I realised that their spontaneous applause was more likely an outpouring of relief. Our second domestic flight in the Solomons reminded us again that we had left the safety net of our sheltered Western lives.

For the first time ever I took particular note of the gauges, clearly visible in the open cockpit. What caught my eye was that the needles for all 14 circular gauges were pointing in exactly the same direction, about half past five, like novelty clocks set permanently for knock-off time. None of the gauges appeared to represent fuel levels because they did not drop at all during the flight despite the strong smell of Avgas suggesting that our fuel storage was being depleted faster than planned. When I yawned, the fuel burned the back of my throat like a shot of Tequila. But the pilots' crisp white lapelled shirts had the desired effect. I trusted them to deliver us to Choiseul in one piece.

After thirty minutes of buffeting in a mass of grey cloud, we touched down at Choiseul Bay, the 'capital' of Choiseul and I could barely contain my muted applause at our safe landing. Apart from a name that included every vowel, Choiseul Bay offered little else of interest. We were amazed that this outpost on a mosquito-infested island adjacent to Choiseul did not have a single guesthouse. Even more unexpected, not a single establishment in this fourth-largest province in the Solomons had a liquor license. There was to be no Solbrew, with which we had just become acquainted, for the next couple of weeks. The Chinese traders had not settled here either. The paltry Gizo shops now seemed like department stores in comparison to the small sheds peddling tinned fish, noodles and rice.

Benae led us up a steep muddy road to the Timber Control Office, where we met Stanley Wairowo. A stocky, incredibly shy man from the eastern Solomon Islands province of Makira, Stanley worked with the Timber Control Unit.

Stanley explained that Benae's case was far from unique; even many landowners who had agreed to logging now sought compensation for unauthorised damages. The Timber Control Unit faced an unenviable task. Asian logging companies turned to Papua New Guinea and the Solomons in the mid-1980s after the more accessible forests of the Philippines and Indonesia had been exhausted and Malaysia had banned round log exports to protect their dwindling forest resources. In 1983 the Solomon Islands Government sensibly decided to follow suit and phase out log exports. However, soaring world prices soon saw this policy shelved and the nation's logging accelerated to more than double the sustainable rate.

Unfortunately, resourcing of Stanley's Timber Control Unit did not keep pace with the increase in logging. International loggers took full advantage. The Timber Control Unit lamented that it could effectively police only a fraction of the international companies logging its forests and calculated that their ineffectiveness allowed twenty-four million Solomon dollars worth of timber to escape royalty payments each year. The logging companies and a handful of recipients of back-hand deals were pocketing the loot at the expense of the landholders and government coffers. Throughout his explanation, which he clearly found distressing, Stanley maintained an infectious smile, accentuated by his broad mouth. I bit my lip as I pondered what it would take to wipe the smile off his face.

Katherine and I grieved at Stanley's desire to circumvent rampant corruption. He faced an insurmountable battle to achieve the sustainable logging practices expected by Australian aid donors who funded his department. The forestry policing section had just been gutted by Solomon Mamaloni, who had resumed the office of Prime Minister for the third time, and apparently supported unregulated logging. Yet despite having access to neither a canoe nor fuel to inspect logging operations, Stanley was keen to assist us if Benae could arrange transport.

The following morning a small fibreglass canoe, then an outboard motor, then a container of fuel materialised from three different sources. We loaded our backpack and gifts of bananas and coconuts from new-found friends into the canoe bound for Benae's village. Benae, Stanley, a thick-bearded driver and several other lads jumped into the canoe with less luggage between them than we would take to the shops back home.

We headed north from Choiseul Bay, our 25 horsepower outboard motor frothing a white line into the warm blue sea. Coincidentally, this line marked the boundary between the Solomons and the large mountainous island of Bougainville, clearly visible to the north-west. Bougainville became part of German New Guinea following a colonial Anglo-German agreement of 1899 that split the Solomons–Bougainville archipelago. Due to its reputation as the most dangerous region of the Pacific, the Solomons were one of the last regions on earth to be colonised. In the late 1800s the Germans and French were rapidly acquiring Pacific colonies as they set themselves up for trade-offs in the more lucrative African colonies. Increasingly isolated in the Pacific, Australia urged Britain to take up the Solomons as a British protectorate, which they did in June 1893. This global colonial chess game saw the Solomons and Bougainville subjected to divergent administrative and political trajectories for the subsequent century.

Despite their colonial separation, the peoples of Choiseul and Bougainville retained strong links. Our broken understanding of Pijin enabled us to decipher Benae's story that during their push for independence many of the Bougainville rebels hid out in Choiseul when they were chased by the Papua New Guinea police and navy. I tensed at being so close to the notorious island that for years had been the most publicised conflict zone in the Australasian region. The thought of spending a couple of weeks preparing damning litigation on the most powerful organisation in this backwater island added to the adrenalin rush.

Sisiro did not appear on the Lonely Planet's sketch of Choiseul. *'Hemi long way go kasim Sisiro?'* I questioned Benae, concerned whether we should be rationing the drinking water in our small bottle. Either my grammar or the reason for my question was unintelligible. I then realised that neither Katherine nor I had ever held a full-blown conversation in Solomon Pijin with anyone. In order to quell my brooding panic I leant backwards to Stanley, the timber control bloke, and tried, *'Sisiro hemi kolosap nao?'* For a frightening few seconds Stanley was quiet but then he whispered an embarrassed, *'Mi no save.'* My relief in conducting the most rudimentary conversation outweighed my concern that our linkman also didn't know where we were going. I stashed the water bottle back into our pack.

In the late afternoon the canoe driver pulled in to a beach. A scattering of timber and leaf houses on stilts with thatched leaf roofs were visible through the enormous beachside trees. The immaculate cleanliness of Benae's village was impressive. Not a scrap of rubbish or even a leaf lay on the ground, nor trace of graffiti. As if our arrival had been announced to the whole village by a secret radio network, four generations emerged from their huts to check us out. A couple of packs of dogs and even a small pig came trotting over for a look. Of all the locals, only the chickens seemed uninterested in our arrival.

Our bags disappeared in a procession of willing helpers into the village and we were unsure whether we should follow them or sit down under a spreading tree with Benae. Following Stanley's lead we squatted down under the tree and waited until a teenage girl emerged from the village. Through his teenage niece Lilian, who was wearing a Bruce Springsteen T-shirt, Benae explained to us that we were to use the beach 'for toilet' and a special place in the river for *was was*. Lilian then led us through the dimming village to a small leaf house where a huge plate of root vegetables and slippery cabbage hidden under a gaudy tablecloth was soon delivered. Three shy women stood aside silently, watching our every move.

'*Tanggiu tumas*,' we half lied to the women, thankful that they had prepared us a meal but 'Thank you too much' seemed excessive for the meal of plain boiled taro with slippery cabbage. For reasons unfathomable to Katherine and me, stodgy tasteless taro remained a delicacy despite being replaced as staple by kumara potatoes that were introduced in the 1840s. After battling with the starch, I blew out our kerosene lamp and peered out through the open wall of our hut. With the exception of dull orange glows in some windows the village was completely dark and silent. With no radio, TV or play stations the village went to sleep quickly and quietly.

The following morning we awoke to the local chicken crowing competition, followed by the sounds of unrelenting sweeping. Every woman and girl in the village was bent over double, cleaning the bare dirt around their houses with brooms of sago palm stalks. The excited chuckle of inquisitive kids who had climbed trees to peer through our open window coerced us from our mosquito-net shroud. A couple of rascals threw large hermit crabs which scrabbled their bulky shells through the leaf roof until they crashed down to the floor. After more taro for breakfast, a morning ritual that soon became Katherine's nightmare, we realised that today was Sunday. Sunday was a day of rest. We were a little unsure of what could, and could not be achieved on the Sabbath, but it was clear that we wouldn't be starting the logging audit. Yet apparently *storying* was fine. *Storying* is a marvellously descriptive Pijin word for yarning or gossiping.

We learned from Lilian that we were in Vurango village, a scattering of a hundred leaf houses occupied by nine different tribes. Benae's two-hundred-strong Sisiro clan moved from their forest down to the coast in 1902 after the missionaries brought an end to headhunting. Although the older generations now felt safe living by the coast, their *piccaninnies* were absolutely terrified of us. As we walked around the village with Benae and Lilian, babies screamed in panic when they saw us, toddlers stared wide-eyed and hid behind their parents' legs. Their older siblings had apparently seen the occasional white nurse or doctor on a clinic run but no *waetfalas* had stayed in the village since World War II, over fifty years earlier.

Benae's mention of the war that had claimed the life of my grandfather in nearby Papua New Guinea sparked my interest. Benae had been about fourteen years old when he carried supplies for the Americans during the conflict. At one stage the Japanese intercepted his group of local porters, whom Benae referred to as *'mifala kanakas'*, so they hid in the bush at the side of the trail. But the Japanese kept going and shot many people in the next village. Most of the Solomon Islanders decided to attack the Japanese with their spears and arrows and some were given guns by the Americans. '*How nao iufala save waswe American or Japanese gudfala or badfala?*' I enquired, intrigued as to how the locals decided which foreign fighters to support. '*Olketa American givim tabako long mifala*,' Benae explained. Tobacco, which had been a key currency for the traders as early as the 1870s, became a more widespread addiction during the war. Benae remembered that everyone, including the Japanese, were happy when the '*bigfala bomb*' ended the war.

While storying away a lazy Sabbath, Lilian translated as the old man explained how he had personally protested against and stalled the logging on his land. Lilian explained that the old man and her mother were particularly concerned about the fighting and jealousies precipitated by the logging in the village. 'The loud men, the ones that could talk to the loggers, took all the money and the outboard motors,' Lilian explained. 'They were our brothers and uncles,' she lamented. 'Now they are our enemies.'

Benae understood that his case against the loggers hinged on proving that Eagon had actually trespassed. Our first task was to map the boundaries of Benae's customary land and then to document any logged areas within it.

Whoaboys and Log Ponds

After a brief but nerve-racking ride in an unstable dugout canoe the following morning, we entered a broad river mouth. 'Vacho River' proclaimed Benae. The forest of huge trees crowding its banks was broken by the occasional tennis-court-sized vegetable garden. Just as pins and needles threatened to paralyse my entire lower body in the cramped canoe, Benae pulled over to the left bank near an enormous tree and pointed with pouted lips, 'Sisiro land'. Leaving the river we stepped gingerly onto the slippery bank and followed three young men along a barely discernible path they were hacking through the jungle. 'Sisiro land,' Benae gestured to us again with a sweeping arm, making sure that we understood that our work should commence.

Once we established that we were standing on the actual boundary of Benae's land, we pulled out our Global Positioning System, or GPS, its first use since we received it as a wedding present. Benae and his boys had never seen anything like it. Apparently our state-of-the-art surveying technology had never tackled forest like this before either. It could not locate a single satellite; much less the four or five required to determine an accurate location.

We looked up. Shielding the sky were several ceilings of green leaves, totally obscuring any satellites tracking past. With our Pijin stretched to its limits we explained, '*Disfala machine hemi laek luk long sky befoa hem waka.*' We quickly learned that if we spoke slowly and threw a few '*falas*' into every sentence our rudimentary Pijin could be understood. Benae barked some instructions and ushered us off to one side. Within seconds the boys had slashed a clearing with their two-foot-long bush knives. Sapling trees with girths like goal posts were de-masted with ease.

Within minutes we had secured our first geographical position and were off, scrambling through the forest in search of another point along the boundary. As we walked, Benae and Stanley pointed out a plethora of useful plants. '*Dis wan fo bele-ran*,' Benae explained, holding a small fruit. Noticing our interest in the uses of plants, one of the lads handed me a severed segment of a Tarzan-like liana vine. He motioned for me to hold it up to my mouth, which I did, not knowing what malady I would be cured of. The juice pouring out tasted like water, an unlikely thirst quencher in the rainforest.

The multitude uses of the forest amazed me. Patches of wild bananas had been booby-trapped with fishing line to snare the mighty hornbills that fed on their small green fruit. Bent green sticks attached to lengths of twined vines snared wild pigs as they trotted along forest trails. Whenever we crossed a stream the boys looked for large snails or small shrimps and if successful trussed them up in leaf baskets to take home to eat. Benae took great lengths to explain that everything they needed had been found in the forest before the company spoiled it. He pointed out trees cut by the locals to carve canoes, build their house, or to make a small garden in the bush. A document that we had scrounged from WWF before we left, and had been reading by kerosene lamplight at night, estimated the annual value of these subsistence products, foods and medicines from the forest at nearly four thousand Solomon dollars per hectare.

At mid-afternoon we found ourselves back at the canoe. After pulling the starter for ten minutes or so the driver checked the fuel tank. Empty. Pushing us off the bank and into the current with his small carved paddle, the driver ushered me onto one of the most fantastic rides of my life.

River ... river in the jungle ...
River in the jungle in my dugout canoe.
Floating ... floating down the river ...
Floating down the river in the jungle in my dugout canoe.

The 1980s classic reverberating ad nauseum through my head perfectly captured the rhythmic buzz of the cicada chorus that throbbed like a Mexican wave through the canopy far above. An iridescent green dragonfly dazzled in the patches of intense sunlight that illuminated our dugout canoe like slow moving spotlights. Big googly eyes reflected no emotions. Like me it didn't have a care in the world. Life didn't get much simpler than this. I relived boyhood dreams of exploring the Amazon or the Sepik, before the age of plastics and engines.

'*Tchweeeee, tchweeeee, tchwooooon,*' sizzled the three sago-palm arrows, the last one arcing downwards well before the two grey pigeons with pastel-green beaks crossed its intended trajectory. One arrow narrowly missed the trailing bird, which disappeared silently into the canopy. Minutes earlier a white cockatoo had screeched indignantly as an arrow flicked its wingtip. The three adolescents at the front of the canoe immediately reloaded from their leaf quiver, awaiting their next target. I watched them keenly. How was it that they were able to stand, turn and fire their arrows without rocking the canoe in the slightest, whereas I threatened to tip us over when I simply adjusted my position to relieve my numb bum.

'*Shhhhplashh.*' I turned in time to see a crocodile's tail, knobbled as a large palm frond, stain the river with a muddy eddy as it slipped out of sight.

Neither Benae nor Stanley seemed the least bit concerned that our overloaded canoe was taking on water that necessitated a rhythmic bailing with a cut-off plastic drink bottle. Even Katherine was relaxed. Her white calves straddled my waist and her toes wiggled casually, only tensing when I inadvertently tapped out the beat of 'The River'. The leisurely pace of the canoe dictated that everyone, except the bird hunters, kicked back and lost themselves wherever the tropical forest took us.

This was perfect. Adventure with a cause. The peace of mind that accompanies the pursuit of a vision. The buzz of placing our lives and comforts with unfamiliar people, who spoke an unfamiliar language and were taking us to unmapped destinations. No phones, no emails nor deadlines. Bliss.

> River . . . river . . . jungle . . .
> River . . . jungle . . . dugout canoe
> Floating . . . floating . . . river . . .
> Floating . . . river . . . dugout canoe

Minutes morphed to hours and the brilliant blue sky was now crowded with pink and orange clouds. I emerged from my trance when a mosquito buzzed in my ear. Suddenly my mind crunched into gear. Dusk means mosquitoes, means malaria. Dusk also means imminent nightfall in the rainforest. I thought back to our outward journey through the sea to the river mouth this morning. Floating down a river in a hollow log was one thing but how were we going to power through several kilometres of sea with one little paddle that was used to steer rather than propel the canoe?

The riverside forest gave way to an impenetrable hedge of mangroves, suggesting we were approaching the river mouth. My adrenalin surged further as our canoe was guided over to the bank and we jumped out into thigh-deep muddy water. Looking around for crocodiles, I sliced my right foot on a mussel shell buried in the mud. Half an hour later, after Benae and Stanley had inexplicably disappeared into the darkness, I found myself alone and scared, limping after Katherine until we were eventually led to the village, tired, sore and very relieved to jump under our mosquito-net in our little leaf house. After a heart-to-heart, we agreed that if we pushed ourselves too hard for our new-found causes we wouldn't make it through the three months together. We would give Stanley and Benae two more days to convince us we could really help them. Otherwise we would try to get back to Gizo and then Tetepare.

Benae was determined that we compile a damning dossier on the logging operation. The next day the old man showed us where the logger's huge fuel tank had washed into the river, the diesel killing shellfish and fish for kilometres downstream. But he was even more incensed at the damage inflicted by the loggers on his *tabu* sites. Although three graves and a sacrifice site had been destroyed, Benae was most concerned about the destruction of the chief's mirror stone. This boulder extended to about Benae's height above the ground and had been used by five chiefs before him. The chiefs created a prized mirror by smudging charcoal into a carved depression in the rock and filling it with water from an adjacent spring. Both the stone and the spring had only been accessible to the chiefs, and now both had been destroyed by bulldozers. Benae was also clearly upset about the destruction of a stone vault that had stored custom money, or *kesa*. *Kesa*, which are extremely important to the people of Choiseul, were carved eons ago from fossilised giant clamshells that are no longer found in this area.

Benae's emotion at his destroyed cultural sites hit a chord with Katherine. While I opted to skip some of the treacherous slides down the hill to view another destroyed site to grant my gashed foot a reprieve, Katherine doggedly followed Benae's boys to every site. Even before we calculated the fines for other breaches of the Standard Logging Agreement she established that damage to the four *tabu* sites on Benae's land was valued at four hundred thousand Solomon dollars. Again swept up by the cause, it was Katherine who encouraged Benae to show us more damage and explain in more detail how the loggers had transgressed.

Benae stopped us at a point along one of the wide logging roads. '*Mi stapim bulldozer long disfala ples,*' he explained. The lads proudly embellished his story. The old man had not merely stopped the bulldozer but had returned on five occasions, three days apart. When the loggers refused to leave he shot at the dozer and broke its windows. Benae's outburst forced the loggers to retreat and the police from Choiseul Bay were summoned to confiscate his war-vintage gun. Ultimately Benae's frustrated rearguard action led to the court case for which we were collecting evidence.

Stanley was patient and dedicated, easygoing yet meticulous. I'm sure he smiled in his sleep. Stanley earnestly coaxed Benae's boys into hacking their way into hundreds of stumps to identify the tree and calculate any waste. Most of the harvested trees were *Pometia pinnata* or *Vitex cofassus*. Even coming from a scientific background where I regularly used Latin names for animals and plants, I found it strange that not only Stanley but Benae's boys also used the botanical nomenclature in preference to common or *kastom* names for these harvestable timbers. Rather than being the teachers, Katherine and I were often the students. Along with serving as our reluctant but patient Pijin tutor, Stanley also introduced us to the language of foresters. Skid roads were the tracks used to drag logs up to the main haul roads, and whoaboys were angled mounds that diverted run-off water from these roads. Log ponds were the storage areas where hundreds of logs were stockpiled.

Together with Stanley we calculated the scale of the claim. While Stanley was familiar with the techniques for measuring waste, we taught him about the sampling and estimating techniques necessary to assess the whole claim. Over a quarter of the standing trees remaining were so badly damaged from the logging that they were either dead or dying. The lack of rehabilitation and failure to leave seed trees or protected species was not surprising given the slapdash and unregulated logging technique for short-term profit. We couldn't believe the number of logs that were left rotting. Again and again after slipping downhill to a patch of wild bananas that concealed a tree stump, we located a massive felled tree base or an entire log. This timber had been lying in the forest for over two years and hence been wasted. Our horror, backed by Stanley's dissent, fueled Benae's interest. Once he realised that the company was obliged to reimburse the landowners for merchantable waste, Benae urged his men to locate every last tree stump. Men from the village who had been employed by the logging company were brought out to the site to help locate stumps and abandoned logs, which we dutifully measured.

Stopping at another huge log that lay rotting in the forest I asked Frank, a former logging employee *'Why nao kampani hemi no takim disfala log?'*

'No eni rod kolosap lo hia,' he replied, touting the unfathomable excuse that chainsaw operators has been sent in early to fell trees that were subsequently too remote from the access tracks to be collected. But hang on, the Standard Logging Agreement stated that 'Construction of main roads should be carried out 3 months in advance of logging operations', thus ensuring that only trees that could be retrieved were felled. After scouring the jungle for nearly a week, we recorded more than five logs per hectare, which raised the value of Benae's compensation claim to in excess of ten million Solomon dollars. *'Dis wan bigfala sumthing,'* Stanley acknowledged rhetorically, for the first time recognising the scale of the damages and the lost financial rewards we had documented.

I did not need any more convincing that the logging had been an absolute scourge for the environment, the landowners and the government. Katherine too had became increasingly resolute in preparing a case that would give the dodgy loggers a flogging and the local communities much needed funds. But, at the same time, we were acutely aware that the loggers and their few beneficiaries would be aware that we were responsible for compiling a dossier that could either close or severely impede their operation. Within a couple of weeks in the tropical backwater of the Hapi Isles we had potentially become targets. Although a little concerned, we felt safe and empowered while we were living among beneficiaries of our work in the village, so we pressed on with zeal.

Throughout our stay at Vurango village Katherine's long strawberry-blonde hair remained a novelty. This attention had its drawbacks, particularly when we were followed by a bevy of inquisitive children while attempting ablution activities in the morning. Whenever we thought that we had found an isolated stretch of beach, kids would emerge from the bush or a fisherman would paddle past. I also tried slipping away in the forest during the day with some toilet paper discreetly hidden in my pocket, but found no freedom there either. We were always being watched and if we diverted from the track or lagged behind, the boys would quickly reappear to see what we were up to.

Releasing the pressure valve was also dangerous. Lilian told Katherine that farting was exceedingly bad form in local *kastom*. Letting go with a *brus*, pronounced 'bruce', used to attract a two pound fine. All the slippery cabbage and fruit that we had been eating had fired up my digestive system and I often found myself either striding ahead of the group or lingering at the rear to avoid being detected sneaking out a *brus*. On these private sojourns my mind wandered to the history of the colonial enforcers of the *brus* fines. Had a particularly vigilant fart Gestapo named Bruce been honoured with his very own word in Pijin? Maybe these apparently trivial indiscretions were the only avenue for revenue raising in a society lacking speed cameras and parking meters. Nevertheless, by the fifth morning a resolution was required urgently so Katherine and I hatched a plan.

We snuck out of our leaf house before first light and took a secondary track to the beach. One of us was to draw the attention of the inevitable hordes, while the other would ablute. Chivalrously I played the original decoy. Through the pre-dawn darkness only one other person was barely visible against the shimmer of the ocean. The dark shadow turned out to be an old man who upon spotting us started walking our way. While Katherine slunk off in the opposite direction, I walked towards him and offered a friendly 'Morning'. He walked straight up to me, stopped and burst into laughter. Oh my goodness, had he deciphered our plan? Could he see Katherine behind me? What was so funny? Finally he questioned me intently in local language. I confided my ignorance of his language with, '*Sori tumas, me save lelebet Pijin nomoa.*' With that he doubled up with laughter again before launching another serious but totally unintelligible line of questioning. Were we using the wrong beach? Were we violating *kastom*? I had no idea. '*Emi orait for go wokabaot long disfala sanbis?*' I probed, which initiated another bout of maniacal laughter.

Enough was enough, I figured that Katherine had by now had sufficient time to complete her business, and the time for mine was rapidly approaching, as it does when one's lower alimentary tract anticipates imminent relief. I waved '*Lukim iu behaen*' or goodbye, and headed off down the beach in the opposite direction to Katherine, hoping that the old man would soon be distracted by her reappearance. No such luck; he followed right at my feet, jabbering and laughing. I decided that pace, rather than rationalising, was the key to my escape. The faster I walked, however, the more doggedly he lumbered after me, tripping over his feet as he maintained his crazed diatribe.

I could not hold out much longer, and definitely could not take the long strides that were required to lose my shadow, so I reverted to plan A. Turning around towards the lightening eastern sky I saw Katherine casually sauntering along the beach, as though in a Bali commercial, while I was being possessed by devils from outside and within. Realising there was no chance of him comprehending, I urged Katherine from a distance to distract my crazy acquaintance. Kids had now started emerging on the beach and I only had a few seconds to spare. The burgeoning crowd ruled out using the shallow water so I slipped into the beachside coconut plantation. With Katherine's distraction techniques having little effect she yelled out, 'You've got about fifteen seconds' as I deposited five days of carbohydrates onto the base of an upturned frond. Relief rapidly turned to panic as I realised that I could not leave the mess there and would have to further abandon normal hygienic practices, pull up my pants and quickly drag the coconut frond into the sea.

Walking gingerly to minimise collateral damage to my jocks, I hurled the frond into the sea as the kids, the crazy man and Katherine closed in on me. To my horror the frond landed upright such that my deposit floated proudly in the current, towards a couple of early morning fishermen in their dugout canoes. Oh my goodness! If *brusing* attracted a fine, I could not imagine what levy would stem from launching my toxic craft. I dived into the water and tackled the remarkably stable coconut frond, wrestling it over as I pretended to be having a morning frolic. The fishermen waved, the kids cheered, the old crazy laughed and Katherine's face turned from shock to hysterical amusement as she pieced together the bizarre antics she had just observed.

On our last evening at his village, Benae asked if we would like to have dinner with him. We were chuffed at the invitation because up until then we had eaten alone. Maybe we had finally been accepted into the village? What greeted us in the centre of the village was amazing. At least eighty people were sitting cross-legged either side of an enormous spread of banana leaves on the ground, their straight backs attesting to the years of paddling canoes and carrying loads of vegetables rather than slouching on lounges. Kerosene lamps and dollops of food including rice, potatoes, taro and boiled bony reef fish, scales and all, had been spaced at regular intervals. Turtle meat, specially hunted for the occasion by David, the village 'turtle man', formed the centrepiece of the feast. Two spaces had been reserved for us next to Benae and Stanley at pride of place in the centre. My amazement turned to concern as I prepared to sit. Sitting cross-legged on the ground was somewhat hazardous for a tall inflexible bloke wearing a *lava-lava* and no jocks.

After a sermon-like grace, dozens of expectant eyes watched us in anticipation as we recoiled from the thought of eating an endangered species that had been killed for our benefit. Eventually I helped myself to a portion of the reddish flesh. Although the consistency was, predictably, 'like chicken', the meat was moist like fish but its taste more closely resembled beef. We asked David about the local turtle population. '*Hemi hard tumas fo findim distaem,*' the turtle man lamented. Those he now managed to spear were invariably small, indicating a family pizza size with his hands. Years ago he frequently speared twenty turtles on a single hunt and they were large, bigger than the circle described by his outstretched arms. Further questioning revealed that David made no connection between the increased harvesting of the eggs and turtles to feed the burgeoning village and the crash in turtle numbers. Katherine and I pitied the fate of marine turtles if their populations were so threatened in such a backwater region. What hope did they have in more populated areas?

We also learned that Solomon Islands custom involved repetitive speeches as every senior man in the village thanked Stanley and Mr John for our efforts. A couple of the more enlightened speeches also acknowledged Katherine. The expectant looks cast my way made it apparent that I should reply in my new second tongue. Then timid Stanley surprised us by his lengthy speech, a prerequisite before the real festivities could commence. A young guitarist named Max accompanied some girls, then boys, for a few gospel songs that they sang and danced to. We then encouraged him to play traditional songs to the delight of the locals who whooped up a raunchy '*Hem nao!*' whenever the beat or volume increased above Sunday-school limits. We felt privileged to be guests of honour at such a feast with impromptu acts enjoyed by the entire village. Several women shyly walked up and presented Katherine with homemade string bags or *billums*. Even more surprise and embarrassment accompanied the gift of three traditional white armbands or *duku*. Carved from the same ancient clamshells as the *kesa* money, these ivory-like bands have been passed down through generations as wedding dowries or as peace offerings. They are crown jewels, irreplaceable prized heirlooms of the village. At first we thanked Benae for his most generous offer but refused to take them back to a foreign culture, explaining that the string billums, feasts and friendship were more than sufficient compensation for our efforts. The shocked looks and silence made it immediately apparent that we had breached a cultural taboo. Lilian explained to Katherine that Benae would be offended if we did not accept his gift, so we proudly donned the armbands that looked paltry on our white skin compared to their black, toned arms.

Back at Stanley's office in Choiseul Bay we calculated the litany of breaches for which the logging company was culpable. Of the seventeen sections in the Standard Logging Agreement that we could retrospectively audit, the Koreans were only compliant with two and had seriously breached eleven. The fines warranted for timber waste and cultural and environmental damages amounted to a staggering twenty-one million Solomon dollar, or ten million Australian dollar, legacy from a fraction of the forest bordering the Vacho River. Much of this fine represented not only an insult and monetary loss to Benae's tribe but also a loss of revenue for the government, which could have used these missed royalties to better equip and pay their forestry staff. Even more tragically, by accounting for two-thirds of the nation's exports, logging royalties should have also underwritten the mounting health, education, governance and transportation inadequacies of the country.

Peter Sheehan, former Professor of Forestry at Melbourne University, had recently been appointed as the Solomon Islands Commissioner of Forests. Katherine arranged a meeting with Peter to review our report before Steve Watt took it to the courts. To our relief he was neither concerned about our lack of forestry qualifications nor surprised by our findings. Another study that he had recently received matched his own experience in the country that the logging practices we audited in Choiseul were by no means unique. Leaving his office feeling upbeat about receiving the provisional blessing of the Forestry Department, we were hopeful that our assessment would make a difference for our new friends in Choiseul and for logging practices in the nation. Back in Gizo we were immediately assigned to two more logging audits, where we recorded similar damages.

Within a month of arriving in the Solomons we had become acutely aware that the destruction of the forests through unregulated logging was not an emotive myth peddled by green activists. Foreign loggers were a cancer turning this idyllic tropical hideaway into a degraded wasteland and precipitating social conflict and capitalistic dependence. Timber harvest rates that had more than doubled in the 1990s were still increasing and the nation's 600,000 hectares of harvestable forests were now being trashed at three times the sustainable rate. A draft map handed to us in the forestry office showed that nearly all of the lowland rainforest in the Western Province of the Solomons was shaded red or orange, indicating land that had already been logged or had logging licences issued; nearly all except for a long green island. We could have easily spent our three-month holiday, or indeed the next three years, travelling from one logging audit to another, making friends in the villages and enemies in Honiara. Instead we yearned for a more tangible legacy by helping with the great battle for Tetepare, the green island. By now we had established that the best place to kick-start our involvement fortuitously doubled as a honeymooner's paradise.

Marovo Wonderland

Take a deep breath. If you can read with your eyes shut, try doing so now.

Imagine a cliff. You are levitating far enough away to appreciate its enormity. The top of the cliff is lost in the clouds and dark abyss engulfs its base. You are neither hot nor cold; there is no breeze and no rain. As you hover closer to the cliff its splendour slowly becomes apparent. Massive columns and chasms, folds and aprons are in turn made up of smaller intricate sculptures. Adorning these sculptures are lumpy beanbags adorned with sequins, lacy umbrellas, statues and moulded figurines. On even closer inspection, lavish gems and delicate plumes compete for your attention.

Throughout this fantastic landscape you thrill to the brilliance of unimaginably vivid butterflies, gaudy parrots and ever changing chameleons. Large-eyed geckoes, flashing fireflies, luminous slugs and finely patterned snails move almost imperceptibly through the kaleidoscope. You are so engrossed by the movements and interactions, the bravado and the bluff within this riot of colour that you forget where you are and what you are doing. Suddenly your senses chill and you glance around nervously to watch a sinister fighter plane zoom past. Instantly your pulse quickens. Short nervous breaths confirm that you are out of your depth in a foreign world. But quickly the danger passes.

You wonder anew at the soaring kites and balloons that merge into and out of your splendid panorama. The cliff conceals a thousand mysteries that you cannot hope to unfold as you float by. The cryptic clues you detect are mere teasers that hint of infinite untold relationships and battles. Your eyes and mind are overwhelmed. You reach that state of hyperbogulation, beyond even those mind-boggling experiences that surpass amazement.

This is no fantastic dream or vision induced by hallucinogenic antimalarial drugs. These scenes are precisely what confront a diver donning a mask in the calm waters of Marovo Lagoon. Over three hundred islands are nestled within and along the hundred kilometre margins of the world's best defined double barrier reef. I was introduced to this improbably brilliant display of life and colour when I learnt to scuba dive at the idyllic Uepi Resort, situated on the outer edge of Marovo Lagoon between Honiara and Gizo.

Whereas the rainforest was reluctant to expose its secrets, the reef boastfully displayed its diversity to the naive onlooker. Kilometre-deep drop-offs, with sharks and barracuda cruising past gave way to colourful 'bombies' of coral that teemed with brilliant small fish. Each piece of coral seemed to support a unique type of fish, shellfish or crustacean, many of them so bizarre and brilliant that I could not have imagined that such creatures existed. At night, with the aid of a torch, I witnessed the change of shift as intricately patterned crabs and shrimps with glowing eyes scuttled past sleeping fish.

Uepi Island was a honeymooner's dream. Powered cabins were linked by long raked paths and manicured hibiscus hedges. Fantastically coloured blue-tailed and lime-green tree skinks dazzled in the sun. Hand-sized butterflies and flocks of scarlet lorikeets frolicked among the orchids and coconut palms. Outside our cabin was a sheltered white beach, shaded by overhanging coconuts, just like the South Seas appears in travel brochures. Yet a two-minute walk to the north side of the island yielded a steep coral wall, bedecked with fans and clams and harmless reef sharks so dense you could almost walk on them. And the best thing about Uepi was the apparent lack of watches or clocks in the entire resort. Breakfast seemed to be available all morning and lunch always appeared at our cabin at precisely the time that we had just finished showering from our morning dive and were contemplating a midday siesta. Evening buffets featuring the lagoon's seafood commenced just after the sunset drinks at the water's edge. Grant and Jill, the Aussie managers of the resort and several of the local staff quickly became good friends. Uepi should have been the most relaxing, idyllic place on earth; the place to atone for the unromantic start to our honeymoon. But it wasn't.

My early morning lie-ins were frustrated by unfamiliar birdcalls. No matter how much I tried to ignore or dismiss them as inconsequential, it bugged me that I did not recognise all the calls of the local birds. As a terrestrial ecologist I felt the ingrained compulsion to identify and explain the critters I saw or heard on the land. Tiptoeing out of our cabin into the frangipani-scented dawn, I quickly confirmed that the wren-like twitter originated from a Sunbird and the distinctive syncopated xylophone solo belonged to the Willie Wagtail which has a markedly different call back home. However, it took several mornings to distinguish the calls of a Myna from a Brown-winged Starling or a Sacred from a Collared Kingfisher. Even then, as I lay in our hibiscus-decorated bed I doubted my identifications and silently chastised myself for caring.

Fortunately, niggling questions that undermined my relaxation dissolved completely in salt water. In the underwater world I was free to marvel, harbouring no expectation to identify everything I saw. Underwater I was transformed from a scientist to a nature admirer. Wonder and awe, two emotions I had seldom felt since childhood, came rushing back. Unwittingly I commenced a quest for the most brilliant, aggressive and brazen fish on the reef. Contenders in the most brazen category were the clown fish, which daringly left the protection of their anemone homes to confront me when I approached. Clown fish particularly interested me because they were one fish that I knew something about, having assisted a PhD student with his study on them a few years earlier. I had learned that the family group of Nemos at an anemone typically comprised several males and only one large female. If the female died the next largest male would grow, change sex and usurp her role.

As I dived down to the anemone homes of these fish and teased them with my finger, I attempted to establish the pecking order. I also wondered what would be going through the mind of the first male in waiting. Like Prince Charles, would he patiently stand by and support his matriarch? I could not help but think that in the back of his little orange mind he would be egging on his big sister or auntie to go the extra yard in chasing away predators or divers, half hoping that she would be knocked off so he could ascend to the throne. At the same time he would have to be watching his small brothers, cousins and nephews, making sure that none of them caught up with him in size and hence challenged him for the role. Their social life would be fascinating. Imagine if the female departs through fair means or foul. How do the males decide on a replacement and how does this mysterious sex change occur. Do two Tarzans square off and the most masculine decide that he will be Jane? Once Jane has rebudded, how does she rationalise a sexual liaison with her bullied smaller brother?

While I was ensconced in my scuba vacuum, Katherine had embarked upon a more zoologically challenging task. Each time she dived or snorkelled she attempted to locate a type of fish that she had never seen before. As she chalked up more and more dives this task became more demanding. Katherine started seeking out well-camouflaged fish to fill her quota. Miniature gobies darted into the holes made by shrimp; sand eels waved in the currents then sucked back into their holes when approached. However, there was little risk of Katherine failing her challenge. Gerry Allen, a world authority on tropical fish, recorded 379 fish on a single dive in the Solomons. He reckoned the diversity in these tropical waters were second only to a dive site in Indonesia, eclipsing the far better known hotspots of the Red Sea, the Caribbean and the Great Barrier Reef. The same regional marine survey found that coral diversity of the Solomons also ranked in the global top five.

Sea water occupies all but four per cent of the Solomons nation and serves as both backyard and supermarket for the locals. Islanders have names and uses for over three hundred local fish species, a hundred shells and seventy distinct classes of coral reef. They know where and when coral trout, or *pajara*, aggregate to spawn and how best to catch them. Some use spears to catch sleeping parrotfish, others net mullet in shallow waters. However, most fishing was conducted by individual men or women in their dugout canoes using bright feathers or small strips of plastic as lures. The rhythmic skywards jerking of their fishing hand became as much a feature of the lagoon as the reef-rimmed islets. In the late 1980s Marovo fishermen caught nearly three kilograms of fish per hour. By comparison, if the bones and scales were excluded, I don't reckon Benae's fisherman mates caught three kilos of fish a month!

The people of Marovo, like those of Choiseul, were outwardly happy and carefree. Depending on their command of Pijin, adults would smile and wave, raising their eyebrows in friendly acknowledgement and welcoming us to their village. Strangers approached us, eagerly asking us where we were from, not simply as a throwaway conversational gambit but through genuine interest. Any friendliness from us was typically reciprocated by offers of bananas or green coconuts. At a village ten minutes canoe ride from Uepi, three young boys with cut-off shorts and bare feet and torsos played games with handmade toys and shrieked with unconstrained laughter seldom heard in Western society where our kids are 'better off'. They didn't have to worry about batteries failing in the chassis of their toy car dragged around on a string. A stray small wheel, possibly from the same toy car, provided hours of entertainment for two other little boys who pushed it around on a stick. Five shiny black *piccaninnies* jumped off a jetty as we putted by in our canoe; a bit further on two naked boys with huge white smiles jumped into the water from sapling tripods before surfacing with grins like synchronised swimmers.

However, their easygoing, apparently carefree attitude masked concerns felt by many of the locals. A government official visiting Uepi boasted to me that the Solomons' population growth would net them a global silver medal. Bountiful resources were dwindling as rapidly as villages swelled. A few of the villages had recently agreed to allow logging companies to provide them with the quick revenue that would have taken them many years to generate from selling carvings or produce from their garden or reef.

An alternative to logging was adopted by a dozen or so villages that had established guesthouses to accommodate tourists. Marovo was a natural drawcard. Not only was it the world's largest double barrier lagoon but Marovo remained one of the most pristine tropical reefs, having largely escaped the devastation of cyanide and dynamite fishing and industrial pollution. Assisted by a New Zealand-based push to declare Marovo a World Heritage site, these guesthouses were linked by radio to assist with bookings and logistics. Sea kayaks and canoe taxis encouraged visitors to stay in the region for a week or more, contributing funds to help locals resist the temptation of logging.

After living it up at Uepi we decided to support these local resthouses to witness how ecotourism may help save both Marovo and potentially Tetepare Island, which was only a two hour canoe ride away. Vanua Rapita ecolodge had been established on a small island near Michi village with assistance from WWF. As our canoe pulled up to a stilted leafhouse overhanging the lagoon a cheerful man strode down to meet us. Freeman, a man of approximately forty with flashing eyes and a short toe on his left foot, escorted us to another small leafhouse, 'our bungalow' where we dropped our bags. Freeman enthusiastically ushered us back to 'the eatery' where a shy woman prepared a jug of squeezed lime juice, surely one of the world's most refreshing drinks. A manky cat rubbed past my leg for the first and last time. The concept of a cat on a conservation atoll disturbed me even more than its weeping sores.

Instinctively appreciating our conservation motives, Freeman's eyes lit up. He wanted to tell his story, or at least the story that he thought we wanted to hear. Freeman informed us his village had embraced the 'ecotourism' preached by WWF because relenting to the persistent offers of loggers would not only strip their land and sea of essential resources but also damage their tourism prospects. He had witnessed firsthand the destruction of the forest on nearby islands, where the locals could no longer access building materials and their reefs had choked with mud, killing the valuable shellfish and fish. Once the easy cash had been splurged and the resulting litter had settled onto the reef, Freeman explained that the pro-loggers would be poorer and more miserable than before. Repeatedly over the next two days, Freeman took any opportunity to repeat his text-book conservation ideology to his sympathetic, yet increasingly skeptical audience. Apart from the title 'ecolodge' and the WWF connection, nothing else at Vanua Rapita suggested that the conservation agenda was anything but a marketing tool. It wasn't just the cat that presumably had accounted for all of the small lizards and birds on the island. Rubbish was thrown into the sea, undersized crayfish were served at meal times, fuel spilled liberally from the leaking outboard and none of the surrounding sea or forest had apparently been protected in any way.

The next ecolodge that we visited was Matikuri, about a half-hour canoe ride from Vanua Rapita and the closest resthouse to Tetepare, which could be seen on the southern horizon. An entertaining, informative host, Benjamin's proportionately large head was needed to accommodate his beaming smile and frequent laughter. Ben's attractive yet shy wife Jilly was the best cook that we had encountered in the Solomons. Her breakfast pancakes drizzed with local honey made a welcome change from rice and Taiyo tuna. They had established the first ecolodge in Marovo with advice and financial assistance from Australians who had befriended Benjamin when he visited Brisbane for surgery. A decade later Matikuri remained the pick of the ecolodges, due as much to the friendliness and experience of Ben and Jilly as its idyllic location, where a panorama of a dozen or more islets revealed no sign of human endeavours. Benjamin courted us with the increasingly familiar pro-conservation and anti-logging diatribe, which obviously met with a sympathetic hearing from most of his tourism clients. But he was less full-on than Freeman and also seemed to be facilitating real conservation initiatives. Benjamin had just hosted a Greenpeace workshop convened to discuss a threat even more damaging to the lagoon than logging.

The Solomon Islands government was desperate for income. Ports, airstrips and large population bases that were the necessary precursors to large-scale industry were limited to a handful of towns, including Honiara, Gizo and the fishing port of Noro. Even more restricting was the scarcity of government land, preventing large-scale developments. As in Choiseul, family groups held customary land tenure over 80 per cent of the Western Province. Some of the rare alienated land was on the volcanic island of Vangunu, which stands like a sentinel one kilometre above Marovo lagoon.

Logging commenced on Vangunu's alienated land in the early 1990s despite local and international concerns that inappropriate development in this area would threaten the lagoon, the food store for thousands of villagers. Marovo tourism also contributed significantly both to the national economy and local wages, a claim that the loggers could not boast. The logging on Vangunu by the Malaysian company Silvania, isolated from the watchful eyes of landowners, was the most destructive logging operation ever witnessed by experienced international observers. On four separate occasions the company's logging licence had been suspended for failure to comply with the regulations but they kept coming back.

Fortunately for the reefs and landowners of Marovo, frequent changes in the national government delayed further logging on Vangunu but the Malaysians bided their time. By the time of our visit in 1999 the Solomons economy was perilous. The SIPL oil palm plantation near Honiara, one of the country's largest employers and revenue raisers, had been closed due to increasing ethnic tensions. The Malaysian tigers smelled a wounded pig. This time their proposal changed from logging the alienated land at Merusu on Vangunu Island to developing an oil palm plantation. It just so happened that the forest had to be clear-felled in the process. In return for their superficially generous offer to bolster the Solomons economy, Silvania requested that royalties should be waived on the timber that had to be felled and shipped to make way for the plantation. This mirrored Indonesian scams, documented by Greenpeace, where the forests had been raped without financial reward to landowners or governments on the promise that great royalties would be forthcoming. In response to the concerns of Greenpeace, Benjamin and others, the government had demanded an Environmental Impact Study.

While this study was being prepared, WWF embarked upon one of their more pre-emptive strikes in the region. Simon Foale served as the conservation manager for WWF at Gizo and was an outspoken critic of the oil palm proposal. As a Solomon-born Australian with a PhD in marine biology and considerable experience in Solomons politics and sociology, Simon had the ideal background for his job. His hawksbill turtle shell earring suggested that, given his knowledge of the threatened status of this species, his affinities for the local culture outweighed his conservation ideals. Jewellery ironies aside, Simon was outraged, yet not surprised, at the proposed plantation. He had seen it all before when decisions by national fishery and forestry departments serviced the greed of key politicians rather than the advice of their own staff, researchers and international opinion.

After we returned to Gizo from our Marovo 'honeymoon', Simon asked us to assist WWF to survey the reefs near Merusu before the inevitable destruction from the oil palm plantation occurred. Maybe WWF could document the damages to both the marine resources and the ecotourism dollar. Righto Simon. It seemed like one of the challenges issued to contestants on a reality TV show. How were two landlubbers going to make any sense of this kaleidoscope of unfamiliar marine species? Our experience was limited to underwater beauty contests and naive fish twitching. We had no idea how this surreal underwater world would be affected by increased sediment loads resulting from the logging erosion. Had it not been for Stanley's local knowledge we could not have completed our logging audit mission and we knew even less about coral reefs than we did rainforests. Simon remained steadfast. We only had to design a monitoring program; the rest was easy.

Simon's half-hour tutorial with a picture book of coral types taught us that the branching *Acropora* corals were more sensitive to silt than the boulder-like massive *Porites* corals or soft corals. Corals that were white, or shrouded by green algae, had already died, perhaps affected by warming of the seas, tidal damage or earlier logging or fishing impacts. A decrease in the amount of live coral or change in the types of coral would be expected if the reefs were affected by the clearing for the oil palm plantation.

We caught up with the WWF field staff back at Matikuri ecolodge, which had already become one of our favourite places in the lagoon. Matikuri's leaf houses looked out upon a cluster of reef-rimmed islands at the mouth of the Nama River. The Nama flowed through an unlogged catchment owned by Benjamin's tribe, who had vowed that it would not be logged. The reefs here would serve as a valuable control region with which to compare the affected reefs on the other side of Vangunu.

Before we commenced the survey, Katherine and I described our proposed monitoring program to WWF Marovo field officers on Matikuri's expansive decking. Glin, who sported a mighty fuzz of hair resembling Bozo the Clown, was as earnest and polite as a forty-year-old Sunday school teacher, whereas his younger compatriot, Perry, exuded an arrogant confidence towards the obviously new techniques that we were explaining.

Old Solomon Airlines magazines spread out on the decking represented branching coral, playing cards were soft coral, newspapers indicated dead coral and the floorboards were sand. We practised estimating the cover of the different corals and substrates with the aid of a one-metre-square quadrat cobbled together from reinforcing iron. Each magazine occupied approximately 3 per cent of a quadrat whereas it took two playing cards to total 1 per cent. We then moved the quadrat five metres down the deck to another scatter of papers and repeated the estimates, just like we would underwater. Ben and Jilly looked on with amazement.

In addition to the coral survey, we also decided to survey marine resources used by villagers. In the same way that destroyed forest products commanded a value that could attract compensation, the value of marine resources had been established through over 150 years of trading. We understood the commercial value of crayfish because Benjamin regularly bought them from local fishermen for Jilly to prepare for our evening meals. Some villagers also eat clams, although their sale had been banned due to conservation concerns. Trochus shells are fist-sized conical marine snail shells that are bought by Asian traders to make pearly buttons and jewellery. A long history of trading bêche-de-mer, or trepang, with Asian traders had elevated these submarine vacuum cleaners into one of the most valuable marine resources in the South Pacific.

Demonstration of a significant reduction in crays, trochus or bêche-de-mer as a result of the oil palm development might motivate the villagers to restrict further unsustainable developments. More importantly, resulting compensation claims would hopefully influence the development company to minimise their off-site environmental impacts. By pretending to swim along a fifty metre tape, our local monitoring technicians counted imitation clams, crayfish, trochus shells, and bêche-de-mer.

Ben somewhat nervously asked why we were counting these resources *'long saed-kam Vangunu'* when he understood that the oil palm was to be planted on the other side, or *'saed-go'*, of Vangunu Island. We explained the importance of monitoring changes in an unaffected region to compare with the area that would likely be damaged by the plantation. If we only monitored the reefs near Merusu we would not be able to separate the impacts of the plantation from natural events like a cyclone or coral bleaching. Therefore the reefs near Matikuri would act as a control for widespread changes that were not linked to the plantation.

Perry lived at nearby Tinge village. He knew the locations and owners of the reefs near Matikuri and was confident that he could take us to six reefs close to the Nama River mouth, six reefs three to five kilometres out and another six out near the open ocean. Glin lived at Penjuku village on the other side of Vangunu, closer to the Ngevella River, which passed through the site of the proposed Merusu oil palm plantation. Glin also claimed that he would be able to find suitable reefs for monitoring on the Ngevella River side and he too knew their owners and guaranteed our access. We loaded the tape measure and quadrat into the canoe, and then Perry navigated us to a reef near the mouth of the Nama River.

Although we had requested that Perry take us to these reefs, they were decidedly unattractive and spooky. Mangroves thrust their gnarly hands into the mud and at low tide their knobbly toes stuck out. Katherine had spotted a crocodile at nearby Matikuri, and Lilian's recollection of her brother being taken was fresh in our minds. To add to our trepidation, as we nervously prepared to start the survey Glin announced that he wouldn't be diving, citing a long-term ear complaint as his reason. Hang on! A WWF marine monitor who didn't swim seemed incongruous, and Katherine whispered to me, 'That's bullshit, he never mentioned it before. He just doesn't want to be eaten by a croc.' Abandoning the survey before it began would send a bad message to the locals and WWF so we agreed that as long as Perry was happy to dive we would continue, with Glin paddling the boat close to our submarine transect for protection. The reefs by the river mouth featured less branching corals, sharks or pretty reef fish than we had become accustomed to at Uepi. We rushed our estimations in the murky water and rapidly hauled ourselves back into the canoe, relieved that all our limbs were attached.

The next day when we were surveying reefs on the outside of the lagoon our black-and-white Secchi disk lowered from the boat typically showed that we could see further than twenty metres into the blue abyss. I had to pinch myself to remind me that our work, albeit voluntary, involved snorkelling in one of the world's greatest reefs. Unlike the murky river mouth sites, these reefs were a thrill to survey, with submarine vistas of huge fish and brilliant corals. Clicks, beeps and crunching accompanied every underwater scene. The chomping of parrotfish on coral was clearly audible. When disturbed, these parrotfish would dart off, jettisoning a cloud of white sand behind them that would eventually form one of the white beaches on the nearby atolls. These open-water sites did, however, have one drawback. When the wind or waves picked up we were choked back to reality by a gob full of salt water as we attempted to yell out our coral estimates while treading water. When I had to exert myself to swim the heavy iron quadrat against the current, the gastric reflux taste of two-minute noodles, which are never buried too deeply in the Solomon stomach, burned the back of my throat.

Three days later we reluctantly left the hospitality at Matikuri to start sampling the reefs around the other side of Vangunu, adjacent to where the clearing for the oil palm 'trial' had just commenced. Fortunately these reefs closely resembled those near Matikuri, which meant that any subsequent changes should be easy to measure. Four more days of snorkelling later and our second mission for WWF had been successfully accomplished.

Solomon Time

Page 163 of our Solomon Island Lonely Planet guide was becoming increasingly dog-eared.

> *Tetepare, also called Montgomerie Island, is 26 km long and seven km wide. It covers an area of 120 sq km, rising to 357 m at its centre. The landscape is rugged, and the island has interesting flora and fauna, including plenty of mud crabs. People from Viru Harbour in New Georgia occasionally come over to Tetepare to hunt crocodiles. The island's saltwater croc population mostly lives along Tetepare's north-eastern coast between Somerville Point and Cape Rice.*
>
> *Tetepare is likely to be the next big battleground between the loggers and advocates of low impact eco-tourism. The issue is complicated by the question of land ownership. It has been unpopulated for three generations, and 30 different villages have laid claim to it.*
>
> *The only way to get to or around the island is by canoe. You may be able to get a ride from Lokuru on Rendova.*

Although we knew nothing else about Tetepare, this tantalising snippet had been enough to stimulate Katherine's and my search for adventure and a cause. 'The next big battleground' intrigued and excited us. After witnessing the damage that logging inflicted on the forests, rivers and landowners of Choiseul, we could imagine the conservation value of an entire unlogged island. The spectacular marine wonders of Marovo lagoon were increasingly threatened by burgeoning populations and the oil palm and logging industries. How valuable could the undeveloped coastline and reefs of Tetepare become in the future?

'*Iu save kasim Tetepare?*' was one of our most common questions we asked around Marovo and Roviana lagoons. We wanted to meet anyone who had visited Tetepare. We learned that the island was not pronounced *Teatpair*, which I had considered an appropriately sexy name for an abandoned tropical hideaway, but *Tet-a-par-ee*, with each syllable receiving equal emphasis.

While based at Matikuri we looked south-west to Tetepare Island. The ancestors of both our friendly hosts, Ben and Jilly, had fled Tetepare and hence they considered themselves to be landowners of the deserted island. Ben informed us that fishermen and hunters occasionally travelled past Matikuri on their way to Tetepare, but that no-one lived there. At another stop on Lola Island, while enjoying the rare decadence of cold beers at the fishing lodge, we were told that there were many Tetepare people from the Munda and Rendova regions who also used the remote island, mainly for pig hunting. Noting our particular interest in Tetepare, Freeman from the Vanua Rapita resthouse suggested that we should meet Seri Hite, his *wantok*, who was the boss of WWF in the Solomons.

Seri was, at the time, considered the elder statesman of conservation in the Marovo area and the first national WWF employee in the Solomons. Surprisingly, despite four earlier visits to the WWF office, we only met Seri after we returned to Gizo from our marine survey. We envisaged a big man with a commanding presence but Seri was anything but big. This shy little man with a Jackson Five-type Afro revealed his perfect rack of teeth in a nervous laugh. WWF fundraising magazines but surprisingly few files on local projects and issues littered his spartan desk and bookshelf. Like nearly everyone that we had questioned about Tetepare, Seri also claimed to be a landowner. More importantly, Seri informed us that WWF had helped a conservation-minded group of Tetepare descendants called FOT, the Friends of Tetepare. FOT had successfully opposed a logging proposal for Tetepare in 1995 and had drafted a conservation strategy for the island. The document he extracted from his in-tray showed only the first traces of rusting around the staple, suggesting that it had only recently been prepared. Katherine and I were stoked that the global conservation organisation had adopted Tetepare. Conservation had won the battle.

We eagerly devoured the draft conservation strategy. Tetepare was reportedly the largest uninhabited island in the South Pacific. An amazing number of archaeological sites attested to the civilisation that abandoned Tetepare over a century ago, and many international organisations had nominated the island as worthy of conservation. We also read with interest the mouldy transcripts of the timber rights hearing, although not knowing any of the players obscured its relevance.

However, there appeared to be very little information on the wildlife of Tetepare. Wildlife surveys, not logging or coral surveys, were our forte. An inventory of critters, particularly unique or rare species, would assist with FOT's objective of deriving income through hosting ecotourists and scientists on Tetepare. Seri informed us that if we were interested in Tetepare we should contact an influential landowner named Peter Siloko in Honiara and that the FOT project was now in the hands of Isaac Molia, who was due to visit Gizo the following day.

An earnest middle-aged man, Isaac's receding hairline framed a pointed face, reminiscent of an elderly dentist. Although he apparently suffered from a sinus ailment causing him to sniffle and hoik alarmingly at the conclusion of most sentences, Isaac was well spoken and, of course, a Tetepare descendant. The FOT coordinator proudly informed us that through his former role as Secretary of the Rendova Area Council he had been instrumental in opposing the 1995 logging claim for Tetepare. This was, Isaac explained, the second of the logging proposals for Tetepare.

In 1984 Danny Philips, the local member of parliament for Rendova and Tetepare, consolidated plans for a logging operation followed by the construction of an international airport and casino for Tetepare. Philips' vision of a tax haven for rich Asians excited 'progress'-seeking locals and cash-strapped federal politicians alike. However, their South Pacific Monte Carlo was thwarted by jilted Lokuru-based Tetepare landholders who were not destined for a share of the profits.

Painfully slowly but methodically, Isaac explained that over the next few years influential Tetepare landowners became increasingly attracted to royalties offered by international loggers, who were systematically working their way through the Western Province. In 1994 the Tetepare Development Company, also spearheaded by Danny Philips, proposed logging Tetepare with the backing of the ironically named Goodwill Logging Company. The Tetepare Original Landowners Association (TOLOA) from Lokuru on nearby Rendova Island threw its weight behind the logging bid and proposed resettling the island after it had been logged. The TOLOA big men were not only aware of the short-term finances and power that logging offered, they also recognised that local opposition to the destructive logging of the dwindling forests on Rendova made the proposal to shift the logging to Tetepare even more attractive.

At that time Isaac was the secretary of the Rendova Area Council, which was responsible for conducting the timber rights hearing for Tetepare. Isaac was miffed that he and many other Tetepare descendants had not been consulted about the proposal. The council subsequently rejected the TOLOA-backed logging application because of objections raised by the Siloko family, Tetepare descendants from southern Marovo lagoon.

Danny Philips, by now the Minister for Foreign Affairs, remained acutely aware of the political gains from instigating a major development on Tetepare. Each of his previous plans for Tetepare had been foiled by disputes between rival landowners. On his third attempt he left nothing to chance. Danny courted influential landowners based in Rendova, Marovo and Honiara, selling his great plans while giving them a taste of their future lifestyles. At the same time, a friend of Isaac's, Peter Siloko along with Solomon Islands' most prominent environmental activist, the dreadlocked Lawrence Makili, shadowed Philips around Marovo, campaigning against the logging of Tetepare.

Danny Philips confidently strode into the timber rights hearing. He had secured overwhelming support for his logging proposal and only had to face two peripheral objectors. First he had to contend with Patrick Lavery, the WWF-funded public solicitor representing the Siloko family. Lavery is a knee-high white socks kind of expatriate, comfortable at the bar of the Honiara Yacht Club, and was almost single-handedly responsible for defending the rights of the nation's customary landowners. Lavery raised a number of technical objections and impediments that he hoped would force the council to stall its decision. Because other landowners who were not present also had customary land rights, Lavery contended that timber rights could not be granted.

Danny Philips was itching to reveal his trump card and Lavery's claim played right into his hands. Not only were the previous objectors to his application now signed as trustees, but also Philips claimed that he could demonstrate that his logging proposal had widespread support. To prove his point he asked senior Tetepare men from Ngatokae, Marovo and Roviana, who had previously objected, to stand and declare their support for the application. They did. For the first time, the far-flung Tetepare landowners had apparently united behind their Rendova *wantoks* to authorise a joint bid.

I can imagine the mood of the court. The masses were swarming behind their charismatic leader, who had overcome their biggest hurdle. The riches of Tetepare, conveniently processed by Asian loggers into hard currency, would soon be theirs. The transcript of the court proceedings of September 19, 1995 at the Munda Council Hall reveal that, buoyed by this support, Danny Philips confidently stated that he could also 'meet the objections of Harry and Mary Bea during the day's proceedings.' This was the final impediment to his claim. Although he acknowledged their input, Isaac declined to expand on the role played by Harry and Mary.

Harry Bea, like Danny, was a former headmaster and a man who commanded attention when he spoke. But after subsequently meeting both men their differences were striking. While Danny's imposing stature is polished and stylish, Harry is an old street fighter, with no more concern for his appearance than tolerance for perceived wrongdoers. A natural orator moulded by years behind the school desk and the pulpit, Harry did not talk, he preached. And if he thought his audience had missed the point he would fearlessly stride towards an ambivalent or disbelieving listener and ram the point home again and again.

The court transcript described faithfully how Harry first asked his daughter Mary to read the Solomon Islands national anthem. He then requested that a world map be displayed to prove that the Solomon Islands compared to other nations were like 'little spots of dust.' 'If Tetepare is so small that you cannot see it on a world map then leave it alone,' he stated. Back on track from his global perspective of questionable relevance, Harry went on to claim, 'God created our islands, so people may live on them and find their daily needs from these rich resources.' Harry strongly objected to anyone logging Tetepare and refused to dispose of, or sell, his timber rights. Harry's brother, Pastor Malon Bea, produced another theological masterpiece. Facing the logging supporters he decreed that, like the story of King Solomon, the real owners of Tetepare would cry like a mother if her baby were to be split in half. By implication, those who had voted to log Tetepare were not deserving Tetepare landowners.

Philips was gobsmacked. He claimed that previous objections were raised about land disputes but now Harry and the WWF-funded lawyer were raising environmental issues. The lobbying continued while the Area Council considered their decision. Meanwhile Isaac explained how he met with Peter Siloko and his cousins, who also opposed logging, Mary Bea and the

WWF representative Seri Hite to establish a coordinated defence against the logging of Tetepare. In October 1996 they established the Friends of Tetepare, complete with a bank account. Isaac was the Chairman, Petrie Sute, one of Peter's cousins and an influential and well-educated accountant, served as the inaugural Secretary and Treasurer. Kido Dalipada, another cousin, who was working for WWF, was appointed Coordinator and Peter Siloko Information Officer.

Although their logging proposal was subsequently rejected by the Area Council, TOLOA had not shelved their plans to develop Tetepare. While the Friends of Tetepare were talking about an ecotourism venture, TOLOA were planning to plant a dwarf mango orchard, employing over one hundred workers. Yet although Tetepare had been used for a youth challenge camp and a training ground for the New Zealand army, Isaac informed us that neither the ecolodge nor the mango plantation had eventuated. The 'next great battlefield' seemed destined to lie waiting until future proposals.

Isaac's main roles, according to the Environment Australia grant that WWF had secured, were to confirm the identity and location of Tetepare descendants and then to encourage them to develop a conservation plan. He had dutifully collected genealogy information from over one thousand descendants from all corners of the Western Province and beyond.

We asked Isaac about FOT's aspirations or plans for Tetepare. *'Mifala FOT like for attractim staka tourists lo Tetepare. Maybe mifala grow rice long samfala place blong island,'* he stated enthusiastically. The detail was even scarier. Isaac envisioned a road for tourists to drive right around his pristine island. He considered rice-growing an environmentally friendly option for Tetepare's lowland areas.

Oh my goodness!

We had quickly learned since arriving in the Solomons to curtail our initial reaction, which was along the lines of blurting out, 'You want to do what? You can't be serious!' Instead we responded that yes tourism would be better for the island than logging, but that driving through wilderness is really overrated. We explained that most tourists would rather walk through the forest or take a canoe ride around the coast rather than drive around a road with a hundred dodgy bridges in unserviced vehicles. The forest clearing, diversion of water and large workforce required to operate a rice farm may also detract from the conservation value and tourism potential of Tetepare, we explained. I'm not sure if Isaac believed us.

Changing the subject, we fired off questions that had intrigued us since we first read about Tetepare. '*Staka crocodiles and pigpig stap lo Tetepare?*' I probed while Katherine simultaneously asked, '*Iu save what kind rare animal stap lo Tetepare?*' We were astounded by his answer. '*Mi no kasim Tetepare yet.*' One of the founding fathers of FOT and the man entrusted with preparing the management plan had never set foot on Tetepare!

Although taken aback by our lack of enthusiasm for his roads and rice paddies, Isaac was keen that we conduct a wildlife survey of Tetepare. He offered to take us there the following week when he planned to visit Lokuru village on Rendova to present a workshop on ecotourism for these 'troublesome people who thought they owned the whole island'. WWF staff, on an earlier Lokuru visit, to discuss the conservation of Tetepare, had been intimidated by their perceived aggression and unnerved by the question, 'Why do WWF have a black-and-white pig as their mascot?' confusing the Panda logo with a rare colour morph of their favourite food. Years later we understood the appropriateness of this misidentification!

Bouncing down the hill from the office of the black-and-white pig in high spirits, we surveyed past the opalescent Gizo reefs to the twin-humped silhouette of Rendova on the horizon. Lokuru village on the far side of Rendova was obscured by the steep island sparsely populated by tribes who spoke a totally different language to the rest of the Western Solomons. We couldn't believe our luck that we had been invited to help on Tetepare, especially at a time when the landowners needed direction and were introducing the conservation agenda to the 'troublesome' Rendova people. A chilled Solbrew or two on the balcony of the Gizo Hotel seemed the appropriate way to celebrate. We mused excitedly about the living museum of Tetepare that dated from the time before bulldozers and chainsaws. For the third time in three months we recognised a problem for which we had ideals and energy but no real idea of what we could do. The island music from the disco further buoyed our emotions. Gizo had become our second home, and as we knew half the crowd it wasn't long before were dragged up to dance. About the only local man who didn't ask Katherine for a dance was a particularly cool dude who danced by himself all night wearing reflecto sunglasses and a Walkman with no batteries.

The following Monday Isaac informed us that his trip had been delayed for one week. We still had a month left of our Solomon Islands holiday so we were not too concerned. In order to brush up on our bird and reptile identifications before our Tetepare visit we started a survey of the wildlife of Ghizo Island. In particular we were trying to establish the abundance of the Gizo white-eye, a small yellow bird with one of the most restricted distributions of any bird on the planet. To kill more time we climbed the mighty Kolombangara volcano that presides, Kilimanjaro-like, above the Western Solomons.

On our return to Gizo we learned that the Lokuru workshop, for which we were supposed to leave the following day, had been cancelled. No explanation was forthcoming for this cancellation. However, Isaac was going to arrange alternative guides to take us to Tetepare for the wildlife survey. He would confirm arrangements later in the week. Although frustrating, the break allowed us to dry our packs and tent and give Katherine a chance to shake a stinky bout of giardia before we ventured to remote Tetepare.

Although no-one had mentioned anything directly, cracks had apparently developed in the relationships both within Friends of Tetepare and between this fledgling conservation group and

WWF, their major source of advice and funding. Payment of grant instalments had been delayed because Isaac had not completed his reports on time. After an adrenalin-filled birth, the small group of descendants working part time with little management had lost momentum. Simon Foale warned us that the noble cause of saving Tetepare, which we had become increasingly excited about, might be too hard. There were simply too many issues and too many descendants who did not trust each other. This 'can of worms' really represented 'mission impossible'. WWF saw the conservation of Tetepare as a worthy objective in a country with few formal conservation regions and a plethora of threats, yet they had neither the money, manpower, nor apparently the enthusiasm to commit further resources.

Fortunately, there are few better places than Gizo to be 'stranded'. We scuba dived down to a hellcat fighter plane and through the wreck of a Japanese cargo ship where a coral-encrusted motorbike and saki bottles remained untouched since the War. However, our favourite dives were on the reefs. Hot Spot was appropriately named and we were awed by manta rays on 'the manta ray dive'. Sitting on the sandy bottom we craned our necks backwards as four graceful rays, each the size of a dining room table, winged silently overhead. Careful not to pollute the water column with bubbles, Katherine and I held our breath in awe at this out-of-world experience. Njari Island, our favourite reef near Gizo, was home to the spectacular 'Grand Central Station dive'. Njari had recently been purchased by Danny and Kerrie Kennedy, who operated the most successful dive shop in town. Corals of every colour could be found in just a couple of metres of water. Whenever a group of divers visited Njari, Kerrie would ask us if we wanted to join them to snorkel at the idyllic location. My favourite spot was a bombie of coral that supported hundreds of pastel-coloured fish that floated out from the coral like leaves in an autumn breeze. In deeper water, vivid yellow pipefish, aggregations of broody groupers, and menacing sharks and barracuda patrolled the reef edge.

Finally news came through from Isaac that we should be ready to depart for Tetepare at 9 a.m. the following morning. With packs and expectations bulging, Katherine and I reached the Gizo wharf at ten to nine. By ten o'clock I was becoming annoyed at voracious flies that were attacking the sores on my legs that had not healed since our Kolombangara climb. These persistent little orange-bummed bastards pushed their heads under my bandaids and into my sores like pig heads in a trough. In their twos and threes, squashed flies accumulated at my feet. By three o'clock I had long since tired of unsuccessfully willing the little purple crabs and primitive mudskipper fish to eat the black cane toad tadpoles that crowded the open drain near the wharf.

What we had been experiencing was not a series of unfortunate coincidences that had conspired to prevent us from reaching Tetepare for the previous three weeks, but indoctrination into 'Solomon time', a normal and predictably unpredictable aspect of Solomons' life. The Hon. Manasseh Sogavare, former PM and current leader of the opposition felt compelled to define Solomon Time in the national newspaper '. . . we are not traditionally limited or controlled by the dictates of time, rather by the achievement of the desired results. Although it may sound 'silly', a Solomon Islander considers himself in control of (his/her) time. According to our way of thinking, things continue to happen along the span of time irrespective of how long it takes.'

This relaxed outlook on time was not a recent phenomenon. Pedro Fernandez de Quiros, chief pilot for Mendana on his second voyage to the Solomons and then the leader of follow-up expedition in 1605 wrote, 'Do not judge the indians that inhabit these countries according to the honour of people here or to conceive of them as affected with the same desires, pleasures, necessities or estimation of things as we hold dear. What they care for is easy living in the world and passing each day with the least pain or perturbation.' Austin Coates, a British commentator of the 1960s, considered the Solomons to be the 'Atolls of eventlessness' and Solomon Time 'an expression of a populace adapted to the time dimension of stone as viewed by society experienced with the time dimension of metal'. Jared Diamond, the famous biogeographer and author, who conducted much of his fieldwork in the western Solomons, reckoned that societies in predictable tropical climates have historically not needed to plan. Fish, root vegetables and fruit were available all year round. This failure to anticipate, along with a cultural reluctance to admit that there may be a problem, conspired to promote 'Island Time' to an art form in the Solomons.

As Solomon Time decreed, just before we gave up, Isaac arrived and we boarded the robust FOT aluminium canoe as the western sky streaked with orange and red. A couple of hours later it became apparent we would stay at Munda that night. A sprawling collection of villages spread out along a coastal fringe. Munda had obviously once been a thriving tourism hub. International flights from Cairns arrived in less than the time it took for divers to take a boat out to the Great Barrier Reef, but the large Agnes Lodge hotel with its inviting open bar and wharves was now devoid of divers. The bird-watching tours were no longer operating, the local carver didn't carve and the hot bread shop wasn't. Isaac advised that we should purchase our supplies for a week on Tetepare from his little store that boasted luxury items like Milo and powdered milk as well as the staples of noodles, rice and tinned tuna. Further inexplicable distractions delayed our departure until mid-morning the following day. From Munda, Isaac steered us south-east through the Roviana lagoon to the islet of Kovu Kovu, where our guide for Tetepare was introduced to us. By his look of surprise, Keto's recruitment as a guide coincided with our introduction. Keto was a typically muscular man with a faded and cracked green plastic canoe. His mate had a 30 horsepower outboard motor, which like the canoe, had seen better days. We had assumed that we would be using the considerably safer FOT canoe to brave the open waters to Tetepare, but Isaac had other plans and promptly departed into the calm lagoon after introducing us to the chief, John Lau.

The chief looked older than anyone I had ever imagined. Dressed only in a *lava-lava* that draped from under his expansive belly, he clutched a tobacco purse and pipe that was dutifully filled by a young maiden hovering nearby. With our new-found guide acting as translator, John Lau claimed to be eighty-eight years old. He was an important Tetepare man, not only due to his status in the local community but because he had visited Tetepare many times and knew many of the remote island's stories. Since we would obviously not be able to find all of the animals on Tetepare during our short stay, this living relic presented a great opportunity to ask about Tetepare wildlife.

We were relieved when John Lau confirmed that *bukulu* lived on Tetepare. *Bukulu* are the prehensile-tailed skinks that were on top of my list of wildlife to see in the Solomons. Found nowhere else in the world and larger than any other skinks, *bukulu* are massive vegetarian lizards with amazing tails that enable them to hang, monkey style, from branches. In terms of uniqueness they were the equivalent of kangaroos to Australia and kiwis to New Zealand and a must-see for any wildlife enthusiast visiting the Solomons. Although Benae had claimed his boys could catch us one on Choiseul and several other guides assured us they could find them on other islands that we visited, we were yet to glimpse these prehistoric beasts.

After receiving the blessing of the chief, we assumed that we were all set to finally depart for Tetepare. Our bags and food were the only luggage in Keto's canoe. No-one said anything but our rapid familiarisation with Melanesian culture suggested that there was a problem. After we started loading the canoe, Keto appeared and suggested that the weather might be too rough. '*Tingting bilong mi, iutufala stap long Kovu Kovu tonaet.*' Arggghh! We could scarcely believe that we had to wait another night before finally reaching Tetepare.

Kovu Kovu islet was rimmed with tightly packed leaf houses perched over the water. Abluting again became an issue for Katherine, with no *smol haus* or secluded beach, nor any woman confident enough to offer direction. Keto showed us to a room in his house that had been hastily vacated by rolling up a couple of sleeping mats. Sunday school posters depicting bible readings of questionable relevance to Keto's daily life and a gaudy wool handicraft were the sole decorations in the otherwise barren room. Just as darkness set, an orange glow signified the arrival of a kerosene lantern and a plate of potatoes and noodles. We heard or saw no-one else until morning.

Keto departed at first light to collect two other guides. A shy bloke in his thirties, Eddie looked the most agile of the three men. Old John T presumably enjoyed his eating more than his hunting and I wondered what value he would be chasing reptiles on Tetepare. With the exception of the Buddha-like chief we had met the day before, John T's belly, which would not have looked out of place inside a truckie's blue singlet, was the match of any we had seen in the Solomons. This big jolly character, who sported a towelling rag tied around his head and a gappy mouth, clearly called the shots among the three men.

As we packed our cardboard boxes of food into Keto's little green canoe, John T checked that we had plenty of tea. We hadn't any. We soon learned that he was not called John T for nothing. Neither Katherine or I are tea or coffee drinkers but Isaac had assured us that the guides would drink Milo. But John T wasn't going anywhere without tea. He explained in rather expressive Pijin that Isaac did not keep tea in his store because he was SDA. For reasons that were unfathomable to both John T and us, Seventh Day Adventists are not permitted to drink tea. '*Iufala SDA?*' John T questioned. When I confessed that I was not SDA but just preferred Milo to tea, I was dubbed John Milo, a joke that was repeated for days.

Following yet another bloody delay to collect tea from another little store on another little island, we puttered off to the south. Keto weaved his canoe through a scatter of forested islands bordered by wave-cut limestone cliffs. Three weeks after we thought we were finally going to reach Tetepare and three days after our departure from Gizo we were finally on our way. Tetepare occupied much of the southern horizon as we left behind the islands of Roviana lagoon and headed out to the open sea.

2

THE LAST WILD ISLAND

'Whoaa!' exclaimed Katherine and I in unison as a huge sailfish jumped clean out of the water in front of us providing a thrilling omen to our long-awaited Tetepare adventure. White terns and black noddies swooped onto the bait fish the sailfish was chasing and evil-looking frigate birds wheeled around, looking for an opening to scab a fish from an unsuspecting tern. '*Bigfala fis*,' John T calmly announced, as if these monsters were an everyday occurrence in these waters. Before we had stopped marvelling at the massive fish and the avian activity surrounding it, the outboard started spluttering and then died altogether. We watched with intrigue, then apprehension, as Keto stripped a midrib from a coconut palm leaf that had been woven into an ingenious potato basket.

Ten minutes later, after unblocking the motor's water outlet with the custom-made cleaner and tugging enough times to crank-start a Tiger Moth, our little outboard spluttered into life amid a pall of blue smoke. We were on our way again. Slowly. Horsepower is a strange descriptor for an outboard motor's power. Any of thirty horses destined for a knacker's yard would have been able to drag our canoe faster on dry land. But horses are not built for dragging crowded leaking canoes through choppy seas. I figured that our motor generated 30-seahorse power instead. Tetepare wasn't getting any closer and trees and huts on the islands that we had left behind were still clearly visible.

Once we left the shelter of the Roviana Lagoon, irregular and increasingly violent waves buffeted our vulnerable vessel. Minutes earlier the radiant blue sky was punctuated only by an isolated dollop of mashed potato cloud forming above the peak of Mt Rendova. But blue turned rapidly to white, then grey. Within seconds the sun was obscured by a seething blackness, with alarming swirls of inky blue morphing through the storm clouds like spice stains in a simmering soup. The crack in the fibreglass seat opened up as the canoe flexed in the menacing grey waves, giving me an almighty 'horse bite' on the arse. Katherine had entered the trance-like state that she uses to counteract seasickness. Then the storm hit. Stinging cold rain pelted our faces and forced me to shut my eyes as if I was riding a motorbike through a locust swarm. Warm thick seawater slopped over us. Then the motor conked out again.

With my eyes shielded from the driving rain I could just make out Keto reaching for the coconut frond basket again in order to fashion another outlet cleaner. Through half-open eyes I could also make out John T and Eddie bailing out water with cut-off plastic bottles. Frantic is seldom an appropriate word to use in the Solomons, but the two men had adopted an unnatural and unsettling urgency. Only then did I realise that my feet and our packs were under water and the canoe was dangerously close to sinking. The top quarter of the waves were breaking into, or over, the canoe which was rapidly filling. I cupped water out of the canoe with my hands while splashing it out with my feet. Katherine inspected the inside of her knees.

Inexplicitly, the old war song 'It's a Long Way to Tipperary' invaded my mind and subconsciously morphed to 'a Long Way to Tetepare', which rhymed with the original destination. While Katherine suffered and Keto battled with the motor, I mindlessly splashed water out of our unstable bath to the tune and wondered whether the original lyrics ever saw the marchers reaching their distant destination.

Finally Keto got the engine started again and for five minutes we lurched through the storm. I had lost all sense of direction while we had been bobbing around, and assumed that Keto was simply trying to gather as much pace as possible to drain the canoe. The rain was driving straight down and waves seemed to be crashing on our small canoe from all directions. Then the outboard died again. Katherine did not once look up. She had reached the palliative state where *nothing* mattered. Without life jackets or any communication or navigational aids we would be totally stuffed when this canoe sank.

Right there and then I conceded that even if the storm abated and we managed to prevent the canoe from sinking, Katherine would never agree to attempt to reach Tetepare again. She was going through hell. The whole thing was a crazy idea; a risky, stupid pipedream. This was not in the script of our South Seas fantasies.

Keto eventually fired up the motor again while we all bailed like crazy. Minutes later the storm abated, and although the waves continued to crash into our little dinghy, the clouds cleared slightly. Amazingly the hazy outline of Tetepare remained straight in front. I had assumed that if we survived the storm Keto would have headed for home but he continued on. John T unravelled his towelling headband, wrung it out, wiped his face and then tied it back on his head again. Unless he did not share my opinion that we had just survived a near-death experience, John T's emotional control would serve him well as a poker player.

As we gradually closed in on Tetepare, the waves diminished, the sun peeked out from the billowing white clouds and life again looked rosy. Fortunately, before Katherine had regained contact with the outside world, we were approaching the calm lee of the island so the decision to continue rather than turning back into the open sea was easy.

The Tetepare forest overhung the shoreline like a verandah, shading the narrow beaches. Silly white cockatoos screeched above the canopy. A pair of brilliant beach kingfishers, sporting a hue of blue normally seen only in tropical postcards, were disturbed by our approach and darted off noisily along the shoreline. In my head I started compiling the bird inventory for Tetepare.

Keto steered the canoe over a shallow sandbank and into a river mouth. 'Raro River', we were told. The trees were enormous. My eyeballs strained as I searched the forest for critters. Admiring scenery is markedly different from prising the jungle apart for cryptic beasts. Our mission to document the wildlife of Tetepare had begun and I was determined to make the most of our time on the island. What rarities would we find on this island that had been shielded from the ravages of modern humanity? A pair of hornbills laboured past. Even one hundred metres away their powerful wing beats, reminiscent of a steam train, were clearly audible over the splutter of the outboard. As we puttered up the river a grey heron and diminutive blue and orange kingfisher slipped along the bank in front of us and disappeared behind a forested bend. Katherine had quickly recuperated and pointed to the telltale mudslide left by a crocodile down the riverbank. The Lonely Planet guide was correct.

Our idyllic cruise stopped where the river bank transformed from a tangle of vines to fern-clad cliffs with little waterfalls splashing noisily into the river. Once we could no longer traverse the shallow riffle of stream-covered boulders, Keto cut the engine and John T announced that we would camp just here. '*Yes, crocodile stop lo disfala ples*,' John T confirmed, without the slightest hint of apprehension. Why should we be concerned? After just surviving the storm on the high seas, a stray reptile was not going to prevent us from exploring the island we had waited so long to visit.

Eddie cleared a site for our little tent, deftly hacking through saplings with his bush knife. In doing so he carefully avoided the wild taro, a *kastom* plant of Tetepare. '*Sapos iu katim disfala lif, devil blong Tetepare baebae kilim man finis,*' he dutifully explained to us. Failure to respect this elephant-ear-like leaf would attract a curse from the spirits of the island, a risk that after fearing for our lives only hours ago we had no intention of taking. While we were still absorbing the significance of these leaves, Eddie tapped a small palm with the back of his knife, '*Deswan hea semsem, no katim.*' Wild betel nut was another *kastom* plant that should not be cut. To keep our tent clear of the mud we laid down a bed of leaves collected from Eddie's hacking, taking care to stomp down the sharp stakes left by his deft swipes. By the time we had our tent up, John T and Keto had fashioned their own shelter by stretching a plastic sheet over a couple of saplings cut from the bush. Four lengths of vine, or *bush rope* supported the whole structure.

The act of clearing our campsite had disturbed a match-sized grey skink with an orange eye. John T called the minute lizard *koko ziolo*, the 'suicide skink'. Historically, or in *taem bifoa*, warriors summoned courage by eating these skinks that were named for their hazardous propensity for running into cooking fires.

Our enthusiasm for catching and identifying the island's critters was not shared by our guides, who were far more interested in John T's attempts to boil the kettle for tea. I had hoped for nimble-footed, quick-handed guides but it appeared right from the outset that it would be up to Katherine and me to find and catch most of the critters.

Before John T had his kettle boiling the torrential rain started again almost dousing his fire. Unlike our guides, Katherine and I were relieved to have the drenching rain to rinse the salt from our hair and clothes. The rain also excited the frogs. John T informed us that the common frogs that were serenading us with their distinctive call of *cree cree cree* were called *kuni* in his Roviana language. Another frog gave a yapping call from among the leaf litter, and we soon confirmed that this poodle-sounding bark belonged to the spectacular horned frog. Darkness quickly engulfed the sodden campsite and we started searching for more frogs by torchlight. Eddie was amazed that we could walk straight up to a frog from twenty metres away when he could only detect them from a distance of about five metres with his excellent eyesight. Then we showed him. By holding his torch near his eyes, he too could see the orange glow of their eye shine in the darkness. A massive brown frog materialised behind a particularly impressive pair of glowing embers as I approached. To my disgust, the monster broke through my grasp and disappeared. Ten minutes later we found another but it leapt an astonishing three metres upstream in a single bound before we approached. The third one that we found an hour or so later was not going to escape. I dived on it and quickly grabbed one of its massive hind legs before it could break free from my hands. With outstretched legs and arms it measured nearly as long as my forearm, the biggest frog I had ever seen. We hoped that this monster would be the first of many special finds that would help us conserve the island by attracting the finances of aid donors and ecotourists alike.

The following morning we asked the boys to take us for a walk through the bush to locate big strangler figs, or *ambalolo*, which might harbour *bukulu*, the prehensile-tailed skink. Our experiences in Choiseul, Kolombangara and Marovo suggested that one reptile we were unlikely to just bump into in the course of a wander in the bush was this pièce de resistance of the Solomons' reptiles.

Ambalolos twine around huge trees, gradually engulfing them as their English name suggests. In the process these figs send down curtains of interlocking roots that form massive living pyramids. The top branches of these rainforest monsters penetrate the forest canopy as green cathedrals that teem with pigeons and parrots attracted to their bounty of fruits. Not only are these figs favourites for many birds, but the cavities in their tangle of roots provide ideal roosting spots for bats, cuscus and the prehensile-tailed skink that we were hoping to find.

John T explained through laboured puffing that the limestone escarpment at the summit of a hill near our campsite signified a *tabu* area, complete with old fortification and nut trees that had been planted by the previous inhabitants of the island. Before the regrowth that now smothered the site, the inhabitants would have had a commanding view of headhunters arriving from Roviana or Marovo lagoons.

On the way down the densely forested hill, the shy Keto did something remarkable. With lightning-fast reflexes he caught a juvenile green tree snake, a darting whip-like snake found throughout much of the Pacific. I was impressed that, unlike most indigenous people I had worked with, Keto was not afraid to catch it. His reaction to the next snake, a thicker yellowish specimen, was quite different. Having previously scanned the Solomons reptile book, which boasted only seven land snakes, I was confident that we had disturbed a *Salomonelaps*, possibly the most venomous land snake in the Solomons.

Bulldozer operators love bulldozing, fishermen love fishing, wildlife biologists love catching critters. I could not help myself and quickly caught the snake, using the thinly veiled justification of requiring a scale count to confirm its identity. Keto and the other boys recoiled with horror when I picked it up. '*Lukaot long tel, hemi foison,*' they screamed, alarmed that their naive visitor was about to be poisoned by the tail of the snake. '*Hemi oraet,*' I reassured them. '*Mi save long disfala snek,*' I lied. What I did *save*, or understand, was the blunt end, not the pointy end, of a snake requires particular attention. The snake proved to be docile in my hands and I was reassured that it didn't possess a strange poison gland in its tail.

The following morning we packed up camp and drifted back down the Raro River to its mouth, our bird watching hampered by misted-up binoculars. Right at the mouth we stopped at a garden the size of a couple of tennis courts planted with spinach-like slippery cabbage. The garden surprised us because Isaac had told us that Tetepare was a wild island completely free of gardens, with the exception of an overgrown coconut plantation on the western tip. A tree with small pink fruits called 'apples' took our eye and we asked if we could try some. This garden apparently belonged to a woman called Mary from Lokuru but we could help ourselves. The 'apples' tasted more like flowers than fruit and there were no seeds or core. The boys were obviously not too keen to hang around in Mary's garden any longer than necessary, although Katherine was keen to catch a rat that we had disturbed to determine if it was a native or introduced rodent.

Eddie steered the canoe out through the river mouth into the calm and idyllic sea that seemed to be apologising for the grief it had given us on the way over. We motored past a little atoll rimmed with white sand that looked like it had come adrift from a tourism brochure. 'Sarumana Island,' announced John T. After half an hour or so of travelling on mirror-calm seas, we rounded the eastern end of Tetepare, where three craggy limestone cliffs formed two deepwater bays. Heading back along the outer, or weather coast, the waves picked up and Katherine's enthusiasm for the speccy scenery quietened down proportionately. A pod of nearly a hundred small grey-and-white dolphins rushed over to greet us and distracted Katherine just before she sank back into her sea trance. The playful dolphins chaperoned us until we broke through a fringing reef and entered a shallow seagrass lagoon. Following John T's lead we made a camp on a narrow black-sand beach.

On the way back to camp from a nocturnal search after dinner we almost walked into a ginger-and-white cuscus, the size of a small cat with a long orange tail and short rounded ears. The Solomons' only marsupial was eating red fruit sprouting from the trunk of a tree at our head height. '*Manue*', we were told but we did not accept Keto's offer to catch it with his knife. Neither of us wanted the first wild cuscus that we had seen to end up in the pot. We also vowed not to make any comments about the limited gastronomic delights that we seemed destined for during the rest of the trip.

Dawn relieved me of another short damp sleep in our little tent. With binoculars in hand I headed off into the forest while Katherine attempted more sleep before the tent transformed into a sauna. The men were already squatting around the fire, their open-sided shelter not conducive to a morning lie-in. I was determined to identify the source of a plaintive, almost painful, tremolo I could hear.

The distinctive call came from a loose flock of small birds moving continuously through the trees. I followed the flock, gradually piecing together the appearance of its members from glimpses of different aspects. By the time I had identified the monarchs I found myself deep in the forest, away from the comforting coastal sounds that provide a direction reference. Fortunately the sun was rising and I could determine the direction to camp by observing the shadow cast by the trees. But I was in no hurry to return to a breakfast of watery Milo and potatoes. For the first time since we set foot on the island I stopped incessantly looking for new critters. Like I did underwater in Marovo, I transformed from a biologist into an awestruck hippy.

Being alone in a rainforest is humbling. The lowland plain where we were camped supported giant trees, far larger than we had seen at our first campsite. Thinking back to Benae's destroyed forest added to my appreciation of my surroundings. I had heard of 'tree-huggers' but had never before been emotionally transfixed by a forest. However, the compulsion to pay homage to these trees became overwhelming. After looking around to make sure that none of the blokes had followed me, I straddled the buttress roots of a giant tree and pressed my chest against it, my outstretched arms barely bent against the huge trunk. Looking up from my awkward face-plant, the trunk went up and up before being finally absorbed by its canopy thirty metres or more above my head. I transcended from walking in a forest to worshipping in a cathedral, the omnipresent buzz of cicadas became an ethereal organ, the dappled ever changing light of the sun filtering through the breezy canopy created a sublime fresco.

Everything seemed in perfect order, even the massive spongy log being consumed by ferns and fungi that had created a sunlit niche for dozens of adventurous saplings and three brilliant yellow butterflies. A massive orange leaf spiralled downwards before crashing noisily into a circular palm leaf which in turn sent a shower of interrupted raindrops to the forest floor. It did not matter, I concluded, what birds or lizards or frogs lived on Tetepare. This forest that had been spared from the chainsaw and bulldozer was special enough in its own right.

On return to camp Keto led me to another black-sand beach at a river mouth where he had just seen the tracks of a huge crocodile. From the other side of the river it looked like a tractor had driven out of the waves. Keto glanced around nervously, so did I. This croc had to be the size of a Tyrannosaurus. Nervously we waded through the shallow stream and up onto the ploughed-up beach. But hold on . . . something looked wrong with the tracks. Then it dawned on me.

'*Hemi no crocodile, diswan hemi bigfala turtle,*' I guessed, trying to convince myself that we had not stumbled on a record-breaking crocodile. To my relief, Keto studied the tracks more closely and agreed. These were not from a crocodile but a giant turtle. I lay down in its tracks that were wider than I was tall. Following the tracks up the beach without apprehension we flushed a large goanna digging a hole. *Regu*, the spirit lizard of Tetepare, had excavated the eggs of this giant. They were huge, far larger than the ping-pong ball size of standard turtle eggs. I raced back and got Katherine, excited that leatherbacks, the world's largest and one of the most endangered turtles, nested on Tetepare.

Our main quest on Tetepare remained the *bukulu*, the giant prehensile skink. On our fifth night of searching, Katherine finally spotted one hanging by its tail only ten metres above her head. Although not in a strangler fig as we expected, the *bukulu* was chomping on the huge vine leaves that we had been told were their main diet. Keto expertly climbed the post-like trunk and caught the massive skink as it retreated a further five metres up the tree. When he returned to the ground with the *bukulu* we could not establish if he was more concerned about the bleeding bite on his hand or the spontaneous excited jig that I had started with Katherine.

Bukulu resembled a big docile blue-tongue lizard, with grey and black flecks on its greenish body and tail. The *bukulu* held me firmly with its long tail curled around my arm and its sharp cat-like claws sliced into my wrists. It was an honour to be scratched by such a phenomenal and increasingly rare lizard. Even in unlogged areas, these unique reptiles have been targeted by the pet trade. In 1989 alone, one of the last years of reliable information, four thousand were exported from the Solomons as pets.

I really wanted to visit the western end of the island to search for reptiles through piles of discarded coconut husks at the small old coconut plantation. Unfortunately the boys were not keen. Apparently that end of the island was the haunt of the Lokuru people and a combination of respect and fear ensured that we would not get close with our Roviana guides. We did not want to strain relations with the Lokuru mob, who were apparently the enemy of the Friends of Tetepare.

Instead we shifted camp to the Kupa area at the eastern tip of the island. A canoe left by pig hunters had been pulled up into the river mouth in a sheltered bay. A couple of hours after we arrived, the hunters returned with an assortment of skinny scarred dogs. They were carrying five pigs, trussed up with vines, to take back to Marovo lagoon for a feast. The dogs inadvertently spooked a nightjar, which flew off from the leaf-strewn upper beach with erratic, moth-like wing beats, revealing its white wing spot. Despite the proximity of the dogs the bird circled close by, so after the dogs and pigs had departed I went back to investigate. A newly hatched chick was perfectly camouflaged in the fallen leaves. We had heard about the Solomon's nightjars, believed by some ornithologists to be a rare endemic species. Tetepare, with few cats and only the stray hunters' dog, could well be a valuable refuge for this ground-nesting species. For the first time since we met him John T was coy when I asked for the nightjar's local name. Eventually he confided that they were called *opopotae*, meaning 'covering its shit', because of the hunched way that they sit on the ground.

The longer Katherine and I spent on Tetepare the more convinced we became of the conservation value of this historic Ark. Although the escalating inventory of critters excited us, what we did not find was as important as what we recorded. We were relieved to see neither sign of water hyacinth nor the poisonous cane toads that are steadily taking over the islands of the Pacific, causing havoc to native frogs and other animals in their wake. We wondered how long Tetepare would remain the near-pristine backwater that made it the 'next great battleground' for conservationists. With only two days left on our three month tourist visa we returned to Nusa Hope, then Munda, then Gizo, then Honiara.

Tetepare Tug-of-War

Before concluding our Solomons adventure we decided to call in on Peter Siloko in Honiara. Peter was a founding member of Friends of Tetepare and according to Isaac had been at the forefront of the opposition to the 1995 logging proposal. I expected to meet an overtly passionate crusader, a flashy-eyed table thumper. But I was mistaken. A quietly spoken, deliberate and well-groomed man, Peter did not seem to have the aggression to take on the might of loggers or their big man supporters. Then we met his wife. Sara had recently changed jobs from being the national Save the Children representative to coordinating English volunteer workers in the country. Being an ex-English volunteer herself she was ideally suited to the role. Her angular shoulders and expressive mouth belied a no-nonsense attitude to wrongdoers.

Peter was a Tetepare landowner with an encyclopedic knowledge of the history and deep sense of responsibility for his island. The determined glint in Sara's eyes left us in no doubt that she too had been thoroughly embroiled by the spell of Tetepare and had helped to inspire and coordinate the fledgling conservation group. Together they made a formidable team.

Hours of tandem dialogue from the pair informed Katherine and me about the phenomenal history and perilous state of the island that we had just visited. Their stories filled gaps in the Tetepare picture that we had compiled from Isaac's draft conservation strategy and mouldy files of court transcripts and ex-plantation managers journals in the WWF office. The key to Tetepare's uniqueness and allure was the reason that the island had been deserted and remains uninhabited today.

Peter ascribed 'the exodus' to a sickness which ravaged his ancestors soon after the arrival of white traders. The Tetepare tribe could well have suffered the same fate as other indigenous people after first contact with Westerners and their diseases. Whalers from London, Sydney and New York plied the waters of the Solomons from the 1820s to the 1860s chasing the once plentiful sperm whale. After the whalers came the bêche-de-mer and turtle shell traders. Either the whalers or the early traders may have exposed the locals to new diseases for which they had no tolerance. European rats and their fleas may have also introduced plague and typhus. Poor hygiene and inter-island raids quickly spread the fatal diseases.

Peter acknowledged that other descendants blamed the fire from the sea. Kavachi, the submarine volcano that has emerged from the waters countless times in recent history to the south-east of Tetepare, may have also contributed to the exodus. Volcanoes have a bad reputation for wiping out civilisations. Unlike the spectacular eruptions that buried Pompei and Rabaul, many people killed by volcanic eruptions die from famines and diseases caused by volcanic aerosols. Maybe gases from Kavachi poisoned or choked the Tetepare people or their crops?

'But why hasn't Tetepare been recolonised in the past 150 years,' I probed?

Peter explained that the spirits of Tetepare are still very strong. Each time a recolonisation attempt failed, stories of vengeful spirits were reinforced when survivors of these Tetepare journeys returned to their adopted villages on neighbouring islands. No matter what the cause or causes of the diaspora, the spirits prevented recolonisation and ensured that Tetepare remains a living museum.

The famous singing dogs of Honiara were midway through their third or fourth chorus and Katherine had retired to bed but I was transfixed by Peter's story telling. Many of his stories revolved around his great-great-great-uncle Kido who hailed from a chiefly Tetepare line. Unlike most of the landholders who fled to Rendova, Kido relocated to Ngatokae Island in the extreme south of Marovo lagoon. About forty years after he fled Tetepare, Kido heard via regional 'coconut news' that his island had been sold by Lokuru people. He paddled his canoe past Tetepare to Rendova to meet with Chief Kevu, who recognised his distant cousin's rights to Tetepare. But it was too late.

Tetepare had recently become part of the newly formed British protectorate of the Solomon Islands. A fledgling missionary outpost at nearby Munda had opened up the once hostile region for white settlers. Soon afterwards the colonists became interested in the island with fertile lowlands and few apparent hindrances to development. The threat of Tetepare's spirits were either not known or revered by the Europeans.

Part of the island was purchased in 1907 by Burns Philp, a north Queensland trading company, for conversion into a coconut plantation. The Tetepare descendants in Lokuru had nothing to lose by selling their haunted island to crazy white men whose enterprise would also surely be thwarted by the spirits. Two Lokuru men, Kodo and Hidi, agreed to take the traders' coins. Kodo was the grandson of Sifu, the last woman to leave Tetepare and hence considered that he had as much right as anyone to the £100 loot. Woodford, the Commissioner for the fledgling colony, recommended the bargain sale as he attempted to attract foreign investment, although his boss doubted whether the price was adequate. Peter's ancestor Kido and the High Commissioner were not the only ones concerned about the sale. Chief Kevu of Lokuru was also unhappy with the deal although Kodo tried to appease his chief by presenting him an umbrella from the traders.

Chief Kevu's father, Ngame, had been one of the great leaders, or *mbangaras*, of Tetepare at the time that the island was deserted. Also a powerful *mbangara*, feared in many villages for his headhunting exploits, Kevu ruled during a period of great change. After witnessing the teachings of the pioneering missionary John Goldie, Kevu preferred the life preached of peace, medicine and schools to the violence that he had grown up with. Kevu abandoned his war canoe and was baptised as Adam. This first Christian chief of the region arranged for his people to gather a thousand coconuts and shell money to pay for the Church to send a missionary to his new village at Rano, just across the water from Tetepare. Kevu was not only concerned that Tetepare had been sold cheaply by Kodo and Hidi but also that his ability to fundraise for the church would be hampered by the forfeiture of much of his customary land.

My notebook was now cluttered with almost illegible four-letter names as I scrawled in the dark, following the flow of Peter's stories. He effortlessly recounted each of his ancestors from Kido down to himself, and explained where the other members of Friends of Tetepare fitted into Tetepare lineages. These descendants were custodians of a myriad of fascinating stories that confirmed their relationship to and ownership of Tetepare. Many of Peter's stories apparently merged the exploits of mythical and historical legends. But I was not to write them down and promised not to repeat them for fear that non-descendants would use these stories to reinforce bogus claims to the island. Peter's storying was relentless, he was in a groove like a well-rehearsed marathon runner and I suspected he could continue all night and the following day. Eventually I had to retire once his Tetepare anthology caught up to Isaac's briefing and the historical records that I had sourced.

The following morning over a breakfast of pawpaw and pineapple, Peter and Sara continued their dialogue. Of immediate concern was the lease of the abandoned Tetepare coconut plantation even though it only occupied 3% of the island. The current unpaid lease should have terminated long before. When it did the plantation would revert to crown land, and the Merusu oil palm plantation provided an ominous example of its potential fate. 'Any kind of big development on the old plantation will spoil the rest of Tetepare,' argued Peter convincingly. But since their relationship with WWF had soured, Friends of Tetepare had no funds or coordination to apply for the lease. Sara implored us to help. 'It sounds like WWF owes you a few favours,' she said, 'Maybe you will have better luck than us?'

We were not initially convinced that their proposed FOT ecolodge was in Tetepare's best interests. Maybe Tetepare had survived the challenges thrown at it for the previous fifty years because it was simply too difficult to develop? Maybe attracting tourists and workers would precipitate resettlement that could ultimately ruin Tetepare's unique status. But from what we had learned those scenarios did not ring true. With Solomon Islands' skyrocketing population, overworked gardens, shrinking forests and plummeting economy, the large uninhabited island was sure to become increasingly attractive to pro-development descendants. Outboard motors had bought the once remote island much closer and the hold of the spirits over the younger people was weakening.

Katherine reminded me of Simon Foale's warning about Tetepare's land ownership being so complicated that any project was doomed. But visions of government plantations and resettlement schemes assaulted our imaginations. Could Tetepare be used to house Middle Eastern asylum seekers, who were being billeted out by Australia to South Pacific nations in exchange for much sought after cash? Even if they were nominally restricted to the old plantation, the implications for the island would be catastrophic. Gardens would be hacked out of the forest, cats and cane toads would almost definitely follow resettlement and the turtle nesting beaches and refuges for coconut crabs and marine resources could be ruined. The Solomon Islands, and the world, would lose their last wild island.

Katherine and I decided right then on our mattress in Peter and Sara's spare bedroom to follow our hearts and not our heads.

Innocence Lost

The Solomon Islands soon become newsworthy of their own accord back home in Australia. Previously only reported in passing during coverage of the unsuccessful war of independence in adjacent Bougainville, the once peaceful little backwater nation now headlined the evening news. There was trouble in paradise. Three weeks after a well-documented coup in Fiji, the Solomon Islands followed suit.

Years of frustration boiled over after Guadalcanal landowners grew tired of the industrious colonists from the Solomons' most populous island of Malaita taking over their land, their jobs and their government. The Guale had not been compensated for land alienated by British colonial rulers for building Honiara and the large oil palm plantation on its outskirts. Militant Guale forced Malaitans out from the capital and surrounding plantations. In a rapidly evolving feud, the Guadalcanal Revolutionary Army changed its name to the more politically astute Isatabu Freedom Movement but their heavy-handed tactics remained unchanged.

The Malaitans did not take being evicted from their houses and jobs lightly. Many had been living and working in Honiara for several generations. Even if this wasn't their land it was their home. Ever since the first days of British rule, and especially since World War II, Malaitans had fought to have their unique customs and rules respected by the Solomons administrators.

More than any other ethnic group in this diverse archipelago, Malaitans had dominated national politics and industry and had no intention of being chased out from the Solomons' capital. The Malaita Eagle Force rapidly gained recruits and firepower from the Malaitan-dominated national police force. Allegations of murder, beatings and property destruction were rife as the two ethnic groups drew their battle lines.

Prime Minister Bart Ulufa'alu was a worried man. Ulufa'alu, a Malaitan, had tried in vain to weed out the institutionalised corruption that had drained his nation's finances and resources. Without recognised party structures or transparent policies, the national government was composed of an evolving kaleidoscope of allegiances. Ulufa'alu's task of squashing corruption inevitably placed him in conflict with some of the parliamentary members upon whom he relied for support. He could not do it alone.

Recognising the pressure cooker developing in his country, the embattled Prime Minister turned to Australia for assistance in preventing the predicted uprising. His request received the cold shoulder. Solomon Islanders felt that Australia was too preoccupied with its peacekeeping in East Timor, and distracted by the recent military coup in Fiji, to come to the assistance of its poor little north-eastern neighbour. Had the international community intervened and allowed Ulufa'alu to enforce tighter regulations on logging, fishing and industry, the Solomons may have got back on track. These finances could have helped the Guales' and Malaitans' requests for compensation. Instead the situation got worse; much worse.

On 5 June 2000, the former 'Hapi Isles' formally lost their innocence. Under the direction of Andrew Nori, the Malaita Eagle Force stormed into the national parliament and took Bart Ulufa'alu hostage. The feeble democracy that began twenty-two years earlier abruptly folded. Under the guise of restoring democracy the Malaita Eagle Force scheduled parliamentary 'elections' for the following week. With Ulufa'alu still held at gunpoint and his supporters intimidated not to vote, Manasseh Sogavare, was elected as Prime Minister.

Coincidentally, June 2000 was also the month that Katherine and I had booked our return flights to attempt to kick-start the Tetepare project. The overthrow of the government precipitated increased lawlessness and violence by both the Malaitans and the Guale. Not surprisingly, most of the country's major industries closed down. Of greatest consequence to us, the only international airport in the country closed.

Despite approximately two hundred deaths, opinions varied as to whether the 'ethnic tension' that had been reported during our earlier visit had escalated to 'localised unrest' around Honiara or full-blown 'civil war'. These definitions became important when our travel insurance refused to reimburse our flight costs because they deemed that Honiara's airport had been closed due to 'an act of war'. We argued unsuccessfully that the Solomons were experiencing 'civil unrest', an issue covered in the fine print. However, the international travel advice warning against visiting the Solomons and the evacuation of expatriates from the country weighed against our claim.

A peace agreement, brokered in Townsville four months after the coup, conferred a weapons amnesty and a means for compensation to be paid to displaced Malaitans. Rather than providing a solution, this agreement precipitated further troubles. Compensation had traditionally circumvented the deadly cycle of payback retaliation by a victim's *wantoks* following a wrong deed. Payment of *kastom* money, jewellery or pigs as compensation, sometimes simultaneously by both aggrieved parties, maintained their honour while preventing an escalation of violence. Malaitans were more enthusiastic users of compensation than most other ethnic groups, and Solomon dollars had become their currency of choice. Instead of signifying a truce, compensation became a weapon. Several young Romeos had confided to me in Gizo that they feared flirting with a Malaitan girl because her brothers or uncles might demand compensation. Setting up a pretty young niece was not their only means of generating compensation income.

The new government was quickly bankrupted through paying out compensation claims to their Malaitan supporters who had been removed from their Guadalcanal homes or businesses. Export sales crashed by 80 per cent, and international aid, the other mainstay of the economy, declined by nearly as much as donors shied away from providing funds that were being siphoned off for unaudited compensation. With no pay, public servants stopped showing up for work.

Compensation was not the only Melanesian idiosyncrasy crippling the nation. Ironically the strong kin bonds that alleviated the need for social security and old folks' homes were diametrically opposed to the capitalistic and legal system that the Solomon Islands inherited from the British. Solomon Islanders share their possessions and unselfishly devote their time and favours to *wantoks*. *Wantok* favours still usually take precedence over government-imposed laws, placing police, customs officials and politicians in a bind. Many police defected or protected their *wantoks* in militant groups. Those remaining were powerless against the heavily armed gangs that profited from the lawlessness. The Solomons were in an economic and security tailspin.

A third tenet of pre-colonial Solomons society that challenged the very roots of their new democracy was the 'big man' system. Politicians and other big men, who were either convicted criminals or simply renowned shonksters, were consistently re-elected because their *wantoks* respected their position of power rather than their performance. A person's ability to acquire, display and redistribute wealth is the basis of being a big man in Melanesia; the source of the funds is less important. While compensation, *wantok* loyalty and big men controlled politics and policing, Solomon Islands democracy, along with the conservation of Tetepare, seemed doomed.

Caution or rational objectivity are not the hallmarks of a bankrupt government. In the mayhem following the coup, the new improved Timber Rights Agreement and Benae's compensation case that we had prepared were thrown out of court, providing open slather to international loggers. A Malaysian logging company took advantage of the 100 per cent government export duty exemption to clear-fell nineteen million dollars worth of timber under the guise of establishing the Merusu oil palm plantation, despite scientific and social advice to the contrary. A desperate government was likely to further push back the limits of inappropriate developments. It was sure to be only a matter of time before development of Tetepare was on the drawing board again.

We waited anxiously for news. There was no response to our emails from Seri or Isaac at WWF. Intermittent contact with Sara Siloko in Honiara confirmed that the situation was bad, but fortunately her family was safe. Eventually, Henderson Airport reopened. Against the advice of the Australian embassy we booked our flights to the Solomons. Tetepare needed our best shot before it was too late.

Solomon Airlines had recommenced twice-weekly flights from Brisbane to Honiara but the schedules were far from reassuring. The date for our flight changed twice in the two weeks before our departure. We were even more concerned about the disarray of the Solomons when we were informed that the currency had been frozen and we were not able to draw Solomon dollars from the foreign exchange booths in either Brisbane or Honiara. With no local currency, no confirmed return flight and no idea whether any Tetepare descendants were still interested in saving Tetepare from its seemingly inevitable fate, our mood upon arrival in Honiara was more apprehensive than when we had first visited as honeymooners eighteen months earlier.

Central Honiara did not look like a war zone. There were no destroyed buildings, bomb craters or gun-toting security forces. The footpaths still crawled with pedestrians as our taxi weaved around the ever present muddy potholes. Despite its peaceful appearance we quickly learned that the residents were frustrated and frightened by the breakdown in law and order. '*No gud iufala wokabaot long naitaem,*' we were warned by the receptionist at the King Solomon Hotel, where we managed to change some money. '*Emi no safe long naitaem nao.*' A disgruntled worker at the Solomon Airlines office explained, '*Kolosap everi dei mi lukim car blong mifala.*' Her car, along with many others, had been taken by thieves, who drove around town with arrogant impunity, knowing that the police would not apprehend them. With a fistful of Solomon dollars and a hastily arranged plane ticket to Gizo, Katherine and I left Honiara before we ran into any of the criminals who were controlling the town.

Flying low over Marovo Lagoon, the square red scar where the loggers had already started clear-felling, for the Merusu oil palm plantation insulted the dark-green forest. Our plane kept getting lower and it quickly became apparent we were to make an unscheduled stop at Seghe. I searched for other landmarks. Uepi Island, our wonderful honeymoon resort, resembled a giant green hammerhead shark out of our right window. I could just make out through the left window the bent dumbbell shape of Matikuri Island where we had based our reef surveys. Just before we landed the hazy outline of Tetepare became visible to the south. We were back.

Under the spreading tree by the Seghe airport shed I noticed Pita, the brother of Benjamin from Matikuri. Pita operated a resthouse at Seghe and recognised us from an earlier visit. '*Iu go lo wea?*' he enquired. 'Gizo,' I replied. 'Ah,' he replied with laughter in his expressive eyes, '*Cheapest buttons lo Solomons stap long Gizo distaem.*' My surprised look at his unexpected statement was the response Pita had been fishing for. He chomped again on his betel nut, shifted his position into the shade and proceeded to *story* in classic Solomons style. Pita explained that gun-toting Bougainvilleans had just stormed the Gizo police station in retribution for the killing of one of their number. Upon hearing the approaching gunshots, the unarmed police scattered like frightened rats and in order to mingle with the townsfolk they ripped their uniforms off, which accounted for Pita's jibe about the availability of cheap buttons in Gizo.

I was confused. The tension was between Malaitans and Guale. What were the infamous Bougainvilleans doing in Gizo? Pita explained, '*Staka pipol frait no gud Malaita takim islands lo West.*' The rich and peaceful islands of the Western Province were under threat from the heavily armed Malaita Eagles, who were setting the political agenda for the country. The Bougainville Revolutionary Army had entered the fray as self-enforced security guards for their friends in the west. The coconut news reported that the BRA had already made their presence felt by disposing of a few outspoken Malaitans. However some of the Bougies felt that they should be better compensated for their 'voluntary' efforts. Strutting around Gizo with big guns and without the anticipated fight, the Bougies became bored, causing more problems than they were worth.

Ethnic unrest had spoiled not only tourism, on which Pita and his brother Ben's livelihoods depended, but had eventually closed the Taiyo cannery that produces tinned tuna for domestic and export markets from the Western Province port of Noro. Westerners had had enough. Some Munda boys had reconstituted old guns and ammunition dumped from World War II to defend themselves against the expected attack by the Malaitans.

Pita lowered his voice, '*Olketa man lo Malaita save come lo West and maritim women blong mifala.*' Marriage gave Malaitans land rights that then allowed them to resettle their *wantoks* and their *kastoms* to Marovo. This was obviously not only a political issue, but was also stimulating grievances at village level. Enough was enough. Pita confided that his Marovo *wantoks* were prepared to fight too.

In Gizo I bumped into Patson, my mild-mannered canoe driving friend, and quizzed him about the ethnic unrest. I was shocked when he equated the Malaitans to Hitler's Nazis. 'Malaitans have always been different,' Patson explained. Originally they respected other cultures but now they considered themselves superior. Tensions between the Western Province and Malaitans hailed back to independence. The pro-independence push had been spearheaded by Malaitans, some of whom had developed their own taxes and laws to challenge British authority. Their wishes came true when the global push against colonialism coincided with World War II, demoting Britain from being the world's largest creditor nation to the world's largest debtor. Yet the Western Province had shunned independence that was celebrated by every other province on 7 July 1978 for fear that the Malaitans would dominate their politics and drain their resources. Talk on the street was that a Western breakaway was now back on the agenda.

Being a staunch Jehovah's Witness and part Malaitan himself, Patson quickly clarified that all Malaitans were not the same, but that the militants and criminals had given them a bad name. The diplomatic and stately Premier of the Western Province, Reuben Lilo, also publicly announced that any Malaitans wishing to remain peacefully were invited to stay, but not everyone was so accommodating. 'They should all go back to Malaita and leave Guadalcanal and the Western Province alone,' was the sentiment of many, obviously frustrated at the effects of the tension on their own lives. The ethnic tussle had become more and more complicated. Displaced Gilbertese vowed to help their landlords in the west. But the PNG-based Spear group, itching for a tussle with their archenemies from Bougainville, sided with the Malaitans.

Gizo, the capital of the Western Province and the hub of the national tourism industry, cowered in the face of developing troubles. Plane and ferry schedules were in disarray and town electricity generators frequently shut down because the government could not afford fuel payments. Even phone lines to many national politicians and senior bureaucrats had been cut because their bills had not been paid. The country had stalled.

The local women's group bravely invited the armed young Bougainvilleans to a meeting. Katherine and I were too scared to attend but we quickly saw the results. One after another the women had stood up and repeated the same compassionate plea. 'We are all *wantoks*. We are mothers like your mothers. Your mothers are far away but we can help you. When you frighten us and our children you are hurting your *wantoks*. Please go back home to your mothers.' Grown men, who hours earlier had strutted menacingly through town with their guns, wept on their adopted mothers' shoulders. These strong women showed that Melanesian culture was the solution as well as the cause of the nation's problems. They had achieved what the police, the politicians and the other 'big men' couldn't. Within days, the last of the Bougies had left town, the Gilbertese concentrated once again on their fishing and dancing, and the pulse of Gizo reverted to its languid pace.

The WWF project on Tetepare had been aborted. It was too hard. Half-finished draft reports, a scattered assortment of radios and an aluminium canoe were all that remained. Our hopes that we could offer assistance to the Tetepare program were dashed. Friends of Tetepare now had no funding to continue their work. With Isaac now off the scene our chances of getting out to Tetepare seemed even more problematic than last time. By phone from Honiara, Peter Siloko recommended that we try to find Mary Bea, who would hold the key to convincing the people of Rendova to conserve Tetepare.

Mary, together with her father, Harry, had been in the frontline supporting the conservation of the island at the Timber Rights hearing. Peter confirmed that she was the same Mary who had a garden on Tetepare. She had a house in Lokuru and was a *wantok* of several TOLOA members including Danny Philips, the federal politician who had been the instigator of the most recent logging proposal.

Eventually we contacted Mary by an intricate Pacific grapevine of radio messages. She agreed to take us to Tetepare in about a week's time. There was a glimmer of hope but we remembered our previous ordeal getting to Tetepare and also Simon Foale's reservations about the project, and did not allow ourselves to get too excited. We had taken leave from work and flown over here to kick arse, and a wasted 'week or so', especially one blown out by Solomon time, was not on our agenda. Instead of holiday dives and picnics at Gizo, we offered to repeat the oil palm marine survey for WWF. Although we no longer naively assumed that repercussions from proven damages could reduce the inevitable environmental damages, we figured revisiting Marovo would enable us to consult more widely with Tetepare descendants.

Since our last visit to Marovo, WWF had also run short of funds and had laid off most of their field staff, including Perry and Glin, who had helped with the initial survey. The Ngevella River near Merusu bled Milo-coloured water as eroded soil from the clear-felled forest deposited onto the Marovo reefs. On three consecutive days I couldn't see my outstretched hand in the muddied sea. Secchi depths that had averaged about twelve metres close to the river mouth prior to the clearing were now closer to twelve centimetres. So polluted were the waters that we did not even bother donning our masks and snorkels, presumably to the chagrin of the local crocodiles.

Back at our favourite Matikuri guesthouse, Benjamin explained how the problems in Honiara had affected Marovo. Most of the other ecolodges had closed through lack of tourists. Many young people who had been working, or simply hanging around in Honiara, fled back to their villages during the 'tension'. Without strong ties to their land and accustomed to luxuries like motorised canoes and videos, these evacuees were easy targets for logging companies. Although Ben's Rodo tribe had already said no to logging several years before, more of the villagers had supported recent offers. Other villages deprived of tourism had been enticed by seemingly generous offers from the opportunistic logging companies.

Not only did large-scale logging spell more bad news for Marovo lagoon, it dealt a devastating blow for WWF. They had invested time and resources educating entire villages about the perils of logging and assisting them in developing alternative resource development plans. But these same villagers had 'fallen' to the loggers. Within months of receiving their pre-logging down payment, the kids had wasted their money at the local shops, the villages were littered with rubbish, the gardens had been neglected and the landowners were demanding their next payment to enable them to continue their new-found lifestyle.

Fortunately it was not only the logging companies that capitalised on the unrest. We were delighted to hear that Benae, armed with our logging report and the court's interim ruling that they were liable for millions of dollars of compensation, had fronted the logging company at their Choiseul headquarters. Since the loggers were unwilling or unable to pay this compensation, Benae's boys marched in and confiscated tug boats, trucks and chainsaws. A bulldozer, which symbolised the destruction of their cultural sites, was driven into the sea. Fuel was distributed among the locals for free and the company was forced to close down their operations in Choiseul. The tenacious and righteous army of little David's eventually wounded the big Goliath.

This rare good-news story could not overshadow the overriding pressures on the Solomons' splendour we had grown to love. Live fish exporters had also moved into Marovo, offering miserable prices for coral trout caught by villagers who were becoming increasingly desperate for cash. The Merusu oil palm plantation had been the final death knell for the New Zealand-funded World Heritage plans for Marovo. We worried about how long the isolated few conservation-minded members of Friends of Tetepare could keep the wolves at bay.

Arghhhh! Katherine and I were so frustrated. Like other 'green' Westerners we could plead and explain and campaign all we liked but from our comfortable lifestyle we were essentially asking Solomon Islanders not to make the same 'mistakes' that our society had made. Like WWF, we were advising locals to relinquish the perceived advantages of development. But who were we to say that they should not try to earn an outboard motor, a generator to power a light, or an education for their kids?

Paying for conservation is contentious. Ideally landowners should look after their land and reefs because they see value in conserving their resources. WWF, Greenpeace and other NGOs concentrated on education, awareness and the buzz concept of 'capacity building' to achieve the conservation outcome that their international donors expected. But unfortunately this worthy approach had failed. Solomon Islanders, like the traditional Aborigines that we worked with in the Australian desert, placed no greater importance on preventing an animal or plant from becoming extinct than they did on obtaining their next meal or stick of tobacco. Extinction, like evolution, biodiversity and conservation are words of fat Westerners who shop in supermarkets. The awareness that the islanders craved was how they could augment their lifestyle with outboard motors, kung-fu movies, chicken cheeseys, school fees and Western medicine.

Another lesson we had learned from Simon Foale was that 'Everyone has an agenda.' Our task was to merge our agenda with those of the Tetepare landowners. Conservation of Tetepare depended upon providing education, medicine and consumables in villages around the province. Attracting finances was of immediate importance. Like the Marovo locals, Tetepare descendants were bound to become disillusioned with workshops and plans if they received no income.

Ecotourism alone would not sustain Tetepare landowners to the degree that logging was perceived to. Due to its isolation Tetepare would be even less viable than the recently demised ecolodges in prime locations in Marovo. But maybe the research station could attract scientists who could help raise the profile of the conservation effort. By establishing a field station-cum-ecolodge we could buy Tetepare a couple of years, by which time, hopefully, the law and order issues would be resolved and tourists and international donors would return to assist.

Peter and Sara Siloko fleshed out the plan. They suggested that Katherine and I should manage the Tetepare project. But we remained resolutely opposed. The first thing I learned about

Melanesian conservation initiatives was that landholders should own them. Under our management Tetepare would be another example of the plethora of *waetfala* initiatives that had eventually failed in the Solomons. Tetepare would only be conserved if the project was embraced by the locals. Peter was equally as adamant. It would only work if outsiders managed the project, at least initially.

None of these plans had any future unless they were supported by the Tetepare landholders in Lokuru, who had most to lose from any conservation strategy. Mary was our key.

Lokuru Connection

Everyone in Munda knew Mary Bea. The two old ladies talking outside a house, the teenage boys riding their bikes and the proprietor of a ramshackle roadside stall all pointed down the road. Our backpacks, filled with snorkelling and camping equipment, became heavier with every step. Sweat trickled down our faces and arms as we negotiated muddy puddles and squashed cane toads on the flower-lined road out of town. Eventually we found the half-painted house on tall stilts, a couple of kilometres from the airport. A young man with an impressive smile confirmed that we had reached Mary's place. We were ushered into a low hexagonal leaf house that served as a church and meeting hall while the smiling man sauntered off to find Mary.

We waited apprehensively. Mary was a founding member of Friends of Tetepare and considered by the Silokos to be integral to galvanising the Lokuru descendants behind the conservation agenda. Yet Isaac had been reluctant to introduce us and Keto and John T had been decidedly nervous about visiting Mary's garden on Tetepare. A generously proportioned and very dark woman in an old red dress strode into the leaf house. Magenta orchids poked erratically from her tight black curls, in a compromise between decoration and non-conformity. Although outwardly reserved,

Mary's eyes burned with a confidence atypical of Solomon women, particularly when meeting *waetfelas*. She held out her hand to us respectfully and, seemingly suppressing an instinct to smile, maintained a somewhat distanced demeanor. In complete contrast, a bare-chested old man with a rag tied around his knee followed her in and offered his hand and beaming grin with an animated '*Leana*.' This man was not suppressing any emotions.

Ever since reading the transcript of the timber rights hearing I had wanted to meet the old man who had stood up to Danny Philips and the other would-be loggers. A scraggly white beard framed Harry Bea's gap-toothed smile. His darting mischievous eyes, muscular arms and torso shamed most men half his age. 'I learn to speak English with Americans in the war,' Harry explained, making it clear to both Mary and me that he did not need an interpreter. I complimented Mary on what good English both she and her father spoke. Harry interrupted, 'I was a teacher most of my life and my daughter attended secondary school in Honiara.'

'Peter Siloko and Isaac Molia have told us how important you both were in opposing the logging of Tetepare,' I offered. Mary nodded without elaborating so I tried a different tack aimed straight at Mary. 'And they said that you were the best person to take us to Tetepare to find out what types of animals live on the island.'

'Tetepare has many kinds of special plants and animals,' Mary conceded, 'and I can take you there tomorrow but you will have to pay two guides as well.'

'That's fantastic, *tangio tumas*,' Katherine I chorused spontaneously, relieved that we were not destined for another Isaac-type wait to revisit the island.

'Do you have a canoe and outboard?' I questioned.

'Twomey has a canoe,' Mary stated, nodding her head towards another man who had slipped into the room and stood at the back without introduction. He was much paler than both Mary and Harry. Only the next day did we learn that this unassuming but powerfully built part-Malaitan man was Mary's husband, Twomey. After our first near-death trip to Tetepare, Katherine in particular was keen that we leave early before the inevitable afternoon thunderstorms.

'We will leave very early' Mary announced, leaning forward to hold Katherine's hand reassuringly.

'If you give me money for fuel and food now I will organise everything'. As we extracted bundles of $50 notes, Mary barked instructions at Twomey, then the smiling man, who both promptly departed, leaving us alone with Mary and Harry.

We were unsure whether Mary knew that Peter Siloko had urged us to assist with the conservation plans for Tetepare, or how she would respond to our involvement. We met under the pretence that she would escort us to complete our wildlife survey of Tetepare. However, our main objective was to suss out Mary and gain her confidence. Were our dreams of helping her dreams of saving Tetepare realistic? How would Mary and her Lokuru *wantoks* respond to the plan that we had developed from the preliminary Friends of Tetepare draft management plan?

Mary was clearly not willing to open up at our first meeting, so we diverted the conversation to old Harry, who needed little prompting to drag me around by the hand, showing me his potato garden and the houses of several of his children and cousins that were spaced throughout the family's land. Mary's siblings were clearly divided into body shapes resembling Harry's leanness and those like Mary with fuller figures.

One of Mary's large sisters brought a tray of rice, potatoes and noodles. We had assumed that we would be walking back to eat and sleep at a Munda resthouse but Mary would have nothing of it. After dinner and an amicable interrogation by old Harry, we were ushered into a bare room in Mary's tall house on stilts. Old pages from a fashion magazine pinned to the walls suggested that we had been assigned to a daughters' bedroom, even though we had not met any children. When we questioned Mary, she brushed off our concerns. 'Domu and Neri will sleep somewhere else,' she stated, as if it was an everyday occurrence that complete strangers would usurp her teenage daughters' bedroom.

The following morning, after breakfast of potatoes and noodles with Harry, we loaded our gear into Twomey's canoe for our second trip to Tetepare. Nearly an hour after passing two small villages on the north coast of Rendova we reached Lokuru. To our surprise, Lokuru wasn't a single village, but a collection of settlements that occupied several kilometres of shoreline. Twomey waited offshore for an imperceptible break in the waves, and then gunned the outboard, propelling us up onto the steep pebbly beach. Several locals had already gathered to check us out. We followed Mary's lead in jumping overboard into knee-deep water and then dragging the canoe up the beach before the next wave swamped us. Local men grabbed round logs to help skid the canoe up the beach in a series of *'Tufi, ehri, hiye, go, go, go'* manoeuvres. Apparently I had not pushed hard enough because the next surge was initiated by 'One, two, tree, go, go, go.'

The rounded pebbles underfoot were nearly as black as the inky locals who congregated around our canoe. Dozens of kids wearing an assortment of clothes in various states of disrepair gathered to watch our every move. Without showing any sign of emotion or engaging in small talk with anyone in the village, Mary marched around the scattering of leaf houses, organising guides and the essential basket of long pink potatoes for our week-long visit. In time it seemed like the whole village had come to meet us under a shady tree where we were both brought a refreshing green coconut to drink. Mary eventually returned with several women carrying vegetables and two lads who were to be our guides. A dozen of our newly made friends helped us to skid Twomey's canoe back down the steep black beach and out into the waves.

We again headed south towards Tetepare. By now the long low island occupied most of the horizon. To the east we could see the mouth of the Raro River where we had camped on the first night of our previous visit. As we approached Tetepare I was staggered at how the western end of the island resembled a giant crocodile's head. Indeed the whole island looked more like a massive crocodile than its namesake, a fighting pig. Rava Point, the southern tip of Rendova, also looked like a crocodile, squaring off against Tetepare like its people had done for centuries.

Unlike the sheltered northern coast, the southern or weather coast took the full brunt of the trade winds from the Solomon Sea. Although Twomey had landed on wave-beaten beaches since he was old enough to sit in a canoe, he was nervous about Qeuru beach where Mary had decided to camp. We puttered up and down one hundred metres offshore, the four local experts debating the merits of suitable landing strategies in their distinctive Lokuru language. Eventually, just as Katherine's sea stomach was threatening to overcome her excitement at revisiting Tetepare, Twomey gunned the canoe for the black beach.

The two guides, to whom we had still not been introduced, jumped out although it was impossible to gauge the depth due to the black sand and white water churned up by the two-metre waves. As soon as they evacuated a monster wave broke over us, washing Mary and Katherine overboard. Pots, potatoes and bags floated in the white water. The next wave crashed into our little canoe, pushing us perilously close to a jagged black rock that protruded intermittently from the angry sea like a massive decayed tooth. With the aid of a stray saucepan I bailed rapidly, still unsure whether our canoe was floating or not. Twomey also valiantly splashed water and stray potatoes overboard as he tried desperately to restart the outboard motor.

Mary and Katherine floated to shore and washed up on the coarse black-sand beach. No-one would know that we were shipwrecked for weeks. Life jackets, spare engine parts, tools and communication links that were prerequisites for this kind of travel in Australia were unheard of over here. I usually found the absence of regulations liberating but right now, in the washing machine of Qeuru beach, I appreciated their value.

Eventually Twomey started the outboard and retreated beyond the breakers as we rhythmically splashed the water out of our salty bath. A stowaway leapt overboard. On the beach, Katherine and Mary stared in amazement as the sodden rat easily swam the thirty metres to shore, ran up the beach and leapt into the forest. My joke to Twomey about our grim fate if the rats had jumped ship was either lost in the translation or in the roar of the waves.

Our second landing attempt was aided by the removal of much of the weight from the canoe. We beached the canoe and rapidly skidded it up the beach on driftwood logs and into a shallow river mouth. All of our luggage was then dunked into the fresh cold water to rinse off the salt.

Upon noticing the guides shaving their tobacco sticks with their bush knives, a habit she apparently abhorred, Mary announced, 'This is Suero, this is Eli. They will help you dry your *calico*.' Both Suero and Eli were Lokuru lads in their mid-twenties but had wildly differing personalities. Eli was introverted and sullen. We were never really sure if he was lazy or just exhibited a pathological lack of confidence. By contrast Suero was a clown. He had a cupid tattoo over his heart, a fish tattooed on one arm and a coconut palm on the other. His closely cropped hairstyle was moulded upwards like a Bobby's police hat. With flashing teeth and bulging expressive eyes, Suero made a joke of every task and every story and in doing so often avoided doing any work at all.

The swamping of our canoe sparked his humour and he re-enacted the whole event in exaggerated detail. Suero dived onto the sand as Mary and Katherine were washed off the canoe and flung handfuls of sand around to imitate Twomey and me frantically bailing the canoe. Flailing around with closed eyes he captured the futile search for fishing lines and pots that had been washed overboard. Only the addition of a long tail and whiskers could have improved Suero's comical rendition of the rat swimming to shore. He then repeated the performance from Mary's perspective, then from Katherine's and finally from mine, each time to increasing yelps of laughter from everyone except Eli and Mary. I immediately liked Suero and decided that if he was indicative of the Lokuru people, we were going to have an entertaining time working with them.

Before Suero had finished his antics, Mary reinforced that she was running the show. This time she barked at Suero to select a place for us to set up our sogalogged little tent on the vines that delineated the reach of high tide. As she pointed in different directions her hefty upper arms flapped like squabbling seagulls under her gaping singlet. She was stern and gruff, a reluctant hostess and a nagging wife. Mary then instructed Twomey and Eli to drape their plastic sheet over two sapling trunks cut by their huge bush knives from the forest to provide both a relatively dry kitchen and sleeping quarters for the foursome.

After we spread our clothes on the baking black sand beach to dry we disturbed a large goanna. This *kastom* animal, called *sosi* in the Touo language of Lokuru, had exhumed a turtle nest and rubbery slithers of white shell were scattered over the hot black sand. Next to a large broken egg was a perfectly formed, yet recently killed black embryo with white pearly ridges down its back. This was clearly a leatherback turtle, the same species that had left the huge tractor tracks on the beach on our first trip to Tetepare. Mary confirmed that this Qeuru beach was their main nesting beach on Tetepare, yet *staka* leatherbacks nested on the beach at Baniata, on the weather coast of Rendova. I was elated that the Tetepare region could provide one of the last strongholds of this incredibly ancient and rare species in the Pacific.

Our first full day and evening on the island were devoted to recording as many types of birds, reptiles and frogs as possible. Kept on a short rope by Mary, Suero was apparently on his best behaviour, restricting his theatrical urges to mimicking birds or frogs we were seeking. Whenever I heard an unfamiliar call I would point in the general direction and Suero, who never seemed to be paying attention, would instinctively mimic the noise. Twomey would invariably point high into the canopy, where he had seen, or suspected the mystery animal was hiding. One call had me bamboozled for over an hour. Suero was adamant that the loud cackle we heard once but that he was repeating with gusto was the call of a snake. I was equally adamant that in general snakes do not vocalise. Maybe we had heard the last gasp of a frog that had been seized by a snake, but we were never able to solve that mystery.

On the second night we tried ascending the steep cliff behind the beach to search for *bukasi*. Afternoon rain had turned the muddy slope into an obstacle course that I slipped down clumsily, bashing my leg against a tree. Mary noticed my discomfort in walking and offered to treat my injury with *kastom* medicine in the form of a hot *boi* leaf. More so than the treatment, I felt most relief that for the first time she was softening her stance towards us. While Mary massaged my leg with the scalding leaf, we sat around the fire telling stories. Our new friends were intrigued by the wildlife of the desert where we lived and were surprised, but not shocked, that we regularly ate kangaroo meat. Mary was also particularly interested in the Australian Aborigines. 'Do they live in the bush or in the cities with the *waetfalas*?' 'What do they eat?' 'Do they own their own land and their own houses?' Mary's line of questioning brought home the marked difference in lifestyles of most Australian Aborigines and Islanders. Living on their customary land and growing or hunting their own food, Mary and her *wantoks* enjoyed a far better standard of living than the largely displaced, welfare-dependent indigenous residents of the 'lucky' country.

Most of the stories around the massage 'table' were not about Australia but about Tetepare and Lokuru. The main storyteller was, of course, Suero. He loved sharing yarns accompanied by hilarious skits that suggested his talents were wasted working for a logging operation on Rendova. Suero told us about his grandfather Kodo, the man who sold Tetepare to the traders nearly a century earlier. Apparently one of the coins from the sale had been placed with Kodo's skull at Difango, not far from where we were camped. Without any trace of reverence, Suero imitated the appearance of his grandfather's massive skull with one of the most impressive acts of facial distortion I have ever witnessed.

Our favourite story was the one about the Korean boatman who fell overboard and drowned near Lokuru. According to Korean custom the deceased's workmates eased him into the afterlife by preparing an offering of copious quantities of food and beer. In true Tetepare style, Suero considered it a pity to waste the smorgasbord so he sat down with the corpse all night and gluttonised. '*Mifala spaka tumas an ful tumas,*' Suero explained as he rolled around on the ground with cheeks puffed like a drunken fat man. Then the story reached even greater heights. Because he worked with the Koreans and was a particularly savvy individual, Suero understood that anyone paying respect to the deceased logger would be rewarded. Although his mischievous gluttony had blown his chances, Suero coerced his mates to walk up to the coffin with their heads bowed. As he had promised, they earned themselves a handful of coins from the appreciative Korean mourners.

Mary had by now totally abandoned her pious pose and was revealing the other aspect of her personality. Her scowl was replaced by sparkling eyes and a smile straight out of toothpaste commercial. Mary's transformation affected the ambience of our little party, after forty-eight tense hours of shadow-boxing we all felt at ease. Clearly amused and proud of Suero's antics, her uninhibited convulsions of laughter encouraged her young friend to even greater elaborations. Every time Suero told a story, Mary, then Twomey, repeated it and with each repetition the story somehow became funnier.

A croaking screech interrupted the *storying*. 'Gooray,' announced Mary to my impending question. I pulled out my notebook and she spelt out QORE. Like P&F and X&J, the letters G&Q were apparently interchangeable in the *Touo* vocabulary of southern Rendova. Mary told us that when they cry at night, like this one had just done, locals tell the *qore*, or night heron to go to their garden to make it fertile. Suero contributed another invaluable fact. *Qore* puts its arse in the water to attract fish, which it then catches by spinning around and jabbing them with its beak. He sprung to his feet and demonstrated this novel fishing technique, to howls of laughter from all of us.

Sensing our interest in birds and their calls, more stories flowed. When *tito*, the crested hawk, calls at night Suero knew that rain would come. Based on my initial experiences on Tetepare, *tito* had the easiest weather forecasting job in the world. Twomey offered that another bird, known in Lokuru as *barughana*, shrieks at night when someone has died. Mary also spoke Roviana language and explained that the same bird, known as *kukuaranga buko*, translates to 'squeal like a pig.' No-one could accurately describe this bird for me, although they believed that it never lands.

Two days later we left Qeuru beach for the calm northern coastline of Tetepare where we set our tents up on a sandbar at the mouth of the small Erava River. Four days of rice and potatoes had worn thin for us all. We fished *men-style* by trolling a lure behind the canoe on a handline. Every few minutes Twomey eased off the throttle at the same instant that Suero commenced hauling armfuls of coarse fishing line onto his feet. Mary would guess '*mamula*', 'kingfish' or 'rainbow' before Suero pulled in four plate-sized trevally and a monster barracuda. Mary then instructed Twomey to land at a narrow beach. 'Slippery cabbage,' Mary announced as she slashed her way determinedly through the beachside vegetation and disappeared into the bush.

'*Gaden stap long hia?*' I enquired of Twomey, knowing that slippery cabbage only grew where it had been planted. '*Gaden blong Mary*,' he replied matter-of-factly.

We followed the slashed trail and found Mary plucking an armful of green cabbage leaves from her garden that was rapidly being consumed by the forest. '*Wae nao iu wakim gaden long Tetepare wea hemi fa tumas from Munda?*' I enquired, eager to learn why Mary would go to the trouble of making a garden so far from her home. Mary laughed off my question, 'Oh it's just a little something, just for slippery cabbage.' But she did not make eye contact. Despite yearning to be wooed by her candor, I guessed Mary's garden was not a little something at all, but I let the matter drop. Not until several years later did I learn the real significance of the now overgrown clearing on the Tetepare shore.

While searching high in an *ambalolo* tree for a *bukasi*, Suero yelped excitedly and flung his arms out. He had found a cuscus and before it could bite him the terrified creature was pulled from its hollow by the tail and flung twenty metres down to the forest floor where it landed with a hollow thud. Alarmed, Katherine and I ran over to the bundle of apricot-coloured fur that concealed a flat face framing huge round eyes. At first we thought the prostrate cuscus had died but apart from losing a couple of claws it was very much alive and demonstrably annoyed by its treatment. As I held the hissing marsupial by its strong prehensile tail a heated argument erupted in two languages.

Mary and Eli wanted to eat the cuscus and Suero, who maintained a colourful dialogue while hastily descending the tree toward his prize, left us in no doubt that he too had culinary aspirations. Twomey was a Seventh Day Adventist and his church had decreed that along with scaleless fish, crustaceans and turtles, cuscus were not to be eaten. He supported Katherine, who was adamant about releasing it. I was torn. I had no problems with catching and eating fish or coconut crab, so why should this furred creature be any different? Nor did I want Mary to think that we were fundamentalist emotional conservationists who would represent more trouble than we were worth. I handed the cuscus to Suero. Eventually intense argument in Touo language saw the possum released and Mary sulking for some hours afterwards. We got the impression that Mary seldom lost an argument and Twomey later confided that after his religious objection had failed to gain traction he told her that Katherine would cry if the cuscus was killed.

Our Erava campsite work plan followed the same pattern as before. We searched for reptiles and birds during the day and geckoes, frogs and *bukasi* at night. While alone in the forest one night Katherine and I both turned our torches off. So intense was the darkness under the impenetrable canopy that I needed to squat down for fear of losing balance. Even after giving our eyes several minutes to adjust to the darkness, we could not see our own hands, let alone each other. One feeble green luminescence, from a fungi, was all I could see. Gradually, like stars in the evening sky, more and more fungi appeared, in patches and lines through the forest. An orange cluster defined a log, which when I inched over to it and poked with my finger, disintegrated like a wet sponge cake.

Abstract shafts of light announced the gradual arrival of Suero's torch. When he spotted us squatting in the dark Suero dived to the ground and peppered us with rattling machine-gun fire accompanied by oriental profanities. Once his laughter had subsided Suero explained that we must be Japs because they too had walked through this rainforest without torches. His uncles had strapped the green fungi we were admiring to their calves so that they could recognise and locate each other at night. Suero also brought good news. He had disturbed a *bukasi* on a '*mighty ambulolo*' and was confident that he could catch it by daylight.

The next day, while cutting a trail to the big strangler fig where Suero had seen the *bukasi*, I felt compelled to lie down on the forest floor. My hips and shoulders had been pile-driven into the ground but my head and legs were floating. Even stretching my legs out straight became difficult and I had to bend my knees to stabilise myself. As I did so sweat trickled down my legs.

After twenty minutes' rest I stumbled back to our little green-and-brown tent while Katherine continued the walk. With a bit of a rest I anticipated I would be OK to check the *ambalolos* at night for *bukasi*, but by the time Katherine returned, my burning fever had switched to a cold sweat. I could barely sit up in the tent and our sheets and thermorests were soaked in sweat. My scrawled diary note read 'I feel as weak as overcooked spaghetti.' Hoping the fever would quickly abate and eager not to reduce our chances of finding rare wildlife we did not tell anyone else. Eventually, Katherine consulted Mary a day later when I struggled to sit up. Mary had no doubt. 'He's got malaria.'

For the first time I had travelled overseas without taking the malarial prophylactic Doxycycline. Because we anticipated spending extended periods in the Solomons, I was concerned about taking an antibiotic for many months at a time. This was the first time I had relied on the less effective drugs Chloroquin and Paludrin. As I lay on my drenched mat I thought back to biology lessons where we learned about the *Plasmodium* parasite that causes malaria. I vaguely recollected that the parasite was released in bursts, which explained why I felt OK, albeit listless at times, and then a few hours later I was sucked to the ground with drifting fever spells.

I cursed the malaria and relayed my frustration to Mary at being bedridden after trying to get back to Tetepare for nearly eighteen months. Although she had never contracted malaria, Mary understood the symptoms and predicted my condition perfectly. She told me that I should take four Chloroquin tablets, instead of the usual one, daily for three days. I would continue to experience fever flushes that would gradually improve until the third day when I would feel terrible. Then I would be OK. She had no doubt about that. That evening Mary relayed that many people had tried to live on Tetepare since the island was vacated several generations ago. Most had become sick because they had defied the rules of the island's spirits. She was remorseful and apologetic that she had not properly explained to the spirits the purpose of our visit and asked them for our protection. I blamed the Paludrin, Mary blamed herself and Katherine blamed the early evenings in the WWF office in Gizo where the disease-infested *Anopheles* mosquito had probably bitten me. I would not have contracted malaria on Tetepare because I had only been here for five days and the symptoms take over a week to develop. In any case there were unlikely to be any malaria-carrying mossies on the uninhabited island as the disease needs a human host.

As I lay prostrate in a tent for a couple of days sweating like a fat man in a sauna, I had ample time to contemplate. I had joined elite company. Many early pontiffs refused to live in Rome due to the prevalence of malaria there, and the exploits of both Alexander the Great and Genghis Khan were undone by the malaria scourge. As recently as 1942, half of the Greek population was infected by malaria, and as little as a century ago, development on New York's Staten Island and the initial attempts to complete the Panama Canal were thwarted by malaria. Had it not been for malaria, colonists would have populated and pillaged the tropics to a far greater extent. On the bright side, I reckoned that were it not for the blood parasites that had relegated my body to an aching jelly, Tetepare would probably not have persisted as the backwater that it remains today.

Mary decided that we would shift camp to Tavara, where Tetepare's main copra drier and coconut plantation manager's house had stood. Rusty tractors, the remains of three generations of copra driers in increasing states of disrepair, old bottles, foundations of workers' quarters and underground tanks were hidden in the regrowth. Tavara supposedly remained the headquarters of the Voseleai copra operation on Tetepare but visitors from Lokuru had pilfered most of the iron and anything else of value. Suero and Eli had helped themselves to the last of the hessian copra bags to use as sleeping mats. The concrete and iron frame of a toilet still perched out over the bay but now it was occupied by an old man goanna, who enjoyed his basking site.

Twomey purposefully slashed a path through the regrowth to the crumbling manager's house. Making the most of a brief respite from my fever, I followed him.

'*Haus blong Mr. Hodge*,' he announced.

Roy Gilmour Hodge had been granted a sixty-nine-year lease for the Tetepare plantation in 1970. However, he was not destined to last even a quarter of that period. About a decade had elapsed since the last original Tetepare descendant had died and Tetepare started to be visited by more and more fishers and hunters from Rendova and Viru, who were becoming increasingly brazen about the lack of retribution by Tetepare spirits. These recalcitrant landowners interfered with the smooth operation of the plantation. To compound matters, Hodge was accused of holding Guadalcanalese and Malaitan workers against their will.

Bullet holes in the door and window attest to the time that Mr Hodge had fired warning shots to quash a revolt by his workers. Suero slunk up to the window then jumped up and threw himself backwards, landing with a thump and a mournful groan. His impromptu recreation of the events took Twomey by surprise, possibly because the gravity of the memory was greater for him since his Malaitan grandfather and father had worked on this plantation. Earlier plantation managers had not been as accommodating as Mr Hodge. Twomey informed us that on quiet nights in the overgrown plantation you could still hear gunshots representing the ghosts of workers shot by belligerent colonialists for not following orders. Early managers were renowned for belting recalcitrant workers with canes. A desperate pioneering Tetepare labourer by the name of Batini Bosuri described the predicament of his fellow indentured workers, who endured beatings, being forced to work on their Sabbath and a shortage of food: 'We want to beat the overseer but our teacher says we don't beat because we belong to God now.'

Following acquisition from the Lokuru men, Burns Philp had set about clearing the coastal lowlands on the western tip of Tetepare. The value of Tetepare's timber was not lost on the Australian traders. In July 1908, Burns Philp's manager Walter Lucas described the planned plantation site as supporting 'Thousands of fine trees forty to eighty feet high, girth ten to eighteen feet growing within a few hundred yards of the coast.' Eventually Burns Philp decided against logging Tetepare mainly due to opposition from Australian timber firms, who discouraged the importation of foreign timber that would affect their home markets. Instead, workers from eastern Solomons were recruited for the laborious task of clearing and burning the forest.

Pagan bush Malaitans, like Batini, made up the bulk of the labourers on the plantation. These men had not experienced the same access to European traders as villagers from the Western Province, nor had they learned the prerequisite Pijin required for more stimulating work. Although they were admired by the Europeans for their working ability, Malaitans were ostracised by many other Solomon Islanders as being unpredictable and aggressive bushmen. Groups of Kwaio and Kwara'ae men from Malaita, along with other workers from Guadalcanal, were encouraged to compete against each other to be the quickest to clear their assigned blocks. Together with their conflicting customs this competitive environment incited many fights among the indentured workers.

Clearing the massive strangler figs, or *ambalolo*, from the plantation area proved to be the most difficult and dangerous task. The men first chopped a path into the centre of the root mass and then worked their way out to the edges. After several days of work the *ambalolo* would finally be felled. One entire group of nine workers was killed when the *ambalolo* they were working inside collapsed unexpectedly. For every ten labourers brought to the Tetepare plantation one would not live to see the end of his two-year term. Yet by 1918, Batini and his disgruntled co-workers had planted 51,784 coconut palms on the westernmost three per cent of the island and a built a base near Lake Tavara where ships could anchor in a deep sheltered bay.

Although not as dangerous as clearing the forest, harvesting copra was also laborious. In the same way that his grandfather and father had before him, Twomey had also been assigned to allotments of the Tetepare plantation to collect piles of fallen coconuts. They prised off the husks using a sharp stake, cracked the nuts with their bush knives and extracted the meat from the split coconuts. Sacks of coconut meat were hauled by hand to the shore. These heavy bags, like the ones now used as bedding by Suero and Eli, were then taken by canoe to the nearest of six copra driers within the plantation. Continual fires dried and lightened the flesh, leaving behind the oil-rich copra for soap manufacture.

Copra yield gradually increased as the coconut palms matured. Seventy workers tended the plantation, collecting the coconuts, drying the copra and looking after the cattle and pigs that grazed under the palms. Within twenty years Tetepare had become one of Burns Philp's most productive plantations. Three hundred tonnes of copra were dehusked, cracked, scraped, dragged, loaded, dried and exported each year. But the good times did not last. Even the remote outpost of Tetepare was affected by World War II.

Burns Philp abandoned the Tetepare plantation in 1942 when the Japanese invasion was imminent. After taking as many cattle and pigs as they could handle, the Japanese trashed the buildings and fences. Pigs and cattle that avoided capture fled into the forest. The cattle did not survive for long because of the lack of grass in the mature forest and the rapidly overgrowing plantation. But the pigs thrived in the rainforest. Interbreeding of these pigs with the smaller wild pigs explains the large size and variety of colours in today's Tetepare pig population.

Tetepare was more than simply a temporary pork supply for the Japanese. The war was fought on, above and around the deserted island. An American warplane engine still sits on the reef on the weather coast of Tetepare, although its wings and tail have now been pounded away by the waves. The pilot made his way to Rendova and was then taken by locals to the US base there. Several Japanese ships were sunk in the passage between Tetepare and Rendova. Mary informed us that Lokuru residents still remembered the massive ships being bombed by American planes before burning fiercely and sinking, smothering the local beaches with oil and debris.

Burns Philp decided against returning to Tetepare, or their other plantations, when the British government failed to grant war damage compensation. Instead, the British Crown purchased the plantation lease for £10,000 with the intention of resettling villagers from Rennell and Bellona Islands who would be displaced if the bauxite and phosphate deposits on their islands were mined. Although mining did not proceed on Rennell or Bellona, Tetepare was subsequently regarded as a logical resettlement location for Gilbertese who were being moved from their overcrowded Kiribati islands in the 1960s. When they learned of the proposed settlement Tetepare landowners effectively thwarted these plans and the Gilbertese were resettled at Wagina, Ghizo and the Shortland Islands instead.

Over the next three decades a procession of expatriate managers, culminating with Mr Hodge, operated the plantation but were not able to achieve prewar production figures because the entire plantation had not been recleared. A fall in copra prices precipitated the end of Hodge's tenure. Once again, in 1978, Tetepare was uninhabited. But this temporary reprieve was destined to be short-lived. A succession of managers from Lokuru, then their neighbours from Ughele, attempted to manage the plantation profitably, yet the state of our current campsite at the plantation headquarters attested to the failure of these ventures.

Suero told us that crocodiles lived in the nearby lake so we rather nervously tiptoed to its muddy edge and followed the guide's lead in climbing a low tree. Within seconds Suero enticed a crocodile to surface by yelping like a crazed dog. The crocodile looked to be a couple of metres long but we were told that a huge crocodile with three legs also lived in the lake.

Katherine and the others went for a two-hour walk out of the plantation and up into the forest while I sweated out another bout of fever. She returned boasting about hearing and then seeing one of my favourite birds. Golden whistlers are striking birds with the rare combination of an arrestingly melodic song and brilliant plumage. The golden whistlers on Tetepare were super special because the famous avian biogeographer Jared Diamond reckoned they were a distinct subspecies from those found elsewhere in the

Solomons or Australia. Suero had masterfully imitated its call to attract the whistler down from the rainforest canopy.

Slowly and gently we broached the idea of the conservation plan with Mary. In marked contrast to the cavalier attitude with which she directed proceedings at our camps, Mary was cautious and noncommittal. Maybe she had seen these ideas too many times without any results. Maybe she second-guessed our motivation for being involved. Of most concern was that maybe Mary resented our interference or had other plans for Tetepare. As if to bury the discussion on the future of Tetepare, Mary announced that she was going out fishing 'woman-style' to catch our dinner. We had been treated to more great trevally, kingfish and barracuda that the boys had caught trolling between our campsites but Mary preferred the smaller, sweeter reef fish that she caught with hermit crab bait on a hook.

With Mary and Twomey away, Suero reverted to Eli's work ethic as they both took the opportunity to relax with cigarettes of shaved tobacco rolled up in the lined pages of a school exercise book. But my fever had temporarily abated and Katherine was anxious to explore. Failing to motivate the guides, we set off alone. Not far from the crumbling copra driers the trail had become overgrown. Undeterred, Katherine took the lead and forged into the regenerating jungle. Even though I was following, the spider webs that she walked under wrapped around my face and the barbed wait-a-while palms ripped at my legs. I mumbled to Katherine, who was a couple of paces ahead of me, that I wished we had a bush knife. Almost immediately she jumped back towards me with a terrified expression on her face. What was wrong? A monster centipede or a charging wild pig? Instinctively I turned to run as well but she stopped me in my tracks with a panicked scream. Now she was slapping and clawing at her legs while hopping around like a burns victim.

Katherine had walked into an infamous stinging plant, although we did not recognise the plant or know if there were more around. On several occasions Benae, John T and Mary had pointed out stinging plants to us but every time they looked different. Some had narrow serrated leaves, others were broader and shaped like a teardrop. I remembered the antidote leaf for the stinging plant was the same leaf that was chewed with betel nut. Looking around frantically while Katherine continued to scream in pain was useless. To my untrained eyes I had as much chance of picking another stinging plant as the cure. 'Let's go back to the camp, Suero can find it for us,' I suggested. But Katherine wasn't listening. Absorbed by the pain she ran off blindly through the bush. As I nervously followed her intentions became clear. She was heading for the beach and ran straight into the sea, boots and all. The salt water provided enough relief to calm her down and return to camp.

Although disappointed at our first solo exploration, we were even more convinced of the need for guides and maintained trails if we were to attract scientists and tourists to Tetepare. While Suero collected Katherine leaves to ease her pain, Mary administered another leaf, called *bihuya*, to soothe my sore throat that had suffered from several days of cold sweats. The cure was worse than the symptom! *Bihuya* made a strong Fisherman's Friend lozenge seem as innocuous as a Lifesaver.

The following morning almost did not eventuate. Neither Katherine nor I had slept much, if at all. She had been sponging me with a wet towel and fanning me with our bird guide. Later she told me that she could feel my heat radiating through the tent as she approached to come to bed. I could barely move. This third morning of treatment was worse than the original fever bout I had endured. Katherine reported on my condition to Mary. 'See I told you that the third day would be the worst,' she replied knowingly. Mary's matter-of-factness did not make me feel any better. The sweet smell of burning fish bones and coconuts on the fire made me nauseous. For the first time in memory I couldn't stomach breakfast. Poor Katherine had to pack our backpacks and sodden tent alone. I slept for the hour-long boat trip back to

Lokuru on top of our bags in the sealed nose of the canoe despite the stifling heat and jarring bumps each time we crested a wave.

While I drifted in and out of a fever-ridden sleep under a leaf verandah in Lokuru, Mary hastily arranged for the big men of TOLOA to attend a meeting with her rival FOT group of Tetepare landowners. Although she had conceded nothing to us, we assumed that Mary had gained sufficient confidence to sanction a joint meeting to determine whether either or both groups were keen to adopt our proposed conservation plan.

An indeterminate time later we left for Munda, where Katherine and I checked into the quaint little Sunflower resthouse. As Mary had predicted, my fever had somewhat abated the following morning but upon Katherine's insistence I visited the dilapidated hospital to seek professional medical guidance. A large, somewhat disinterested doctor prescribed Quinine tablets for three days, despite the fact that the Chloroquin was bringing the fever under control.

After a couple of days of quinine my ears were ringing like a swarm of miniature cicadas had invaded my cranium and I was as listless as I had been at the height of the malarial surges. Mary came to visit to inform us that the meeting between the rival Tetepare landowner groups would be held the following day. Upon hearing that I was taking quinine, Mary frowned. 'That stupid Dr Panadol,' she cussed. 'You don't need quinine. That will make you feel worse. Your medicine is already working'. Huffing and puffing like a dejected four-year-old, she confiscated my new tablets. True to her word, by the following morning my head had cleared. Mary's manifestation of compassion reminded me of a story she had told us on the island when we quizzed her about her unlikely days as an air hostess. 'One time,' she reminisced, a *spaka* man had mouthed a sly remark to her, and then touched her as she squeezed down the aisle. Mary spun around and pointed at him with her finger. 'Shut up,' she yelled, and apparently he did. Mary didn't last much longer as a hostie.

Mary intercepted the TOLOA men from Lokuru before they reached our guesthouse, which they had selected as the location for the pivotal meeting. She spoke at length with them, particularly a short man in a loud unbuttoned orange shirt and reflecto glasses. Whoever this dude was I was going to remember him. Eventually he extracted himself from Mary's lecture and strode up to where we were making small talk with the other men. Tilting his head slightly askew he paused to ensure that everyone was listening. 'Mr Jack Daniel' he announced grinning while exaggeratingly shaking my hand. Falling into line behind Jack was a bearded man of similar stature but opposite demeanor. Through deep-set concerned eyes framed under a protruding furrowed brow he announced quietly, 'Seda ... Henry Seda.'

Jack had been involved in logging operations on Rendova and was the Chairman of TOLOA. A mischievous midget, Jack had given the impression that he had not concentrated on what Mary was saying, and was not interested in holding a serious meeting about the future of Tetepare. However, he surprised us. Waving a copy of the draft conservation proposal at us, the unlikely leader displayed his support with a flashing grin and an exuberant 'Very nice.'

Jack gestured me away from the others. Through an intensely beetle-nut stained grin, he frankly admitted that on previous occasions when TOLOA had managed projects like this that much of the loans and all of the profits had gone down his and his mates' throats. Assuming an unconvincing seriousness, Jack proposed that if the groups decided on supporting 'their' Tetepare project, then we should manage it. Despite being thrilled at Jack's willingness to support the concept I remained opposed to managing the project for them. We were enthusiastic about advising and assisting the descendants to secure funding but this was not our land, or our fight.

I suggested to Jack that if his TOLOA group were considering merging with Friends of Tetepare they should reach some resolutions in the next day or so to assist us in seeking funds for a collaborative environmental project. Jack didn't hesitate. With a cheeky smile he replied, 'You come back from Australia with a bottle of Jack Daniels for me and I will sign the resolutions on the bottle right away.' With that he sauntered off to get a smoke and that was the last we were to see of this charismatic rogue for the rest of the two-day meeting.

Concerned that his leader was avoiding the seriousness of the meeting, Henry confided, 'We have had many developments on Tetepare before.'

'Do you support this one?' I asked.

He replied in near perfect English, 'Yes, it is good but we will only give it two years to show that it can make us money.' True to their reputation, the Lokuru men were pragmatic. This two-year deadline for monetary success added pressure to the fledgling conservation agenda.

While the TOLOA contingent seemed content to allow FOT to take the initiative, Peter Siloko, Mary, Isaac and the rest of the Friends of Tetepare met until 3 a.m., determining what their stance would be at the next day's meeting. Did they trust and want to work with TOLOA, or retain their independence? Poor old Twomey sat under the verandah like a loyal sheepdog while Katherine and I retreated to our room. Although only a couple of panels of palm fronds separated us from the mixed Marovo and Roviana dialects interspersed between bouts of fast Pijin, the FOT meeting sounded like another world away. The smells of the Solomons were heavy in the air; the insect repellent that we had smothered on our legs and arms, the dank sheets that never dry. Maybe I had become accustomed to the malaria-induced sore joints, listlessness and my chest infection. As Mary had promised, my symptoms must have abated because for the first time in a week Katherine could lie close to me.

'What are you thinking?' she asked; a common conversation starter we both use when we are reflective and not ready for sleep. 'I'm not sure whether I want the two groups to agree,' I admitted, surprising myself. 'How about you, what's on your mind?' I asked. '*Sem sem*,' Katherine replied, reverting to Pijin. It was not the first time that we had consistent thoughts, the opposite of what we had discussed and agreed upon. In clarifying, Katherine conceded that offering to help the landowners felt good, but if they agreed to the plan and really needed us to manage it, we would be committing ourselves to at least two years of frustration in a project over which we had little control. Tetepare would absorb all of our spare time and energy and we had been warned several times that it was too hard. Should both groups decide tomorrow to say 'Thanks but no thanks' we could sign off our little Melanesian adventure with a clean conscience.

TDA IS BORN

Ten minutes into the meeting the following day Katherine and I were cognisant that we had strapped ourselves in for a rollercoaster of emotions. Every project or business that we had witnessed in the Solomons was fraught with logistical, political and financial woes. The added pressure of providing tangible benefits to thousands of Tetepare landowners who had by now become accustomed to lucrative logging royalties compounded the challenge. Odds were clearly stacked against success and we were aware that many landowners and interested observers felt that the 'conservation project' would fail like previous development attempts on Tetepare. By pinning their collective hopes on Katherine and me at their combined meeting, Friends of Tetepare and TOLOA had issued us the greatest challenge of our careers.

Like most other development in the Solomons, conserving Tetepare initially depended upon securing funds from international donors. The panda emblem on our grant applications would greatly enhance the funding opportunities and the local WWF office could also provide Tetepare descendants and their reluctant expat managers with valuable advice and an inaugural office. Before returning to Australia we worked with supportive local staff to apply for funds from three international agencies. Once signed by WWF managers, the applications could be posted in the stamped envelopes that we had left on their desks.

A few months back in Australia filled out my shorts, which had slid off my waist after my malaria. Unfortunately, replies from prospective donors informed us that law and order, civil society, health and education eclipsed the environment as priorities for international aid. The unofficial two-year deadline ate away at my patience. Two years was both the limit of the landowners' patience for this strange conservation 'development' and the time frame that we were prepared to commit to Tetepare. We had already used up four months and hadn't got past first base. Simon Foales' warning that Tetepare was too hard and too complicated resonated louder and louder as the weeks passed.

Any doubts we harboured about the worthiness of the Tetepare battle were dispelled by a most unlikely source. Walking past the TV one night Katherine's attention was caught by familiar-sounding Pijin. 'I think this show is about the Solomons,' she announced. We flopped down on our couch as grainy old black-and-white footage gave way to a colourful village scene. Recognising several faces from Lokuru on the screen bolted us upright. The Haforai tribe was self-imploding with distrust about the misuse of funds from their logging operation. Jack Daniel, the flippant larrikin, was portrayed as a serious, worried man. He and his tribe were clearly under considerable stress. Subtitles indicated that logging royalties had not been distributed fairly and fingers were being pointed aggressively. We perched on the edge of our seat when a slightly younger and skinnier, but unmistakable Mary Bea filled the TV. Staring straight down the camera lens in the same determined stance that we had experienced, Mary accused the local men of being too scared to stand up for what they knew to be right. Instead she encouraged women, the real lifeblood of the village, to make a stand against logging. The documentary then moved to Tetepare, with Mary and others explaining the values of this last unlogged island. Mary's stirring performance in *Since the Company Came* convinced us to throw everything behind her fight against the logging of Tetepare.

As far as we could establish, our joint applications with WWF had still not even been lodged. Rather than pinning Tetepare's hopes on the whims of the local WWF management we decided to apply directly to the donors on behalf of the descendants. As a result, glowing reports on the value of Tetepare by international conservation authorities and statements of commitment by landholders, rather than the Panda stamp, supported our new round of grant applications.

Within weeks a New Zealand-based donor agreed that the Tetepare project was probably worthy of funding but only if we had the backing of a recognised international organisation. A quick phone call confirmed they were happy for us to increase the value of our grant application to accommodate WWF's overheads. Despite this news, our letters, telephone calls and emails to WWF in Gizo remained unanswered. Before long we got another bite. The European Union, or EU, which supported many village-based initiatives in the Solomons, showed interest in funding the Tetepare project. An additional benefit of EU funding was that they could endorse residency status for Katherine and me, allowing us to stay longer than permitted through our annual three-month tourist visa. But the EU had not swallowed the hook either. Both potential donors advised us against heading back to the Solomons before Tetepare landowners were represented by a single association and funding was approved. Yet we knew that FOT and TOLOA would not merge unless we returned with funding. With two big fish nibbling away at our bait and our time running out, we decided that we had little option than to ignore the advice of the donors, the Australian Government and our concerned families and friends.

In December 2001 the Solomons held fairer elections than the post-coup sham of eighteen months earlier. Hopes were high that incumbent Prime Minister Sir Allan Kemakeza could lead the Solomons out of their rut. Air Vanuatu was the third different airline servicing the Solomons on our three trips. Opinions were divided on whether Solomon Airlines had pushed Qantas's patience and finances too far or whether the Australian airline had deserted the South Seas community at the same time as it capitalised on the demise of their domestic competition, Ansett.

Flying in over the unbroken canopy of the Guadalcanal rainforest we were reminded of just how special the Solomons were, in stark contrast to flying over the ravaged hills of Madagascar and south-eastern Asia. This was the documentary-style vision of unspoilt rainforests. But the first step out of the air-conditioned plane thumped us back into reality. The thick, oppressive air drained our energy and moisture seeped from every pore as we made our way across the unshaded tarmac. Perhaps because we had committed ourselves to a long association with Tetepare, we began to view the country through residents' rather than travellers' eyes.

Our loyal taxi driver's car reminded me that taxis provided a microcosm of Solomons' decor. Ben's dashboard was festooned with wobbly-headed plastic dogs and strings of gaudy plastic flowers. Arriving as cooks or builders for the traders, the Chinese soon became storekeepers, and by 1920 the fifty-five Chinese in the Solomons had established the country's decor. We grew to despise the Chinese imported hanky-sized bed sheets that invariably peeled off onto our sweaty backs because they were too small to fold under mattresses. Chinese cutlery was fashioned from the softest metal known to mankind, and rolls of white crepe 'toilet' paper stretched into deformed ribbons in your hand when you attempted to tear it yet offered no resistance at all when put to the task for which it was marketed. 'ABC' batteries, the typical brand found in most little stores, were so named because your torch beam dimmed in the time taken to recite the first three letters of the alphabet.

The realities of living in the Solomons took the gloss off the postcard images universally associated with the South Pacific. A leaky cold shower with resident cockroaches soon becomes a luxury after washing half clad at a tap in the middle of a village or with a plastic cup in a mossie-infested stream. An unbroken kerosene lamp, with kerosene and a dry match to light it, became coveted items.

Wandering down to the Honiara market reminded us that in a country virtually bereft of refrigeration, diet reflects both the season and the weather. Locals seldom plan meals in advance, except for the occasional feasts when special efforts are made to hunt pigs or turtles. Unlike in supermarkets back home, Islanders don't get duped by out-of-season artificially ripened tasteless fruit. Mussels and cockles are found at nearly every market in July when low tides allow them to be harvested but were rarely seen at other times. Rough seas that prevent fishing effectively close fish markets and prevent the Simbo and Savo communities bringing their megapode eggs to market. Big rains prevent many farmers from harvesting, starving the following day's market. Living in the Solomons forced us to be aware of the vagaries of the weather.

Despite limited access to any media, many Solomon Islanders were astute followers of world news. Ian Thorpe's efforts in the Sydney 2000 Olympics were commented upon by most people we met and the remotest villages speculated wildly about 'Ben' Ladin's latest plans. On the rare occasions that papers did reach the villages their phonetic spelling provided as much amusement as information. One noteworthy headline in the national paper screamed 'BIRTH OF A NEW ERROR' following a change of government in the early 1990s. Another Freudian slip 'GIZO HOSPITAL AIMS TO ELIMINATE MALAITA' was a typo heralding an anti-malarial campaign that coincided with fears held in the Western Province that Malaitans intended taking over the Western Province.

After giggling at the latest paper in Honiara, Katherine and I headed down to Gizo. We flew out west over the magnificent Marovo Lagoon that we first witnessed three years earlier. But now red scars of the logging roads and the new oil palm plantation bled into the bays, where the previously opalescent fringes of blue and green were now brown and blotchy.

Everyone in Gizo seemed down in the dumps. Even Tony, the ever smiling diabetic husband of our delightful landlady, had his foot amputated after an infection that would have been treated routinely back home. He got off comparatively lightly. The medical students at Phoebe's Resthouse told me of a diabetic who was sent to the Honiara hospital to have his gangrenous leg amputated. While in the country's main hospital, a rat bit his other leg, which also became gangrenous and the poor bloke returned to his village without any legs.

The 'black-and-white pig' was also suffering further from the unrest. All WWF field staff had now been laid off and the remaining office-based staff had little to show for their efforts. Seri Hite, the manager, could still not commit to long-term support of Tetepare but fortunately he did find funds for another meeting between the rival groups of Tetepare landowners to discuss a potential merger that was a precursor to securing both grants.

We had hoped that our like-minded FOT friends would arrive first, so that we could hone our tactics, but it was the renegade TOLOA representatives from Lokuru who fronted first. Jack Daniel led the delegation and only half-jokingly asked for the bottle of his namesake that he assumed we would buy to secure his support. His eyes flashed confidence without assuredness and brazenness without purpose. Depending on which way he swayed, Jack's considerable charisma seemed destined to either cement the success or precipitate the demise of the merger talks.

Along with the serious Henry and several other faces we recognised from our earlier brief meeting was a paler man, with a Mexican-like moustache and straighter hair than his *wantoks*. Lloyd Hodge was the local MP for the Lokuru region. His father had been the Australian-born Tetepare plantation manager and his mother was a Tetepare descendant. Although younger than the rest of the delegation, Lloyd's intelligent eyes and neat clothes conveyed a sense of responsibility for steering the future of the island to which both his parents had been inextricably linked. Guided by his political instincts, Lloyd had clearly been contemplating how to capitalise on the new conservation agenda, which seemed destined to receive international support, with development. His notions of a large resort, serviced by a village of resettled descendants on Tetepare, raised the interests of his compatriots.

Although we suggested that commercial resource extraction and resettlement were unlikely to be viewed favourably by environmental donors, we stressed to Lloyd and the other men that these issues were the decision of the landowners. Jack clarified, or rather muddied the waters, by stating that TOLOA wouldn't have any disputes with FOT or *'iu tufala whiteman'* because his organisation was originally established to conserve Tetepare and to unite landowners. They had 'gone off track' with the logging plan and now had no funds to operate. Led by Jack, the failed developers were keen to merge with their smaller but better resourced rivals. Yet despite his persuasive manner Katherine in particular harboured concerns. Jack did not have a good record of championing successful inclusive projects. Would he coerce FOT to adopt another short-sighted project for Tetepare? Which group would need to concede the most compromises?

Not since Tetepare had been sold to the traders a century earlier had such important decisions been made about the fate of the island. Would resettlement be allowed on Tetepare? Should the island be owned and managed collectively or should each tribe or family group own their traditional area? Would commercial resource extraction be permitted on Tetepare? Prior to this meeting I had considered constitutions to be boring legal documents, usually referred to in passing at equally boring annual general meetings. Yet most members of both landowner groups were more familiar with the process of developing a constitution than Katherine or I, perhaps due to the plethora of associations that had been established since independence. On a personal note this constitution would decide whether Katherine and I would continue our involvement. If we did not agree with their policies we had no qualms about leaving Tetepare and finding another cause.

As Solomon time decreed, representatives of the two factions sequentially appeared and greeted each other cordially but reservedly. Kido from WWF and his accountant cousin Sute were the last to arrive. Despite the meeting scheduled for one o'clock, it was not until after four that Isaac opened the meeting with a thoughtfully prepared prayer. For the first time in years I closed my eyes and embraced the prayer with its noble, yet predictable aspirations of mutual respect and togetherness for the benefit of '*olketa descendants blong iumi*'.

Our ESP emitters were red-lighting well into the evening of the merger meeting but they may have been almost unnecessary; since our discussion a few hours earlier Lloyd Hodge had prepared a draft constitution that showcased his political nous. A little prompting was all it took for Lloyd to articulate a set of rules that I had only dreamed of. With surprisingly little dissent, the two groups agreed on a list of objectives that were diametrically opposed to TOLOA's previous plans:

(1) To unite the landowners of Tetepare and promote and encourage cooperation between members and tribes.
(2) To manage and own the entire Tetepare Island collectively by Tetepare descendants.
(3) To conserve the natural resources of Tetepare for the benefit of present and future generations of Tetepare Descendants.
(4) To prevent commercial resource extraction from Tetepare Island and surrounding waters and prohibit poaching of resources by non-descendants of Tetepare.
(5) To research, locate and document natural resources (including tambu sites and traditional artifacts) on Tetepare Island in order to adopt and enforce resource management orders to ensure their adequate protection.

(6) To research and document the genealogy of individuals, families and tribal units descended from Tetepare and their history, traditions, stories, myths, legends, songs and art.
(7) To discourage the settlement of Tetepare Island by descendants and prevent the migration to or resettlement of Tetepare Island by non-descendants.
(8) To establish a trust fund to further the objectives of the Association and to assist and encourage members to undertake sustainable ventures within their existing communities (outside of Tetepare Island).

Point 2 was a very brave and valuable step. Collective management provided a unique opportunity for Tetepare. Possibly for the first time in Melanesia, decisions were to be made communally for an entire large island. Katherine and I naively felt that the battle for Tetepare had suddenly become one-sided and we only needed to tweak the details.

Dark sweat lines were still oozing across the creases in the sleeves of my shirt at midnight but at least now the perspiration was through the heat and humidity and no longer through concern about the objectives. It was already tomorrow by the time that the decision on a name for the united association was addressed. In a bizarre bout of Melanesian shadow-boxing, Kido from FOT suggested that the new group should be called TOLOA because they were the Tetepare Original Land Owners. In response Lloyd Hodge, from TOLOA, pointed out that the acronym was nonsensical because they were not the original landowners but their descendants. A dozen permutations were dispelled, and eventually the Tetepare Descendants' Association got the vote but the ensuing discussion on the placement of the apostrophe necessitated further debate. Eventually the acronym TDA was used for the first of thousands of times.

Jack Daniel was unanimously elected as the interim Chairman. No-one else nominated for Chairman and the decision had obviously been stitched up in advance, which aroused our suspicions.

We worried about Jack's commitment to the newly endorsed objectives and his record of flitting from one failed venture to another. Unlike the other delegates, who seemed willing to extend the meeting until dawn, Jack took over the reins and rapidly wound up proceedings with characteristic off-hand eloquence, although there were still many core issues to discuss. Jack made only one decision. He immediately appointed Mary to the Communications and Registrations role, which gave her the freedom and authority to inform and recruit far-flung descendants to TDA. Her first target was to travel with *'tufala whiteman'* to her local communities on southern Rendova, the people with the most to gain and lose from any developments or regulations on Tetepare.

Mary's first awareness talk at Hopongo village concerned Katherine and me greatly. After a twenty-minute monologue in local language, Mary translated that she had told the village, 'If you join TDA you agree to not log Tetepare, which means you will get money from overseas.' Perhaps her eagerness to recruit TDA members had blinded her responsibility to restrict promises. Sensing our unease with Mary's approach, John Aqarao addressed his people. 'This man is a conman,' the local big man and FOT member pointed at me alarmingly, but then went on with a smile to explain 'a conman to help TDA get money from overseas.' Fortunately John also raised a serious issue. 'How would you feel if the government decided to resettle Gilbertese on Tetepare?'

John Aqarao was the son of John Kari, buried in a prominent location in the centre of the village. A former paramount chief, Kari had been responsible for uniting the landholders of Tetepare to form TOLOA and introducing Christianity to many Rendova residents. The great man also became a war hero when he was pivotal in the rescue of John F. Kennedy after his PT109 boat had been rammed and sunk. Half a century later Kari's son was instrumental in paving the way for TDA converts.

The next village we visited was Havilla, a twenty-minute canoe ride south along the Rendova coast. This quaint village, nestled into pretty gardens between the escarpment and a black-sand beach, boasted one of the best grass soccer fields that we had seen outside Honiara. Symmetrical cassava crops and tangly purple potato vines were bordered by spiky pineapple plants and taller banana palms and fruit trees. A massive green-and-yellow birdwing butterfly clumsily pursued his even larger but less colourful mate across the path. Mary strolled through the village as if she had lived there all her life, making small talk with the locals but never stopping or deviating. She made a beeline for a hut near the centre of the village with myself, then Katherine, a few paces behind, and with Twomey our boat driver nowhere to be seen. We were completely unprepared for what followed.

A rotund middle-aged man casually emerged from his leaf house and took up a position on a waist-high verandah. Without introducing us, Mary addressed the bare-chested man in his language for a couple of minutes. I watched the man intently. He was presumably the main man of Havilla, a big man in every sense of the word. He did not look at Mary while she spoke, nor did he acknowledge our presence. With an air of total disinterest he stared into space but as soon as Mary stopped talking, the big fella let rip.

At a hundred miles an hour and a thousand decibels, the big man made no secret of his mood. Pointing back in the direction we had arrived, we were presumably being evicted from the village. Katherine and I looked at each other in shock. We had always been welcomed in every village in the Solomons and were not anticipating any problems. After all, most Havilla residents were Tetepare descendants who stood to benefit from the new association. We had suggested that Mary tone down the financial benefits that TDA could deliver but assumed that the reasoning used by John Aqarao of increased control over Tetepare would also win converts here. What was even more remarkable about the chief's outburst was that no-one from the assembled throng showed any emotion at all. Everyone seemed very interested in their feet. Except Mary.

Before he could finish, Mary barked at the chief, forcing him to make eye contact. She then unleashed a tirade of her own, while at no point breaking her wide-eyed stare. I nervously edged backwards a couple more steps but the big man was not easily subdued. With his village looking on, he upped the ante, leaving no-one except Mary in any doubt that he was the one who called the shots in Havilla. Whatever Mary had proposed was not on his agenda. Mary retaliated banging her fist and pointing aggressively at the chief, her shiny black skin rippling with anger.

Oh my goodness. Despite not understanding a single word, it was clear that we had just instigated or rekindled a civil war. Was Mary, along with her two white companions, about to be lynched on the order of the angry chief? Of less immediate concern but equally worrying was that the villagers would not support the new initiative just forged by their 'representatives'.

As I was contemplating the gravity of the situation the storm clouds cleared as rapidly as they had formed. The chief waved his hand down the path and Mary's hackles and volume declined immediately. 'This is William,' Mary announced to us as they both acknowledged our presence for the first time. 'We are going to hold a meeting to explain about TDA.'

I was still shaking with adrenalin as Mary casually sauntered over to the meeting hall, a leaf house slightly larger than the others in the village. 'What's the problem?' I asked Mary nervously. 'Oh, no problem,' she beamed with a smile like an angel. 'We always fight first but now I will story with the village about TDA.' Years later I learned that William still held a grudge against Mary for opposing the logging on Tetepare. Like many other big men he was keen on the royalty payments from the island and Mary's new plan appeared less lucrative.

The Havilla village listened attentively to Mary. I listened to the local dialect with plenty of e's and o's which were reminiscent of the related language of the indigenous Yolnu from northern Australia. Instead of 'Yo' for yes they used a similar sounding 'Eyo' delivered with the same acknowledging nod seen in Arnhem

Land. Occasionally Mary reverted to Pijin so we could trace her story about the formation of TDA, the plans to conserve Tetepare and the $5 membership fee. Despite murmurings about paying $5 to have a say about their own island, the overwhelming response from Havilla was 'Very nice plan.'

As we approached the next village, Katherine and my concerns about the reception we would receive were overridden by how we would land on the beach. Baniata occupies a rocky point that bends waves into aggressive conflicting patterns. Twomey's face was blank as he powered our canoe towards the whitewash. Just before we were hit side-on by an errant wave, Twomey expertly swung our canoe hard left and then hard right. Amidst the cappuccino seas was a protected passage that allowed the locals to land in almost any weather. In keeping with the other villages on Rendova, Baniata did not have a wharf. Instead we powered along on the crest of a low wave and onto the steep black-sand beach.

Children and fishermen materialised within seconds and helped us drag the canoe up the beach and onto the baking sand before we were swamped by the next wave. Mary instructed the wide-eyed kids to carry our bags, which almost started a fight as they jostled to determine who would porter our belongings. We even threw our sandals on the ground so that four more pairs of hands could assist. As we followed the throng along the narrow path leading into the village I quietly asked Mary if she was expecting any trouble here. 'No problems, John. These are my people,' she beamed with the confidence of a boxer.

A balding old man with crazy teeth and excited eyes introduced himself as Livingston, the 'village organiser'. Mary spoke with Livingstone briefly, who then diverged from the track, only to catch up with us further on with a large conch shell in his hand.

'Meeting, meeting, we will hold a meeting,' Livingston announced before pursing his lips and producing a foghorn from the shell.

Slowly the village responded to Livingstone's call to the meeting under an enormous shady flame tree. The meeting commenced with a prayer in Touo language accompanied by clapping and chanting of 'New Life'. After Mary's now well-rehearsed awareness talk, several senior men responded. Katherine and I studied their faces intently, assessing the response of the village without understanding a word. One old man stood up and addressed the crowd in an animated tone that drew embarrassed laughter from some of the listeners. Twomey whispered to me, 'Only 75 per cent.' Later on the women explained to Katherine that one of their number was 'half normal'. Sanity was apparently measured in percentages here in Baniata.

A smiling bloke wearing a cropped ladies green coat with padded shoulders stood up and everyone started sniggering again before he had even opened his mouth. Billy, who liked to be called 'Chief', was the reluctant village clown. Although he was never likely to be a key decision maker in Baniata and struggled to write his own name, Chief Billy eloquently summarised our one-hour awareness session in one minute. He stated that 'Eco-two-reason was given that name because two reasons for bringing tourists were income for villagers and looking after the environment.' Despite the laughs that this statement initiated from his fellow villagers, I was impressed with Chief Billy's lateral thinking or amazingly accurate faux pas.

Twomey translated some of the earlier conversation for me. 'Two men asked why the donors don't pay the TDA membership fees.' 'How did Mary answer that?' I questioned, thinking back to the debate about the membership fee in the TDA merger meeting where the leaders decided that a token payment would confirm descendants' commitment to TDA's ideals. 'Mary asked them if they wanted donors to feed them and take them to the toilet as well,' Twomey smirked. With Mary prepared to stand up for TDA's ideals in such a manner we were confident that the recruitment drive and Tetepare's conservation agenda were in good hands.

While Katherine and I were introduced to our new hosts for the night, Mary signed up new members under the glow of a kerosene lantern and collected ever broadening family trees to confirm new members' ownership of Tetepare, setting a pattern for our visits to villages across the Western Province.

More than a Name

Every new village we visited with Mary on our TDA recruitment drive and every new family who signed up to TDA's conservation agenda left me scrawling more notes into my increasingly crowded notebook. For in the Solomons, one's name is nowhere nearly as important as the names of one's forebears, every last one of them. Two years earlier there was no way I would have predicted that the most important aspect of the great environmental battle was collecting thousands of names.

Genealogy is a sensitive subject in indigenous communities, where tracing one's forebears is proof of land and resource ownership, as well as a complex web of mutual obligations and responsibilities. Land ownership was a ticket to riches when royalties from logging companies started flowing in the 1980s, and disputes over land inheritance since the commencement of large-scale logging were the most common cases taken to court in the Solomons. Less lucrative opportunities, such as those we were offering on Tetepare, also relied heavily on closely guarded family histories. Before I became involved with the Tetepare project I did not even know how to spell genealogy. However, from our honeymoon several years earlier I had already developed a perverse interest in Solomon Islands names.

The first Marovo man we met was the Uepi resort's boat driver. This wiry middle-aged man introduced himself as Lady. Presuming that I had misheard him I asked him to repeat his name. There was absolutely no doubt about it. I bit my lip. What were his parents thinking? Were they hoping for a girl? I could imagine the grief that Lady had endured at school. No wonder he was a more solemn fellow than most other Islanders.

The dive master at Uepi was a rotund smiling local who was as outgoing as Lady was reserved. 'Deliva,' he announced loudly, leaving us in no doubt that we had heard him correctly. I wondered what was going on. Was there some tradition of using off beat names in this part of Marovo? Did Deliva's folks decide on his name during the final throes of his birth? Maybe he had an older brother Stan? For the first time in my life I developed a fascination with people's names. Not casual nicknames conjured up in schoolyards and footy clubs, but real names bestowed upon *piccaninnies* at christening ceremonies. As sensitively as possible I asked many of the locals about their family's names and I never failed to be amazed.

Ben and Jilly from Matikuri laughed about a tribe from the nearby Zaira village who maintained a particularly colourful nomenclature. Chief Green Jina was aptly named as he was one of the few local big men who remained steadfast against the loggers and the immediate yet transitory benefits that they offered him. But others in his village were named 'Brown', 'Yellow' and 'Black'. A generation of girls from the same village were blessed with 'Red', 'Blue' and the less than flattering name of 'Grey'. Maybe it was a family joke that got out of control, but I can still not fathom how a jet-black *piccaninny* girl could be named 'White'.

The most interesting names, at least to my sense of humour, were those that reflected the exposure of the Islanders to Western influences. Jack Daniel, TDA's inaugural Chairman could have formed a likely partnership with 'John Wayne', who presides over an ecolodge on Marovo Lagoon. Other Marovo names signalled the first time their parents had been exposed to traders' consumables. 'Milo' is not a bad sounding name and could almost pass as conventional if it wasn't for the fact that 'Milk', 'Tea', 'Coffee' and 'Beer' were also christened in the same period. Elsewhere I met a 'Jelly'. These unfortunate souls must have cringed whenever people called out to storekeepers who generally only stocked their namesakes along with a few cracker biscuits and tinned meat. Solomon names are not only inspired by food and beverage products. 'Motor Car' and 'Eveready' were self-explanatory and 'Evinrude' was endowed with the brand name of outboard motor favoured in his village.

Mary's extended family boasted an impressive botanical nomenclature. Along with Naqarita, who was named after a local flower, Mary's cousins included Lotus, Cedar, Kauri, Oregon, Hickory, Alpine, Willow, Pinus, Sycamore and Fig. Poor Fig. I reckon Fig rates as a pretty ordinary name for a girl, especially due to the transposition of F's and P's. Figgy was a striking, effervescent teenager who played representative netball and drew longer than usual glances from the teenage boys of Munda. Fig more closely resembled Venus Williams than Miss Piggy, who her name sounded like in the local dialect.

'Marvelous' seemed an appropriate name for the son of 'Darling' and I noted that 'Merry Love' was no relation to 'Virgin'. Other names seemed unrelated to a theme. I could not rationalise why 'Endless' had younger siblings or why 'Beginning' was the sixth child of regal-sounding parents, William and Elizabeth. 'Cradle' may well have outgrown his name but hopefully 'Lucky' did not. Eghiness's daughter lucked out in the naming stakes even more than her mum when she was christened 'Loveless'. Poor old 'Nameless' may have pondered why more conventional names could be found for his six younger brothers and sisters.

Other names heralded historical events. Peter Siloko told me that his brother 'Aldrin' was named after one of humanity's greatest achievements that was as far removed from July 1969 life in the Solomons as was possible. 'Argentina' was born during the Falklands war and 'Freewill' was born in 2001, the year when the whale video with a similar name reached Rendova villages. 'New Year' celebrated her birthday a week after 'Happy Christmas'. It was no surprise that 'Abba' was born in the 1970s and 'Stallone' in the 1980s. One of the strangest names that I heard was when I asked some proud parents in Lokuru the name of their little baby. 'Stone Cold,' I thought the shy mother said. She repeated it three times for me, each time a little more apprehensively. Surely only a stillborn baby would be called 'Stone Cold'. Later on, when I commented on this unfortunate name to some other locals they informed me that he had been named after a glamour American TV wrestler, whose name somehow filtered through on the coconut news to Lokuru.

When our turn came, I found that naming babies generated as much stress and strain as the temporary inconvenience of childbirth. For months prior to the big events the name of the expected babies dominated discussions in our household. Favourite names of one partner reminded the other of undesirable acquaintances; other potentials had already been taken by a friend's, cousin's or celebrity's child. With the world's second-highest birth rate, this stress would be expected to be a regular feature of Solomons villages. But hang on. How could worried parents concoct 'Yellow', 'Milk' or 'Fig'? There had to be another explanation.

All was revealed one morning while staying at Baniata, when we woke to the news that a baby had been born overnight in the neighbouring leaf house. The baby was the first-born son of Livingstone's niece. Livingstone, the conch-shell-blowing village organiser, had named the baby 'Jason' after a turtle researcher who had accompanied us and only met Livingstone the previous day. Baby Jason's arrival, as well as thrilling our turtle mate, also taught me a couple of lessons about baby naming that in hindsight seem obvious. Firstly, it is rarely the parent who names the child. More often a village elder, grandparent or respected visitor is charged with that responsibility. Secondly, spur-of-the-moment decisions are not uncommon.

What started out as a laborious task to document Tetepare descendants turned out to be both interesting and often amusing. Even more noteworthy than the amazing names was the encyclopedic memory and knowledge of the villagers. In some cases seventeen generations were effortlessly recited, a feat made even more impressive considering that fourteen of these generations had been pre-literate. I was frequently amazed that these people could list hundreds of cousins, their spouses and children and humbled that I could not name four generations of my own ancestors.

The stories behind the naming of some of the Tetepare descendants were even more interesting than the bizarre names that cropped up. Poor 'Koukana' may well have required counselling. Meaning 'left over' in his local dialect, his twin died at birth. 'Veira' and 'Vaira' have a more heartening story. When Nairy and John finally managed to bear children after years of trying they ecstatically named their twin boys 'Veira' and 'Vaira', which translate to 'we got it' in Vangunu and Marovo languages respectively. The most original geographical name that I recorded was coined by George Hite from Baniata. George's daughter had married an Indonesian and hence George named their boy 'Indopart' in recognition of his part-Indonesian heritage. Other Solomon Island names, including 'Melbourne', 'Brisbane', 'Albany' and even 'Royal Charles', were inspired by hospitals where those naming them had been treated.

I could not help but exclaim when a parent listed their ten or twelve children. Having been exposed to contraception and population awareness, several of them quipped '*Mifala famili planting not famili planning.*' Family planting had definitely been successful in the past century. The British had resigned themselves to importing Indian labourers to fulfil their vision of lucrative commercial plantations in the Solomons because they believed the sparse Solomon Islands population was doomed. C.M. Woodford, appointed by the British as the nation's first resident Commissioner, stated in the early 1900s, 'My opinion is that nothing in the way of the most personal legislation or fostering care, carried out at any expense whatever, can prevent the eventual extinction of the Melanesian race in the Pacific.' But C.M. Woodford did not count on the effectiveness of twentieth-century family planting. By 1951 there were 95,000 islanders and the 2002 census revealed that the ranks had swollen to

450,000, owing to the world's second-fastest growth rate of 4.7%. Approximately one and a half centuries after Tetepare was deserted, Mary was among the 749 descendants who could trace their lineage to Sifu. Although Mary often digressed to stories about many of her ancestors, it was her story of Sifu, the last resolute woman left on Tetepare following the diaspora, that captured my imagination.

•

Sifu had peered from the cover of the forest. A knot tightened in her stomach as she watched the unfolding drama on the beach. On a normal day Sifu would have taken her daughter Nido to harvest taro from their irrigated ruta fields deep in the rainforest. But this was no normal day. No-one had gone to their gardens, nor fishing in their dugout canoes, nor hunting for pigs. Most of the Tetepare tribe had gravitated towards the Hukata beach where the chanting throng gathered for their annual marriage festival.

Traditionally, an expectant damsel selected by the elders had waited across the sea on Sarumana Islet's little white-sand beach. I was sitting on this beach, looking back towards Sifu's hideout on Tetepare, as Mary recounted the story. Would-be grooms proved their worth by racing to swim the stretch of water between Hukata beach and Sarumana Islet that was renowned for its fearsome sharks and crocodiles. With gaudy parrot feathers in their tightly curled hair, bands of kastom leaves tied around tensed biceps and heavy shells jangling from stretched earlobes, the bachelors worked themselves into a frenzy. Survival, rather than prenuptial nerves, forged adrenalin through their wiry bodies.

Although the Hukata marriage ritual had been a Tetepare institution, Sifu had boycotted that final festival under the mighty tree at Hukata beach, where reluctant women were arranging freshly cracked Ngali nuts along with fish, pork, taro and fruits on platters of wild banana leaves. Instead she had cowered in the forest, a confused frightened stranger in her own land. Sifu's life had been turned upside down since many of her relatives were slain by brawling tribesmen and raiding headhunters. Despite experiencing untold atrocities in the past year, not even Sifu knew that this would be the last Hukata festival ever held.

Sifu's once great Tetepare tribe had imploded. Gossiping women had fuelled fights that escalated to murders. In the ensuing mayhem scores of Tetepare men were killed defending their honour or as the victims of payback killings. Upon witnessing such destruction to their people, the Tetepare tribe felt betrayed by their spirits. They abandoned rituals and customs that had structured their lives and those of their ancestors. The surviving Tetepare warriors transformed the Hukata marriage festival into a sordid abuse of women captured on one of their own inter-island raids. Petrified, the huddled captives waited helplessly to be shamed by their captors. The quick death afforded to their men folk back home was a blessing by comparison. Rather than risking the sharks and crocodiles by swimming the three hundred metres to Sarumana Islet, the men paddled across with impunity to consummate their success in full view of their tribe. In the ensuing orgy no-one seemed concerned about one of the terrified girls who lay like a rag doll in a pool of her own blood and excreta. The idyllic little atoll where we were sitting suddenly took on a squalid ambience.

Within weeks of the sordid festival, several babies from Sifu's Siokodi village also died a horrible bleeding death. Fever-racked toddlers turned the sea red when they *toileted* in the morning. Grandparents contracted the same sickness and wailed helplessly from their leaf huts. Red-eyed blue flies swarmed around the stinking mess that spread from the beaches to the villages. Customary medicines were impotent against this sickness, the likes of which had never been seen before.

Within days of the first deaths, over half of Siokodi village had either died or become bedridden. Sifu was too distraught and exhausted to maintain the all-night sing-sing ritual that traditionally followed the death of a loved one. News from *wantoks* evacuating other parts of Tetepare indicated that whole villages had been deserted as their occupants surmised that the spirits were punishing them for losing their respect. Word was that the catastrophic illness had been inflicted on them by a holy man on a neighbouring island in retaliation for deaths inflicted by Tetepare spirits. Other panic-ridden survivors believed that Kaluvesu, one of the eminent spirits of Tetepare, had cursed the island because no-one helped him battle a giant clam that had been terrorising fishermen.

After being devastated by the infighting and sickness, Sifu's family then faced the coup de grace. Early traders conceded that the Solomons was the most dangerous region in the Pacific and that the people of the region immediately adjacent to Tetepare were the terror of the Solomons, the most ferocious of the ferocious. Perhaps unwittingly, these traders promoted the demise of the Tetepare civilisation. Iron tools, traded for turtle shell or bêche-de-mer, enabled villages with access to these tools to create gardens, build canoes and fight more effectively than those without. These rare and coveted new commodities diluted the power of chiefs and elders in favour of ambitious leaders who controlled the distribution of iron. Headhunting, once a regulated means of honouring spirits by collecting the heads and consuming the souls of warriors, became a no-holds-barred inter-island contest to control these new commodities. Tetepare became embroiled in a regional massacre of Rwandan proportions.

Lokuru people from neighbouring Rendova Island embarked on a series of unprecedented headhunting raids, returning time and again to Tetepare to wipe out the tribe. Since the day her husband Nguvi was killed, Sifu had deserted her leafhouse and cradled her daughter throughout terrifying sleepless nights in a neighbour's outdoor kitchen. She had watched blankly as the few Tetepare survivors obscured the entrance to the great cave where the skulls of their ancestors were kept. In a final act of defiance before fleeing their island, Sifu's distraught relatives also smashed their traditional shell money so their enemies could not benefit from the spoils of their destroyed civilisation.

But Sifu didn't want to leave. She had nowhere to go and trusted no-one. Together with Nido she abandoned her now vulnerable Siokodi village and hid in the bush near Tetepare's rugged weather-coast. Angry seas protected them from raiders on all but the calmest days. Mother and daughter eked out an existence eating taro, bush yams and the occasional fish. From their hideout they watched raiding parties sweep through Tetepare searching for them but leaving empty handed, spreading the word that the island was deserted.

Mary explained that a fisherman had spotted the last Tetepare survivors near the beach on the rough weather coast. Although they tried in vain to hide, Bina caught up with Sifu and Nido and pleaded with them to return with him to Baniata, on the far side of Rendova. Bina confirmed Sifu's suspicion that no-one else remained on Tetepare and that she was not safe alone with her daughter. Reluctantly the pair allowed Bina to take them back to Baniata. The Tetepare evacuees gradually stopped speaking their native tongue and learned the strange Touo language of southern Rendova. Eventually both Sifu and Nido married Baniata men and raised children in their adopted village.

Although Sifu's ordeal was a survival epic, other Tetepare victims had even luckier escapes, which Isaac Molia learned about while collecting genealogies in Roviana lagoon. Sisters Doavoja and Zarorega had been captured by warriors from Roviana for their chief, Bene. Both girls were destined to be *vealas*. *Vealas* were kept immaculately clean and well fed so they could be sacrificed to honour ancestors. Chief Bene traded Doavoja to faraway Vella la Vella Island. Years later, the people from Vella la Vella were invited to bring their *veala* for the feasting ceremony to commemorate a sacred *tabu* site on nearby Ranongga Island. Doavoja had grown into an attractive girl and her looks saved her from the cooking pot. At first sight the son of the Ranonggan chief lusted after her and they married, with Doavoja bearing children for the chiefly line.

Zarorega had an even narrower escape. She was traded for traditional shell money to a village on Kolombangara that was mourning the death of their chief. The distraught child was taken to the sacrificial altar wrapped in *kastom* leaves. Her petrified wailing caught the attention of the chief's widow Vinia, who begged to see the child before she was dispatched. Vinia's quick thinking ensured that the child would be unfit for sacrifice. She dirtied some roasted taro between her legs and fed it to the wailing child. Having spoiled the *veala*, Vinia successfully suggested that a pig be sacrificed instead. Zarorega was adopted by Vinia and also grew up in a chiefly family and learned their magical spells. But Zarorega never saw her island or her sister again. Indeed it was to be five or six generations before the Tetepare people were reunited.

I was happy to compile the series of Tetepare genealogies that began with Sifu, Doajova and her sisters and about twenty other survivors. Identifying landowners was essential to establishing who could make decisions about the island and also share in TDA's opportunities. However, I soon learned that a genealogy was seldom sufficient evidence to prove that an individual was a Tetepare descendant. The knowledge of Tetepare *kastom* stories was often required before families could confirm their ties to the island. Some lineages recalled detailed stories about how they were descended from the Great Snake or other spirits of Tetepare. Others claimed knowledge of the now defunct Tetepare language, the location of the hidden skull cave on Tetepare, or even the power, passed down through generations, to summon the island's spirits.

Even recalling Tetepare stories and tracing one's genealogy back to an ancestor from Tetepare was still not enough to convince some of the elders that an individual was a legitimate Tetepare landowner. *Kastom* decreed that had one's forebears been captured and forcibly removed from Tetepare during headhunting raids, they and their descendants forfeited their landowner rights. Likewise the offspring of prostitutes or sibling marriages were not recognised by customary law. To confuse matters even more, some individuals born on Tetepare were also disqualified because their ancestors were not true Tetepare people but had temporarily occupied the island following the evacuation. In the years after the great exodus, several Tetepare families, sometimes accompanied by unrelated individuals from their new villages, attempted to resettle on Tetepare. However, the spirits had not forgotten or forgiven. Sometimes the settlers' crops failed or they became sick again. Each budding new village was foiled. The ultimate test of a claimant's rights to the island was knowledge of the location and nature of *tabu* sites, most of which had been consumed by the jungle in the generations since the island was abandoned.

The TDA constitution, drafted in the all-night Munda meeting, decreed that all descendants are equal, no matter which lineage they are descended from or how many generations they have been separated from Tetepare. This even playing field meant there were at least four thousand prospective land owners, all with rights to decide the island's fate. This also potentially meant that four thousand people, many of whom did not know or trust each other, might be asking for a share in any royalties, training or employment that we could generate from the island. Katherine and I had to be careful that our role didn't mutate from facilitators to adjudicators. We also promised not to repeat 'secret' stories that could be used by non-descendants to fake land ownership.

The dysfunctionally large TDA membership was paradoxically one of the potential saviours of the island. There was little chance that a majority of the TDA members would agree to any particular commercial extraction from the island without financial compensation, yet few commercial interests could provide meaningful incentives for more than four thousand descendants. Through the work of Isaac, Mary and the fledgling TDA committee, many of these land owners were now aware of their rights. Maybe this unwieldy bureaucracy representing thousands of distant relatives would be the most effective barrier to logging or resettling the island.

Our third Solomons visit achieved the prerequisite set by both potential donors, which included establishing a united Tetepare landowner group with a shared vision. When our visas expired we returned to Australia, upbeat about Tetepare's prospects and eager to complete the applications to enable the project to commence in earnest.

Reality Check

While we fine-tuned the proposals for the ecolodge and ranger station with the aid of functioning computers and printers in Australia, I also grappled with our potential impact on Tetepare. Since the last incarnation of the coconut plantation a decade earlier, Tetepare had been deserted. For the first time in nearly a century, the island had reverted to the largest uninhabited rainforest island in the world. Maybe the spirits and the lack of any well-coordinated projects offered the best possible protection for Tetepare.

TDA's plans were going to change all this. We were going to attract visitors to Tetepare and train locals to work for them at our new field station and ecolodge. Maybe we were encouraging the very threat that we were trying to avert. Would the field station that was owned by all descendants be the conduit for resettlement of the island? By buying boats and fuel, would our rangers exacerbate the hunting of turtles and overfishing of reefs that they were employed to prevent? Any development, even 'green' development, could be a two-edged sword.

The donors did not share my concerns. Eventually we learned that our grant application to the New Zealand-based Pacific Initiative for the Environment had finally been approved. An informal name for this grant body was the 'Rainbow Warrior Fund' because it dispersed French compensation money paid in atonement for the sinking of Greenpeace's flagship. The *Rainbow Warrior* had been in the forefront of the campaign against the destruction of Muraroa atoll by French nuclear bomb testing and hence I reckoned it was appropriate that this money was now helping to protect one of the Pacific's jewels. Buoyed by securing one of the grants we were chasing but apprehensive about the consequences of this work, we flew back to Gizo.

Within hours of hearing that we had returned Mary greeted us in Gizo like long-lost friends, with the ever loyal and smiling Twomey 'holding the motor' of the original FOT aluminium canoe. We stashed a couple of weeks' supplies of noodles, rice and tinned tuna in the waterproof bow of the canoe, carefully arranged a motley assortment of plastic containers of fuel at the stern, and headed off for Tetepare.

As soon as we sighted Tetepare my fears of the project causing additional impacts on the island were turned inside out. Bright yellow and white plastic sheets screamed out from the normally unbroken line of forest on the unadulterated coast. The island had been resettled before our project had even started!

'Who is this?' I asked Mary, who pretended to ignore the beachside tents.

'Oh, just some fishermen,' she responded offhandedly, waving her hand vaguely in their direction.

When we reached the shore, camouflaged leaf shelters were also revealed among the trees. Together with the plastic tents they constituted a small village. Women and children strolled around on well-worn paths, and chainsaws growled from within the forest. The soil at our feet was buried in rain-softened woodchips strewn around like big yellow confetti.

'Making canoes,' Twomey responded to my unasked question.

Freshly carved yellow canoes were perched atop piles of wood shavings. Trails slashed through the regenerating plantation indicated where rough-hewn logs had been dragged down to the makeshift village where they were being rhythmically hacked into canoes by bare-backed men. While Mary chatted nonchalantly with her Lokuru friends, Katherine and I wandered around in shock.

Fishermen and women returned in their canoes with their booty of bêche-de-mer and undersize trochus shells. Marga, a dumpy jovial lady, approached us. Together with her husband she had collected a bowl of piddly black lollyfish, which suggested that more valuable bêche-de-mer had already been stripped from the waters. Marga and her husband had been camped on Tetepare for six weeks. The canoe carvers must have been here for just as long to generate so many woodchips and convert a dozen logs into new yellow canoes.

As the tide receded, another even more alarming story was exposed. Table-sized piles of hundreds of fresh *tutufa* clamshells were dotted along the shoreline. I was intrigued. During all our snorkelling and diving in the Solomons we had never seen densities of these foot-sized clams that could have supported such intensive harvesting.

'*Staka tumas stap insaed lagun,*' Marga beamed with an irregular smile, after noticing my interest in the piles of shells.

'*Mi laek traem disfala tutufa,*' I asked Marga, confident that given the hundreds of shells lying at our feet there would be a spare mouthful to sample.

'*Sori nao,*' Marga lamented, '*Evri tutufa finis nao.*'

Apparently since the camp had been established the clams had been wiped out from the lagoon. While I stared almost disbelieving at the piles of now scarce clamshells, two more fishermen paddled a large dugout up to the beach. Overflowing from the canoe were enormous *topa* fish. These bump-headed parrotfish were endangered in many tropical waters because they were large, tasty and slow. The coin-sized scales of other topa on the beach indicated that many more of these huge fish had been consumed at the makeshift village on Tetepare.

Katherine and I were confused and frustrated. Tetepare was hardly uninhabited. Mary had not informed us that, although we had sourced funds to look after this virgin island, her *wantoks* were systematically pillaging anything they could find. She had known the camp had been on Tetepare for months. The fact that Mary feigned surprise, not the fact that a few blokes were carving traditional canoes from the overgrown plantation, worried me most.

When we asked more questions about timber harvesting we were told that for the past decade or so high-value trees such as rosewood had been felled from Tetepare. Because there had been no rules there was no way of controlling timber extraction, Mary explained. Scattered batteries and rubbish also insulted our notions of a pristine island. The risk of cane toads or cats being inadvertently or deliberately introduced and more gardens hacked into the forest had also increased markedly with the establishment of this semi-permanent village. Tetepare had become the free-for-all breadbasket for anyone motivated enough to visit the island.

Wandering around in the regrowth forest behind the campsite we found fishing line nooses draped over low branches.

'*What nao disfala?*' I asked an inquisitive teenager who had followed me.

'*Kasim kara,*' he replied without any trace of guilt.

Kara, the magnificent green and red Eclectus parrots, were being trapped to sell to exporters at Munda for SBD$50. The few terrified birds that survived their smuggling out of the country would subsequently net US$500. Katherine and I had once driven six thousand kilometres to far northern Queensland to see these spectacular birds that were exceedingly rare in Australia and hence no matter how often I saw them in the Solomons they always made me stop for a moment's indulgence.

Reality shattered my idealism. Spirits and the honourable objectives of the TDA had not overridden the need for Tetepare landowners to make a living. Of course it hadn't. Tetepare wasn't the protected bubble that we had been led to believe, and that we in turn had convinced our donors. In time these camps would become villages and timber harvesting would lead to full-scale logging. We were wasting our time. To compound the problem, we were told that one of the canoes had been ordered by Mary. We had been duped.

This time Mary heard my unasked question. 'They will all leave when they can see the project working,' she suggested optimistically.

Was this another lie, another example of being told what we wanted to hear rather than the truth? I did not believe Mary that the camp would be abandoned once the Field Station was built. But we had committed to the project and so had the New Zealand donors. We had no option but to give it a go.

Mary explained that the ethnic tension had driven many people from Honiara back to their villages, either for their own safety or because the crumbling economy had cost them their jobs. The economic situation was no better in the provinces, especially those that had depended heavily upon copra exports. In the past twenty years copra sales had slumped from an average of $173 to less than $3 per person. The per capita GDP in the Solomon Islands had halved since 1996 to only US$500 in 2002. Tetepare landowners were harvesting their resources because they now had few alternatives to generate income for school fees or to buy rice, soap or kerosene. Many had worked on the Tetepare plantation; some had even lived nearby at copra drier number 4. What I saw as secondary rainforest bordering a pristine wilderness, Marga and her *wantoks* considered to be an overgrown plantation. Our reefs and lagoons were their supermarket and cash crop.

If the scale of the harvesting that we were witnessing continued unabated, Tetepare was doomed both as a food source and a conservation zone.

'I was thinking,' announced Mary, reaffirming my faith in telepathy, 'we should find out how many *topa* and *tutufa* people are catching then we should make some rules.'

Tetepare's reefs and forests would only be saved if TDA could establish and enforce sustainable harvesting rates. Mary volunteered to interview hunters and fishermen and record their

Tetepare catch, and the location of their favoured fishing or hunting grounds. Over the next few days we honed our interviewing methods and Mary accumulated an enormous inventory, just from those camped on Tetepare. Before the end of the month Mary could account for over three hundred pigs, over one thousand crayfish and nearly as many coconut crabs, all harvested from Tetepare over the previous six months. The canoe making that we witnessed at our campsite must have been replicated elsewhere on the island because at least twenty-one canoes had been carved from Tetepare trees. However, despite their appeal, neither the pigs, the *tutufa* clams nor the canoes were the principal reason that most people visited Tetepare. Ten thousand dollars worth of bêche-de-mer, four thousand dollars worth of trochus shells and a staggering seven thousand kilograms of fish had also recently been taken from the island's waters by the locals.

Fishing techniques varied from traditional methods to potentially more exploitative modern techniques. Mary and Marga preferred the small sweet reef fish that they caught by jerking a small baited hook up the face of a reef. Some of the men used a traditional variation of reef fishing. After collecting armfuls of fist-sized rounded cobbles they anchored their canoe next to a deep drop-off. Their hooks were concealed under a palm lure and dropped in an expertly crafted sling of coconut frond weighed down by the stone. Once the stone reached the ocean floor the men jerked the lure free from its coconut frond sling and then rapidly hauled it upwards, hoping to catch a prized *pajara*, or coral trout.

Marga's husband and some of the other men favoured spear fishing, where they could sneak up on an enormous *topa* that would feed their family for several days. The recent advent of waterproof torches had enabled the men to spear sleeping fish and these enormous fish were in danger of becoming as rare on Tetepare as they were throughout most of their former range. Night diving also increased harvest rates of trochus and bêche-de-mer. Fortunately no-one that Mary interviewed had used or witnessed the devastating cyanide or explosives that are used for fishing in other parts of the Pacific.

Camped at the outskirts of the temporary village, the evening humidity was stifling. Another drawback of our campsite was, unlike our other Tetepare campsites, there were no rivers where we could have a good wash. Instead we scooped water into a handleless saucepan from a slow-flowing shallow stream. After five days I had already started developing all-too-familiar skin eruptions. Even my smallest cuts required immediate disinfecting to prevent them swelling into weeping sores. Typically after a couple of weeks of camping in the forest my golden staph population was so vigorous that it did not even need cuts or bites to initiate mini-volcanoes that provided an irresistible smorgasbord for persistent orange-bummed flies. To fight unwanted biodiversity my travel doctor suggested I stick Savlon up my nose every evening, which did little to endear me to Katherine on our sweaty tent-bound nights!

Mary convinced us that since most of Tetepare's harvesters hailed from Lokuru we should hold another meeting there and convince the locals that the newly funded project was about to commence. Mary and Twomey owned a small three-roomed hut near Twomey's parents' house in Bangophingo, the Seventh Day Adventist section of the village. Followers of the United Church lived at the other end, called Vanikuva. John Kari, the founder of TOLOA, had named the Methodist village after the North American island during his first posting as a missionary in Lokuru in 1930. The division between denominations within the village was marked by a flower hedge. I was intrigued by this separation. How could two churches have such a strong effect on the layout of the village given that Christianity had only been introduced to Rendova three generations earlier?

Alan Tippet Bero, a Lokuru man whose grandfather had studied the rise of the local mission, explained that the introduction of several strong denominations to Solomon Islands could be better attributed to colonial trading than to the zeal of the early missionaries. John Goldie was the pioneering Methodist missionary who established Christianity in the Munda region and paved the way for the conversion of much of the Western Province. Goldie's arrival in 1902 coincided with the most significant social upheaval that the Solomon Islanders had ever experienced. Centuries of customary law were being forcibly replaced with British law by the fledgling colonial authorities. This changing of the guard provided a perfect opportunity for a leader to replace the revered warriors who had ruled in the 'lawless' headhunting days.

Goldie quickly gained converts and became revered in almost god-like fashion by standing up for the Islanders against unfair treatment by the authorities. To fund his burgeoning flock, Goldie's Methodist mission became involved in copra trading. Conversion to Christianity and the copra business both responded to Goldie's vigour like wildfire. Within a decade Goldie boasted over six thousand regular churchgoers. In his own words Goldie claimed that 'No other mission has done so much to instruct the natives and encourage them to plant up their undeveloped land.'

Wheatley, a copra trader who had married a Roviana woman, resented Goldie's entrepreneurism, which was eroding his business. He attempted to gain support from landowners by supplying headhunters from his region with illegal firearms. When this failed, he invited first the Salvation Army then the Catholics to the district in order to break Goldie's Methodist monopoly on the copra trade, but neither became established. Eventually Wheatley's third choice, the Seventh Day Adventists, established a successful mission at nearby Viru in 1914. The SDA mission, who dutifully supplied copra to Wheatley, quickly spread to Marovo, largely because the SDA pastors promised to teach their converts English.

Today's division of Lokuru and many other villages stems from those early colonial days when families opted for one or other denomination. Because children traditionally build on their forefather's land, historical artifact rather than deliberate segregation has resulted in the modern layout of these villages.

Mary organised another meeting with the 'troublesome' Lokuru mob. Jack Daniel worked the floor of the church hall like a preacher, yet somewhat disconcertingly seemed to be addressing me as often as his people. He proudly announced to the gathering that TDA had now received funds and that local workers would soon be employed to build a field station that would then be staffed by local rangers, guides and cooks. This prospect of work turned the trickle of registrations into a flood. Mary worked much of the night filling out forms and issuing receipts. TDA was up, up and away.

The following morning Mary asked Matthew Suka, one of the local TDA committee members, to introduce Katherine and me to two important men while she busied herself registering more TDA converts with Goldie-like zeal. Matthew led us to 103-year-old Solomon Ebokolo, who was a generation older than anyone else I had ever met. Ebokolo, whose birth predated the sale of the Tetepare plantation and the arrival of the missions, was the last man on Rendova with the enormously stretched earlobes that were characteristic of his day. We then met Matthew's father, Jonathan Suka, who was as talkative as old Ebokolo had been reserved. Suka *storied* about the special powers that he could summon from Tetepare spirits and about his dream of finding the hidden skull cave on Tetepare.

Mary had excelled in motivating and registering her people on Rendova but TDA also needed disciples on other islands where Tetepare descendants lived. By radio we confirmed earlier arrangements to travel through Marovo lagoon and New Georgia Island to appoint local communication officers. Casper, an ex-WWF field officer who we had befriended during our second oil palm marine survey, was to transport us in his canoe.

The following morning an excited conference of women had congregated outside Twomey's house where we were staying. Mary strode over to us from the gathering and snorted, 'They say it is too dangerous for you to go to Marovo.'

'Why?' Katherine inquired.

This was the first time that we had ever heard the word danger mentioned in the Solomon Islands. The women had heard that a white couple had been kidnapped by rebels at sea between Rendova and Marovo.

'When did this happen?' I asked, concerned.

'Yesterday,' Mary replied gruffly, clearly not believing the women's story.

'What should we do?' Katherine questioned.

'Of course it is safe, they are just talking,' Mary replied. 'When Casper comes you will go with him to Marovo,' she instructed.

After Mary had left, the women called Katherine over. They were convinced that we were in danger and that Casper would not come because everyone knew the rebels were after us. We had expressly asked our Marovo friend to reach Lokuru early so that we didn't have to cross the open sea in the afternoon when storms were more likely. But Casper didn't come. By now we had become accustomed to Solomon time, but the wait for Casper took an eternity, especially with the ever embellished stories about us being targeted by pirates. Our frustration was eased by an impromptu singing concert by the local kids. Although shy at first, the makeshift choir that congregated around Twomey's house sang Sunday school songs in both English and Touo with gusto.

Mary was annoyed that our schedule had been interrupted. She arranged for Eric, a Lokuru man, to take us to Marovo at first light the following morning. The local women reported an update that the kidnapped woman had been killed, but despite their fears we decided to trust Mary, as we had become accustomed.

A couple of hours after our bags were packed the following morning, Eric turned up at Mary's leaf house with an outboard motor on his shoulder. We followed him to a small fibreglass canoe on the beach. As is typical, one of the blokes who helped us push the canoe down the beach jumped in at the last minute. He had no bag, clothes, food or water. After a couple of minutes of unconvincing splutters, the engine blurted into life and we headed off, waving to nervous huddles of new friends on the beach.

Less than a kilometre from shore the outboard motor coughed and then cut out. Eric pulled and pulled to no avail. The dark figures who had just disappeared back into their houses reappeared on the beach. Before we commenced our Solomons odyssey I considered photocopiers and old lawnmowers to be the most unreliable and frustrating machines ever made. Outboard motors are definitely up there on the medals dais, particularly given that paper jams or unkempt lawns are rarely life-threatening.

'*Iufala garem eni tool?*' Eric asked his empty-handed crew and us together. We had just set off to cross the same open water where we had been stranded in the storm with Eddie and John T on our first visit to Tetepare two and a half years earlier. I admired Katherine's nerve, particularly when we were possibly running the gauntlet of pirates, when she rummaged her pocket-knife out of her pack and handed it to Eric. The unlikely mechanic then cut the drawstring from his rain jacket to tie up something within the outboard motor. After another twenty minutes or so, all the time scanning the open sea for menacing craft, we resumed.

Not long after the beachside houses and churches of Lokuru had been absorbed into the distant forest I spotted another canoe, heading straight towards us. While trying to look as inconspicuous as possible, I watched the canoe and Eric's face intently. What would we do, what could we do, if we were intercepted by pirates on the high seas? I had a pocket-knife, but neither Eric nor his mate even carried a bush knife. It didn't matter, because the canoe's path gradually veered away from ours.

As is typical of mid-sea encounters, both drivers simultaneously pointed in the direction they were travelling and threw their heads back acknowledgingly. Then, having sorted out that they were heading in opposite directions, both drivers, as if by mirror image, pointed exaggeratedly in the direction that the other was travelling and repeated their mirror image laughing acknowledgement. It never ceased to amaze me how predictable the response of canoe drivers was to a passing *wantok* but how different their interpretations of the same response could be. Sometimes when I asked I was told that 'His wife has just had a baby in the hospital so he is taking her some potatoes from her sister's garden' or 'He is trying to get his opposition to the timber rights hearing to the forestry office before it closes' all from a point and a laugh. This time I was extra keen to hear the interpretation of this point-and-laugh charade. Was the other canoe evading murderous pirates? 'No,' Eric explained, 'The schoolteacher was returning to Lokuru after spending some time in Marovo with his *wantoks*.'

After a couple of tense hours Eric steered us towards an almost imperceptible gap in an imposing cliff. We entered a narrow channel that had been modified using World War II ammunition to create a shortcut into Marovo Lagoon. A fifteen metre high white cliff, dripping with icing-like stalactites overhung the narrow waterway. With heightened awareness I conjured up a James Bond canoe chase through the meandering channel with rebels firing at us from the jungle. But there was no chase nor pirates. When we met up with Casper we learned that he had not picked us up because both his outboard and his radio were *bagarap*. We pieced together the source of the fears held for our safety in Lokuru. A white couple had gone missing while diving at the erupting subterranean Kavachi volcano but had subsequently been rescued twenty-four hours later. In another separate drama, that had been morphed by the coconut news with the missing divers, a senior New Zealand diplomat had apparently been tragically stabbed at her Honiara home.

Katherine and I spent the next few weeks travelling around Marovo and New Georgia, staying with Tetepare descendants at a different village every night. We appointed TDA communication officers, who were issued receipt books and registration sheets, compiled ever more detailed genealogies and yarned with far-flung descendants about their aspirations for Tetepare.

Although still clothed by green, bare tree trunks and red–brown scars, clearly evident from the sea, attested to the sparseness of the canopy in the recently logged forest that was spreading like a cancer around Marovo lagoon. From our base at Matikuri ecolodge we were woken by the insult of screeching metal as excavators chewed up live coral to extend an already enormous log pond on adjacent Vangunu Island. Aggressive groaning of diesel compression and the wheezing airlock brakes announced another truckload of freshly felled logs winding down the steep muddy roads. Previously we had woken to the distant screech of lorikeets, the indignant squeak of a wrestling gecko or the comforting drum of rain on a leaf roof. The panorama for which Katherine had coined the word 'serenic' was now anything but. Three logging operations were clearly visible and audible from our rough hewn timber deck that had, only three years previously, framed an unspoiled wilderness.

Benjamin lamented the destruction that he was powerless to combat despite the effect on his ecolodge. His family were also now bitterly divided by logging opportunities, and this division was the Achilles heel that the loggers capitalised upon.

'*Supos mifala mill timber seleva, no any dispute, no any problem bi stap*,' he stated. Greenpeace had offered Benjamin's tribe and other Marovo landowners an alternative to the relentless destruction of the international logging. By carefully selecting, milling and exporting their own timber, they could generate more income and preserve their forests and social cohesion. But few islanders, indeed few landowners in developing countries, were prepared to forgo the possibility of quick easy money for a more labour-intensive alternative. Although he did not admit it himself, Benjamin knew that neither he nor any other members of his tribe would stick their neck out to champion the hard-work option of arranging their own milling rather than bowing to the pressure for logging that his brother favoured. While international demand for cheap yet unsustainably harvested round logs persists, Matikuri's devastating experience will continue to be replicated throughout Melanesia.

Eventually we worked our way back to Munda, met up again with Mary and travelled with her back to Gizo. The news back in civilisation was dominated by speculation about the cause of Brigit Nichols' death. The New Zealand Deputy Commissioner had been found with a fatal knife wound just days after completing a report suggesting a revamp of the corrupt national police force. Due to increasing frustration with the situation in Honiara that had been highlighted again by this incident, Western Province politicians told us openly about their plans to secede from the troubled nation. Despite the enthusiasm for TDA's plans among descendants, it seemed likely that the national unrest would continue to thwart plans for a sustainable ecotourism venture on Tetepare.

Katherine and I were worried, very worried. Although we wanted to help Mary at this vulnerable time for the fledgling TDA, we were forced to leave because our annual three-month tourist visa had expired. I pleaded separately to Mary and Twomey to keep the faith. I promised that we would return once we had secured our residency visa and that in the interim we would continue to apply for more support and work on the genealogies while back in Australia. Little did we suspect at that time that the immediate threat to the preservation of Tetepare was not from political or social forces, but from within the ranks of descendants.

Operation Suicide

April 2002 found us cooling our heels in Australia. Our inability to return without a residency permit was compounded by lack of news from the Solomons. Like many Islanders we were frustrated that the only functioning facet of Solomons' bureaucracy effectively thwarted well-intentioned expatriates.

The European Union, or EU, held the key to securing our residency, which would allow us to spend more than three months a year in the Solomons. However, the EU was reluctant to support Tetepare and hence arrange our residency until the concerns of a disgruntled landowner had been sorted out. One Nathaniel Soto had written to the EU expressing his opposition to the conservation plans for 'his' island. Fortunately, after a series of emails, the understanding staff at the EU office trusted that we could organise a retraction letter from Nathaniel if only we could get back into the country. As soon as we received our EU sanctioned residency visa, Katherine and I booked our flights to kick-start the Tetepare project.

Unfortunately Nathaniel Soto was not our only impediment. Just before we left Australia we received our only contact with any Tetepare descendants since we had left the Solomons five months earlier. A fax from WWF informed us that a Tetepare descendant from Ughele village on neighbouring Rendova Island had commenced an export logging operation on Tetepare. Worse still, accompanying this shocking news was a letter signed by four senior Tetepare landowners based in Lokuru, including the two paramount chiefs of Rendova.

The Chairman
Tetepare Descendants Association
Lokuru, Rendova Island

29 April 2002

Environmental Propose Project on Tetepare Island.

We the registered Tetepare Original Landowners Association (TOLOA) Trustees on the power rested on us in Toloa's constitution do oppose the above project initiated by TDA with WWF support and perhaps with overseas financial support.

Please advise your overseas co-ordinators of the above project to call it off and keep future environmentalists out of Tetepare, as we are concern that our accessibility to the island might be restricted and our survivability and livelihood on the resources of Tetepare will be affected.

Leave Tetepare under TOLOA. Thankyou.
Cc: WWF Gizo
Cc: Chief W.Lianga – Ughele

I was flabbergasted, annoyed and scared. Logging just months after TDA had established its conservation agenda was the worst conceivable scenario for Tetepare. Furthermore the chiefs' letter suggested that the logging was not the work of an isolated renegade, but had been sanctioned by key Tetepare powerbrokers. By uniting with the Ughele people, the Lokuru elders were articulating their preference for logging rather than the conservation agenda of TDA. The signatories were all close relatives of TDA committee members, including the brother of TDA's Chairman Jack Daniel. What was going on?

Surely Mary and Jack were aware that their community leaders had asked, or maybe told, us to abandon the Tetepare project. Yet why had they not contacted us to explain? Had WWF tried to intervene or simply passed the message on to us, accepting defeat? Was this the typical non-confrontational way of being dumped in Melanesia? This dramatic about-face mirrored Solomon international diplomacy. We had witnessed aid donors being courted by senior politicians agreeing to requirements with which they had no intention of complying. The farcical simultaneous commitments made to opposite factions of the international whaling fraternity that frustrated Australian and New Zealand politicians and conservationists were another classic example. Had we too been lured by hollow 'commitments' that were superseded when more immediate logging royalties were offered?

But we had been captured by Tetepare's spell and had toiled for months writing grant applications, entering genealogy information and arranging our work commitments in Australia to allow us six months unpaid leave each year for the foreseeable future. One thing for sure was that we would not get to the bottom of the issue without returning. But this time both the key Tetepare landowners and the Australian government were advising us not to return. Throwing caution to the wind, we decided to go regardless.

As soon as we arrived in Gizo we caught up with Peter Siloko's cousin Kido at the WWF office. Like his great-great-uncle of the same name, Kido had taken on a leadership role with Tetepare landholders, at least on paper, by being a founding executive member of TDA. Yet neither Kido nor WWF had challenged the logging on Tetepare, nor convened a meeting to rectify the issue that threatened to scuttle TDA's plans. Developments had stalled during our absence. TDA had not been registered, its bank account had not been opened and apparently Nathaniel Soto, who was on his deathbed in Honiara, had not retracted his complaint to the potential EU donors. Kido also informed us that the flamboyant politician Danny Philips was campaigning to convert Tetepare into a US naval base!

Despite the dark storm clouds hanging over both Gizo and Tetepare we noticed an easing of the post-coup atmosphere. The New Zealand police had publicly confirmed that the NZ Deputy Commissioner had not been stabbed in Honiara but had died from a freak accident. Expatriates bravely believed this verdict. Kids playing soccer on muddy Gizo roads emulated their heroes Ronaldino and Renaldo after an astonishing number had been able to watch the soccer World Cup on pirated videos. My Gizo sounding-board and willing boat driver, Patson, agreed that life was reverting to normal and half quipped, 'Maybe everyone is just getting used to the situation.'

We needed to contact Mary to find out what was really happening on Tetepare and whether we had a chance of reinvigorating the fledgling project. Our only avenue was through her brother Hukata, who worked at Agnes Lodge in Munda. The vagaries of Solomon Telekom eventually aligned and I was able to speak with Hukata. As far as he knew Mary was in Lokuru but all the radios there were *bagarap*. A few days later his answer was the same.

Katherine and I were going crazy in Gizo. No matter how hard we tried we couldn't make contact with the key Tetepare people from Lokuru to confirm that the project had been canned. We had no option but to broadcast an appeal for Mary over the national radio.

The windup radio on the verandah of Phoebe's Resthouse crackled into life. Music and drumming introduced the announcements segment known as Radio Hapi Lagoon. 'Tonight we have three messages. First one is for Mary Bea to come to Gizo by canoe as soon as possible; expenses will be reimbursed in Gizo.' Even if Mary was not listening we were hoping that one of her *wantoks* would pass on the message.

Amazingly Mary arrived the next day. Our relief in meeting her again was matched by her obvious joy in our return. Mary brought welcome news. Although she was unable to convince the Munda police to enforce the Forestry Department's ruling requesting the Tetepare loggers to stop, her *wantoks* had taken matters into their own hands. Fewer than one hundred trees had been felled before the loggers had been forced from the island. Importantly, Mary informed us they had used portable mills rather than the destructive bulldozers and trucks like we had been led to believe. 'Tetepare is still OK,' Mary beamed, although her frustration with waging the battle almost single-handedly was apparent.

'Tetepare may be okay,' I acknowledged, 'but what about TDA?' Apart from Mary, no-one else seemed to have lifted a finger. Mary explained Jack Daniel had privately repented to her and was now 'very strong for TDA'. Following his recent birthday, Jack had confided that he had reached fifty without noteworthy achievements and now he was determined to put something back into his community. TDA's current predicament offered him an important opportunity to do just that.

'If Jack turned a blind eye to the logging and the letter sent to us,' I probed, 'are you comfortable about him representing TDA?'

'If a leader is cast out he can do much harm,' Mary explained. 'We elevate responsibility in a leader who has gone astray. It is better to have him with us rather than against us.'

In accordance with this Melanesian approach, we authorised funding for Jack to fly to Honiara with Henry, his serious sidekick who had been appointed as the Secretary, to register TDA and secure the retraction letter from Nathaniel.

Despite our fears, TDA was still alive, so we arranged with Mary to head straight to Tetepare to ensure that the loggers had left for good. The sight of felled trees lying along the shore like fallen soldiers brought home the reality of the threat to Tetepare. Although several Lokuru lads had been given work, community dissent against the few beneficiaries galvanised the Lokuru descendants against logging. Mary's scary *wantoks* had stolen the loggers' boat, fuel, remaining timber and even their clothes. The loggers got the message. We got the message too! Hopefully this grassroots defence would be a turning point, another one, in the history of Tetepare, and that the backlash against taking forty-nine trees would be the catalyst to protect the islands' US$20 million forest resource.

But simply chasing away one gang of renegade loggers was not going to secure TDA's long-term objectives in the eyes of the ambivalent but observant descendants. We needed to initiate activities; the training and income generation we had spoken about. A couple of mates from WWF in Gizo agreed to visit Lokuru to train a dozen local divers and fishermen to be marine monitors. Mary's daughters Domu and Neri decorated a small shelter at Lokuru with coconut fronds and flowers where local women brought platefuls of food for the hungry students. Like Perry and Casper from Marovo, these lads recited the names of dozens of fish, including the eight indicator species used by the 'reefcheck' system to assess the condition of coral reefs throughout the tropics.

At night, after returning from the training sessions on Tetepare's reefs, TDA committee members held awareness talks in Lokuru.

I questioned a couple of the signatories to the letter asking us not to return. To my surprise these men all claimed that the letter was written by the logging supporter, not them. 'Why nao iu saenim disfala leta?' I probed, determined to learn their motivation for shunning TDA and our involvement. 'He paid us $50 to sign it,' was the unanimous response, with no remorse. The men had been paid for their signature, not their endorsement of the letter!

Having witnessed the reefcheck training, where the importance of managing and monitoring marine resources was explained to local fishermen, Jack Daniel uttered an offhand yet remarkably prophetic quote, 'The hardest resource to manage is people.' Although he had finally spearheaded the local awareness sessions, Jack had not registered TDA when he visited Honiara with Henry. What seemed to be lost on our Chairman was that registration was required before TDA could secure the lease for the island to prevent further logging. 'No problem,' laughed Jack. 'Mary will collect the trustees' signatures and my deputy Kido can register TDA,' he decreed.

We were in high spirits when we returned from Tetepare to the WWF office in Gizo. Within a few weeks of fearing that TDA and the Tetepare forests were finished, donor funding was now flowing and WWF had now formally agreed to work with us. We began busily planning for TDA's inaugural annual general meeting, the first gathering representing far-flung Tetepare descendants for at least five generations.

A phone call shattered our spirits.

'The Chairman is very worried,' Mary announced ominously from Munda.

Apparently Jack had just 'intercepted CIA intelligence'. Chief Willie from Ughele was not going to support TDA or the plans to build the field station and ecolodge on the overgrown Tetepare plantation. Even worse, he was planning to reinvigorate the Voseleai company and crank up the plantation and timber extraction again. By successfully dealing with the chiefs' letter asking us not to return, chasing away the loggers and securing funding, we felt that we had overcome TDA's major teething problems. Yet this news was worse still.

Another complication was that Mary now realised that Henry, TDA's secretary, held the TDA constitution in Munda, I had the trustees' signatures in Gizo but the application for the lease was lost in transit. All three needed to be presented together to register TDA. We couldn't hold the AGM or start to implement plans without registering and then securing the lease. Jack was 'so concerned' that he had travelled to Munda with Henry and Mary. Was this a well-executed excuse for Jack and Henry to have another all-expenses-paid trip to Honiara? Was it another delaying tactic? Once again we were frustrated and confused. But one thing we were convinced of was that TDA needed to secure the vacant Tetepare plantation lease before Peter Siloko's fears were realised by Voseleai or another opportunist.

Jack decided that Henry, who had influential *wantoks* in Honiara, should accompany me to register TDA and secure the lease. WWF could not advance us any funds for flights because one of the three signatories required to clear their cheques was out of the office. Katherine calculated that we had just enough cash for plane tickets for myself and Henry so we agreed to the plan.

Within an hour of deciding to fly to Honiara, my plane from Gizo touched down on the huge Munda airstrip and taxied to the terminal, where I searched in vain for the TDA secretary. The pilot did not shut down the far propeller because we were only stopping to load passengers. I sprinted over to a shady meeting tree where I found Henry. 'Come quickly!' I implored as I ran back to the airport and asked the local Solomon Airlines manager if I could pay for a ticket. 'The plane is leaving,' he said, exasperated. 'You can't buy a ticket now.'

Henry eyeballed the pilot, who was, of course, his *wantok*. The pilot gave Henry the thumbs up. Then the most remarkable thing that I had ever witnessed in the Solomons occurred. Henry actually RAN to perch on the scales. Another Solomon Airlines' staffer, after being barked at by his annoyed boss, RAN to his office to scrawl out a ticket. Of course they did not have change. Someone else in a Solomon Airlines' shirt volunteered change from his pocket that was thrust into my hand as I stooped into the plane. For a couple of brief minutes I witnessed a scene that could be described as urgency and even efficiency, two concepts that were as foreign as snow to the Solomons.

Jammed into my seat with perspiration streaming down my face and my soaked shirt sticking to my back, I calmly enquired of Henry why he hadn't registered TDA last time he went to Honiara. What I really wanted to ask was, 'What the fuck's going on?'

I was annoyed and frustrated, and not only because I worried that I was being manipulated by the Lokuru mob while they defied the conservation agenda to which they had supposedly 'agreed'. My thoughts were also with Katherine. Half an hour earlier as she waved me off from Gizo she announced, 'I think I might be pregnant'. Oh my goodness. 'You think or you know,' I asked blankly, not knowing in that instant whether to call off my flight, to go to the hotel to celebrate, or to sit down under a tree and take in the enormity of those six words. 'I'll find out when you get back' she replied stoically and followed with, 'Good luck and stay safe' as she waved me towards the plane.

Henry broke my thoughts. 'I have never seen a plane hijacked before,' he quipped, his erratic beaver-like teeth smiling through his nicotine-stained moustache. This was the first time I had seen him smile; maybe he no longer had to maintain the serious persona that characterised his meetings with his more jovial comrades. I wanted to show him my annoyance with our predicament and that this was not going to be a joy flight. I only had a couple of hundred dollars and had left Katherine in Gizo with $10, which would have to last her the whole weekend until the bank opened on Monday. My ploy didn't work. Henry tapped his top pocket that predictably revealed two protruding cigarettes. 'I only have three dollars,' he laughed. I had to laugh too. I could not maintain my attitude with this likeable leprechaun. I had no choice but to trust him and make the most of our time in Honiara. 'We will call this Operation Suicide,' Henry quipped. Operation Suicide indeed.

Over the drone of the twin-engined Otter, Henry told me that years ago he had been the Honiara-based administration officer for the Development Bank of the Solomon Islands. Through his bank contacts Henry became aware when Mr Hodge's Tetepare lease expired and reverted to the Commissioner of Lands. Fearing that a consortium of Malaitans were poised to take over, Henry arranged for his Lokuru *wantoks*, led by his old mate Jack Daniel, to manage the plantation. A few years later, following the conversion of the bank loan into Solbrew, which lubricated the throats of TOLOA's big men, Henry was called back to Lokuru to take over. In the mid-1980s Henry commenced replanting the Tetepare plantation and applied for additional bank loans to replant the remainder of the plantation and to introduce cattle. He was only operating in the area close to the main Tavara copra driers, while the rest of the plantation continued to be overrun by the regenerating rainforest. Yet Henry still found it difficult to maintain the productive coconuts and motivate the local Lokuru labourers. Novice canoe operators broke outboard motors and Henry smirked as he told me the story of one frightened bloke who crashed a tractor after he mistakenly 'stepped on the speed' while lounging on an idling machine. Another new tractor became *bagarap* within a week when oil was placed in the petrol tank and vice versa. Unsurprisingly, TOLOA were unable to repay their loans from the shambles.

Fearing again that the bank would hand the Tetepare plantation to Malaitans, TOLOA encouraged their *wantoks* from Ughele, on the northern shore of Rendova, to take over the lease. Ughele people had just been the recipients of the first logging royalties from Rendova and hence were temporarily cashed up. Voseleai Company, which comprised Tetepare landowners from Ughele, became the leaseholders of the plantation in the early 1990s. However, like their Lokuru *wantoks* and the Australians before them, Voseleai were also unsuccessful. The plantation and its meagre buildings again fell into disrepair.

After we landed and made our way into downtown Honiara, Henry and I found out even more about the Ughele-based company that still officially held the lease for the Tetepare plantation. Voseleai had not repaid their bank loan and indeed had never paid their annual lease fees since they acquired the Tetepare plantation in 1992. Their ship used as collateral on their loan had sunk. However, due to a series of oversights or possibly *wantok* intervention, Voseleai had neither been bankrupted by the bank, deregistered by the Register of Titles, nor had their lease terminated by the Commissioner of Lands. Unless registered, TDA would not be granted the lease and could not build the ecotourism base. More worrying, the future of Tetepare was in the hands of the Commissioner of Lands, who could grant the lease to any suitor he pleased. Jack Daniel's 'intelligence' was that TDA's plans had rekindled Voseleai's desire to regain control of Tetepare.

Henry and I waited in the queue at the Registrar of Titles office until a blackout stopped work for the day. I found myself a room at the cheap but immaculately clean Melanesian Brothers' Resthouse and bought a bunch of bananas for dinner that stretched my stomach without shrinking my wallet. Henry said he would board for free with Danny Phillips. Although helpful for our tight budget, I harboured misgivings about the role of this entrepreneurial *bigman* at such a delicate time for TDA. The following morning I walked back to the government offices before 8 a.m. so I would be first in the queue. I carried a torch in case another blackout thwarted the search for files. At 8.20 a clerk, then a cartographer, arrived, neither of whom had been paid for six weeks.

'Must be strike,' my new acquaintances surmised, glancing at their watches and the empty building in front of us that should by now have housed at least fifty staff. Eventually, Henry wandered up with another helpful *wantok*, who promised to process our registration as soon as the offices opened.

While we waited I decided we should visit the EU office to arrange funds for TDA's inaugural AGM planned for the following week. Henry introduced me to Honiara's confusing but incredibly efficient public transport system. From what I could establish, a procession of minivans travelled along the coastal side of the main road towards the airport until they ran out of passengers. The small cardboard destination sign nestled among plastic flowers in the windscreen was apparently redundant. The buses then turned around, chose another random destination and all travelled the same reverse route until all the passengers, picked up along the way, had departed.

A rasta, resplendent in dark glasses and a bandana, noisily wrenched open the door of the minivan. After stooping into a seat I asked the disinterested dude what the fare was, but he continued to ignore me. Henry found a seat at the back of the bus where he casually looked out the window without paying. No wonder he could make SB$3 stretch for three days! Then, after a minute or so, I witnessed a bizarre ritual. One by one the passengers surreptitiously slipped the ticket collector a two-dollar note. No-one made eye contact. No acknowledgement was made of payment or those who had not yet paid. I followed suit and covertly slipped the bandit a five-dollar note, the smallest denomination I could squeeze out of my pocket while wedged in the cramped seat. A full thirty seconds later a hand suddenly appeared at about knee height with SB$3 change, clasped by a grotesque curled nail painted with purple sparkly nail polish. In the time that it took me to pay my fare and receive my change, the van had stopped three times at scheduled or random locations, on each occasion the driver responding to a hiss from Mr Bandana. Despite their aloof initial persona, bus drivers and conductors turned out to be incredibly accommodating. One subsequent fare collector, wearing an upside-down woman's golf visor that spooned his enormous Afro upwards like a flower arrangement, diverted the driver several kilometres to the Minister of Forests' office on my behalf.

The European Union office was a different world from the humid chaos outside. Not only was the office air-conditioned and spotless but it was also equipped with functioning computers, printers, faxes and even photocopiers. The contrast between this office and the government offices was as striking as that between the affluent European countries and the struggling developing country they were assisting. No sooner had we stepped inside than Danny Philips mysteriously arrived and whisked Henry away. Apparently Nathaniel Soto, whose letter had delayed our EU funding for over six months, had just died in hospital. The timing of his death and Henry's sudden departure with Danny Philips on a pivotal day for Tetepare rekindled considerable suspicion. I smelt a rat, a big one and raced back to the government offices.

Without Henry around I had no idea who our potential competitors were but I was sure that Henry was not the only Tetepare landowner in town trying to secure the lease. All of a sudden, everyone loitering around the closed offices looked suspicious. Maybe one of the men in the haphazard queue was the bloke Mary had just stopped milling timber on Tetepare or the representative sent by Voseleai to beat TDA to the lease. I had no doubt that they knew exactly who I was and my motives, and that was dangerous.

Never before in Honiara had I felt threatened, but then again I had always made a point of informing everyone that I was a tourist. Knowing that conserving Tetepare was a contentious issue, neither Katherine nor I had ever told anyone that we were now spearheading its conservation agenda, yet now I found myself having to inform an increasing number of strangers of my motives. Two expatriates had recently been killed in the Solomons because their well-intentioned actions were not appreciated by renegades. Suspecting that I was going to become a father further heightened my apprehension at loosing my head to a disgruntled logger. Conspiracy theories raced through my mind like a thriller movie as I studied everyone walking down the scuffed corridors or sitting under trees outside. I recalled Henry's announcement of our suicide mission and hoped he wasn't psychic.

A handwritten notice placed on the locked door of the Registrar's office since we had been there this morning spelled out 'Open after 1 p.m.' I propped myself against the door so no-one could walk in or out without me moving. The polish had all but worn off the floorboards leaving a narrow fringe against the walls. One of the pink metal shutters adjacent to every door, except the Registrar's, was missing. As I scanned the corridors for conspirators I noticed the public servants reaching through these shutters to open the locked doors. If only I could break into the Registrar's office I could grab our new registration certificate, photocopy it and then return it without anyone knowing.

The secretary departing for an early lunch looked at me incredulously as I somersaulted backwards into her office. Why would anyone sit against a door with a sign that clearly stated that the office would not reopen for another two hours? I locked the door behind me and told her that I only needed to collect a registration certificate that had been processed this morning by Henry's *wantok*. 'Oh yes,' she replied, 'the Tetepare registration is complete,' before ambling back into the catacombs of her office. Ten minutes later I was still standing in the waiting room, wondering how it could possibly take so long to retrieve a certificate that had just been typed. There must be a problem. Maybe she had snuck out of a back door and was sending some boys around to discourage me from pursuing the TDA registration?

Eventually the secretary sauntered back with the typed certificate, signed and stamped by the Registrar, confirming that the Tetepare Descendants' Association had been registered today. There was no way that I would hand this prized original certificate to the Commissioner of Lands, so I took it across the road to the Australian embassy where my *wantoks* obliged with prompt and free photocopies.

Back outside the Commissioner of Lands' office was the biggest, meanest looking thug that I had ever seen. Built like a Samoan front-rower, his imposing presence was accentuated by an intricately tattooed head. With my heart pounding I squeezed past him in the shallowly confident manner that you use when walking past a snarling Rottweiler. Although I was early for our appointment I took my chances, not knowing when another blackout or strike would stymie our chances of securing the all-important lease. The Commissioner, looking as professional as any public servant in the Solomons, beckoned me forwards to his desk. He recognised me from earlier visits, sparked no doubt by the several phone calls I had made from Gizo during the week.

After scrutinising TDA's registration certificate the Commissioner announced that he could not issue TDA the lease today but assured me that it would be available on Monday. Disgruntled, I left the office and bumped into Henry, who was waiting outside. Despite visiting the hospital and Nathaniel's house he and Danny Philips were unable to confirm whether or not TDA's nemesis had died. Even more intriguing and concerning was that Danny Philip had an appointment with the Commissioner this afternoon, although Henry assured me that his meeting was unrelated to the Tetepare lease. Furthermore Danny planned to send his son to pick me up from my resthouse this evening so that he could meet me. What was going on?

Danny Philips was as polished as expected from someone who had graced international diplomatic circles for over a decade. Like many other Rendova men, Danny was far blacker than most Honiara residents, a fact accentuated by his crisp white shirt. His generous girth and the ease with which he carried his gold jewellery testified a big man accustomed to the good life. The assembled throng of Rendova powerbrokers who boarded at his house listened intently to Danny's stories of meetings with Clinton and Howard and his recollections of getting drunk with Jonathon Major, who was a closet party animal once you got to know him well enough. Henry's mates agreed with Danny's opinions, laughed at his jokes and hung on his every word.

After making the appropriate comments about his worldly experiences I asked the big man his impressions of TDA's objectives. In polished political overtures Danny praised the Tetepare project. He was particularly excited about a fanciful drawing that Lloyd Hodge had drafted of a major resort complete with several pleasure craft, five-star accommodation, fancy restaurants, dive shops and an expansive manager's residence. 'That can be your house,' he announced to me, stabbing his finger at the two story mansion. 'Was this the vision that I had for Tetepare also?' he enquired, eagerly. The pressure was on.

I replied that Katherine and I were simply helping descendants to achieve their goals as long as they were consistent with the conservation of the island. Small-scale ecotourism was readily achievable but more elaborate opportunities were potentially available if Tetepare was protected from logging and resettlement. I lauded environmental trust funds and even carbon and biodiversity trading as opportunities for the Solomons, and particularly Tetepare, to generate hard currency income. Henry and his mates looked understandably amazed when I explained, with more confidence than conviction, that the forest could be worth more to them intact than if it was logged. It had been Danny's ideas to establish a casino and a US military base and I felt it was important for a selection of the Lokuru powerbrokers to be exposed to greener alternatives.

Almost sheepishly and with a lavish rubbing of his boot-polish-black face, Danny admitted that he had wanted to log 'that bloody island.' 'If it wasn't for my 'sister' Mary I would have done it too,' he reflected.

'Thanks to Mary, Tetepare now has the opportunity to provide more lucrative and long-term income for all descendants,' I exaggerated to appreciative acknowledgement by Henry and the others. Danny was charming and friendly but I could not decide whether TDA had gained an influential supporter or whether he was planning to use the new association to progress one of his alternative plans.

The following morning, a Saturday, while waiting at the airport for hours on end with Danny's son, who had been appointed as my driver, I lamented the unreliability of Solomon Airlines. I was booked to return to Katherine in Gizo, and Henry was to fly direct to Munda after securing the lease on Monday. Through months of experience, I reckoned that I had an even chance of catching a booked flight within a couple of hours of its departure time. On those frustrating days when luck was against me the Eagles song *Hotel California* played relentlessly in my head, inspired by the line 'You can check out any time you like, but you can never leave'.

Returning to the airport the following morning I was amazed to see three planes, the entire national fleet, on the tarmac. Temporary relief proved ill-founded when a fellow passenger surmised 'Must be strike.' Like the teachers and police and public service, the Civil Aviation Authority had finally reacted to the failure of the government to pay their salaries for several months. Domestic and international flights had ground to a halt. So too had my chances of returning to Katherine for another day. Was she okay? Was she now convinced that she was pregnant? On the advice of the sole Solomon Airlines clerk I booked both Henry and myself on every scheduled flight for the next three days and continued to play the waiting game.

The Commissioner of Lands was again difficult to meet on Monday, this time because the national superannuation fund, to which his office owed three million dollars in rent, changed their locks on the weekend, keeping out all government workers. Eventually we tracked him down and negotiated and paid for TDA to lease the Tetepare plantation at a bargain price. With a stamped and signed receipt in hand we had eventually accomplished our mission, or so we thought.

Tuesday morning found Henry and me sitting on the same dirty bench where I had spent the weekend strumming my air guitar to John Fogarty's *Hotel California* riff. The CAA had permitted a limited number of flights and we were the third and fourth listed standby passengers on a flight to Munda. I managed to ring Katherine, who was going to catch a canoe from Gizo to Munda in time for this afternoon's inaugural annual general meeting of TDA. With so many passengers booked on three or more flights, there was a better than even chance that we would be issued a seat. Then Mr Nice arrived with his entourage.

Mr Nice wasn't. He was tall for a Korean but I quickly learned that he did not live up to his name that was scrawled on several boxes that were also marked Eagon Company, a company I remembered well from our logging audits. Mr Nice treated the patient waiting passengers and Solomon Airlines staff with the same contempt that his company treated the government and the nation's forest. He followed staff into their private room where the apparently arbitrary decision as to which standby passengers would be granted tickets was made. Then Mr Nice aggressively moved his luggage to the front of the queue. I was incensed. This rich bully was bribing his way onto the flight in front of several locals who were patiently queuing and following the rules. As keen as I was for Henry and I to make the flight, I was determined not to displace the first-placed locals.

Instead I stood in the doorway to the departure gate as still as a basketball defender about to take a charge from a sprinting opponent. Through three decades of playing this 'non-contact' sport, I had perfected the art of knocking the wind out of an incoming opponent with a last second thrust, while appearing to the umpire to be standing still. I waited for Mr Nice to push through and visualised him sliding backwards across the floor and into the non-flushing toilet. Instead he avoided my trap by sneaking through the private door. Fortunately for us and the other waiting passengers, another flight to the Western Province was scheduled for a couple of hours later and Henry and I arrived in time for the big meeting.

Mary was rushing around Munda organising the catering and accommodation for over a hundred delegates. Minutes before the meeting started she reappeared wearing a new purple floral dress with a matching purple orchid in her hair, a flashback to her days as an airline hostess. Jack Daniel was also in his element in front of the assembled throng. Followed by a pregnant pause designed to ensure that everyone was listening, Jack announced in typical style that he had been 'inspired by the past and called to shape the future'. He went to inordinate lengths to reinforce the historic significance of the meeting where all Tetepare descendants were again reunited after many generations.

Jack then abandoned his notes and stepped out from behind the table where he had been seated with Henry and myself. 'I will tell you a story about TDA,' he announced, then turned around and laughed mischievously at me.

'Once there was a centipede,' started Jack, 'that was writhing near dead on the ground.'

Katherine and I looked at each other nervously. We had no idea where this story was going.

'Some insects walked down a tree towards the centipede and tried to drag it away to eat it. But other insects were coming down other trees and they too wanted to eat the centipede. The centipede was pulled to the east and to the west, to the north and to the south'. Jack really cracked himself up when he added, 'Some insects even climbed on top and burrowed underneath and pulled from those directions too! For hours they struggled but none of them got to eat the centipede.'

Relieved that we could see where Jack's parable was headed, I relaxed and watched the congregation hanging on Jack's every word.

'Then a *Pitikole*, which had been watching the struggle, flew down and took off with the centipede and the bugs got nothing'.

'For years,' Jack stated, 'Tetepare descendants had been squabbling over the island from different directions but had never achieved anything.' If we are to stop someone else coming in and taking over our island we must not be bugs! We must work together.'

Spontaneous applause reverberated around the hall and Jack waved his hands in the air 'Adjourn, adjourn,' he said as he strode out for a beetle-nut break. After reconvening, TDA's objectives received universal support from the far-flung descendants, who repeatedly expressed how pleased they were to have their land ownership recognised by the new association.

As is customary at the conclusion of big meetings, everyone of status felt compelled to make a speech. Old Harry Bea, with a couple of lonely teeth left in his top jaw, pointed his finger at me and delivered a serve. 'Don't you lead us astray. You must be good not evil.' At first I was offended but then he walked up and shook my hand and laughed, along with the rest of the gathering. Then Chief Leban Sasa, the most senior big man from Lokuru, made an eloquent speech asking Mr John and Kathy to stay for ten years. Six months ago when we first met him he seemed deeply suspicious of our motives and had barely uttered a word of Pijin. Three months ago he was one of the signatories to the letter warning us never to come back to Tetepare. Our lingering doubt as to the viability of the Tetepare project and our involvement evaporated within minutes.

After securing the lease and the support of the Tetepare powerbrokers, our Tetepare roller-coaster was thrust skywards. The landowners and government both now 'agreed' that the island should be conserved by TDA. Once again, for a few brief weeks, we thought that the battle had been won.

Olisogo's Curse

'John!' Katherine screamed as her nails ripped into my arm.

For a split second I thought that one of her pet hates, a spider or cockroach, had penetrated the sanctuary of our mosquito net.

'What's going on? Who is it?' she panicked, as I woke suddenly to a loud hollow boom, followed by a crash, as we were thrown around on our mattress. Twomey, in the room next door, woke with a scream. Twomey never screamed. I was shit scared.

Another boom was followed by a second violent shudder that sent crockery crashing to the floor. Dogs barked, neighbours yelled out in frightened Roviana dialect. As if paralysed by fear, we lay prostrate on our mattress as the house shook violently for a third time. Katherine, who had been half awake when the assault started, visualised a crazed man smashing Mary and Twomey's Munda house with an axe.

'Kathy, John get out of the house,' Mary yelled from the darkness, snapping us out of our groggy haze. We realised that we were not under assault but that lying in a house perched on five-metre concrete stilts was not the ideal place to surf out an earthquake. By the time I found my jocks, the violent shaking had stopped but Katherine was already down the stairs. Mary kept repeating nervously, 'That was the biggest one.'

There had been no time to find or light any kerosene lamps. Darkness intensified the fear and Katherine and Mary's adrenalin-charged minds were racing. 'Was it Kavachi?' The submarine volcano had been simmering off the weather coast of Tetepare for weeks. The locals attributed the torrential rains, in normally 'dry' July, to Kavachi's eruption that had been emitting clouds of steam and a red glow at night.

'Will there be a tidal wave?' A couple of years ago, at about the same time that a tsunami had flattened a community in Papua New Guinea, monster waves initiated landslides and stripped the sand from Tetepare beaches. Canoes were tipped over in the normally sheltered waters of Roviana Lagoon. 'There will be a big wave and we must not travel tomorrow,' Mary instructed. We had planned to travel from Munda to Tetepare to visit important cultural sites.

'That was the biggest one,' Mary repeated again, still coming to grips with the violent shaking exacerbated by the tall, now cracked, stilts. Old Harry, woken by the quake in his house next door, confirmed it was the strongest he could remember in his seventy-seven years in the Western Province. About twenty minutes after the quake Twomey checked his watch. 3.50 a.m. I made a mental note to remember 3.30 as the quake time. What damage had been wreaked in villages on Rendova and Vangunu that were closer to Kavachi? What had happened to Qeuru, the black-sand beach on Tetepare where we had crash landed on our second visit? Qeuru beach had only recently accumulated enough sand since the last tsunami to again provide a nesting habitat for endangered leatherback turtles.

After more earthquake talk but no earthquake action, we gingerly climbed the steps back into the house, figuring that the malarial mosquitoes presented a greater risk than the house collapsing. Inexplicably, Katherine fell asleep straightaway. I could not. Every time Mary, Twomey or their teenage daughter Domu moved or rolled over, the whole house shuddered. Alert to the point of paranoia, I could feel the house vibrating to my pounding heart.

Compounding my heightened sense of awareness, we had gone to bed that evening fresh from Harry Bea's Tetepare stories about the supernatural acts performed upon, and by, his ancestors. Now, humbled by the erratic power of the Earth, I readily visualised how terrifying an earthquake would be to people without 'Richter scale' or 'plate tectonics' in their vocabulary. Their spirits were sure to be punishing them for transgressions. The earthquake had added reality to Harry's stories that followed my simple question: 'What is so special about Tetepare?' He was also a landowner on Rendova and New Georgia but was clearly most attached to Tetepare. *'Hemi spirit aelan, hemi wild aelan,'* Harry explained, reverting to Pijin for extra effect. Continuing the global perspective that he first raised in the Tetepare timber rights hearing Harry added 'Maybe the last wild island.'

The eastern extremity of Tetepare, those cliffs we had rounded on our first visit with Eddie and John T, is known as Kupa Point.

Legend has it that Olisogo, one of the main spirits of Tetepare, used to live at Kupa Point. At some stage, possibly because someone mocked her elephant-like ears, Olisogo became angry and ordered the decapitation of the head of the fighting pig island of Tetepare. In the Tetepare language, Kupa means 'cut off the neck'. Coincidentally the French translation of Tetepare has the same meaning. The village that had been built to the east of Kupa was cut off and drowned in the sea. To this day, divers from Lokuru still avoid diving in this area cursed by Olisogo. Fear of the region was accentuated several years ago when a visiting scuba diver reported seeing the remains of the old village under the sea.

Harry's story of the creation of the western end of Tetepare was equally dramatic. Tetepare used to be linked with Rendova, the larger island that lies to the north and west. Rava, the closest part of Rendova to Tetepare, once supported so many people that albinos were not uncommon. Harry told us that in *taem bifoa*, approximately one in every thousand children was born albino and that the presence of albinos attested to the large population on both Tetepare and Rava.

Legend has it that the people of Rava wanted to borrow some fire from Tetepare so they could light their cooking fires. A Rava woman asked her two sons to walk to Tavara, on the western tip of Tetepare, to ask the queen for some fire. Because the people from the Tetepare region spoke a different language from the rest of Rendova, the mother informed her sons that the Tetepare word for fire was *maekesu*.

On their walk along the beach to Tetepare the boys forgot the word for fire. Several hours later they returned to their mother without any fire. Sheepishly, and presumably with a bit of a giggle, they admitted to their mother that they met the queen of Tetepare but must have guessed wrongly the word for fire. Mum instantly imagined what had transpired when her boys admitted they had asked for *maekeso*, instead of *maekesu*.

While her husband was performing kingly duties elsewhere, the lonely Tetepare queen had taken the two lads up on their inadvertent request for carnal liaison. The boys' mother feared that the king of Tetepare would angrily seek retribution from his westerly neighbours once he returned to his violated queen. Fearing their imminent fate, the Rava elders summoned their spirit, the giant shark, to cut the peninsula and forever separate Tetepare from Rendova. To this day the Sagomuvo Passage serves as testimony to the uniqueness of the Tetepare people and their language. Possibly as a result of this transgression, the people of Tetepare and Rendova always wanted to fight each other.

The separation of Tetepare from Rendova and the antagonism of Tetepare peoples to their neighbours probably strengthened their cultural bonds and the importance of their stories. One story claims the name Tetepare means 'come out' and originates from the command of the chief angel Hiburu to Tabarabara, the great snake angel. Accordingly, Tabarabara placed Olisogo at Kupa on the east side of Tetepare and another spirit named Kalevesu at Lelei on the west side. Kaluvesu was responsible for the sea and Olisogo, the spirit that decapitated Kupa Point, had supernatural powers in the bush of Tetepare.

Kaluvesu's name was derived from the eight (*vesu*) hairs (*kalu*) on his head, but hairstyle wasn't his most impressive feature. After a gestation of 18 months, Kaluvesu was born with such propulsion that he penetrated straight through the buttress roots of a giant rainforest tree. Right from the moment of his birth, Kaluvesu's amazing powers were a source of wonder for the Tetepare people. So strong was their eight-haired wonder that the Tetepare people asked him to subdue their greatest threat.

A giant clam terrorised fishermen and seafaring warriors in the waters between Tetepare and the Hele Islands, a string of atolls that leads towards Marovo Lagoon. By summoning powers from under a *nedala* stone and killing the mighty clam with a spear, Kaluvesu proved his legendary status among Tetepare people. Although his most famous conquest occurred to the east of Tetepare, Kaluvesu lived at Lelei, on the western end, where the coconuts were subsequently planted. His traditional stone-carved canoe had been left at Nabo Point, from where his massive footprints can still be seen in the stone heading across Sagomuvo Passage from Tetepare to Rendova and then again between Lokuru and Baniata.

The fantastic powers that enabled Tetepare's spirits to battle giant clams and collapse entire villages into the sea could still be harnessed by Tetepare's people. Empowered individuals can *haro*, or call upon, Tetepare spirits to either cast magic spells on their enemies or to summon outrageous strength for battles. It was Harry's accounts of the powers retained by Tetepare people that kept me awake after the earthquake. John Kari, one of the last paramount chiefs of Tetepare origin, once fought off one hundred workers at the Tetepare plantation who wanted to kill his wife and house girl. He escaped but was later followed to Lokuru and the workers produced their best boxer to exact revenge. John Kari beat the boxer and in the melee that followed, a couple of the plantation workers were killed. As Harry bluntly told us and Mary subsequently confirmed, once Kari had summoned Tetepare powers it was impossible for any number of people to hold him down.

Jonathan Suka, the old storyteller from Lokuru, could also call the spirits' powers, although he confessed to not putting *haro* to the test for many years. Suka's powers included the ability to call sharks but he feared the consequences of calling large sharks now that he lived in the densely populated Lokuru village where dozens of *piccaninnies* typically played in their first dugout canoes.

The dawn chorus of brown-winged starlings and self-confident roosters relieved me from trying to salvage more sleep after the earthquake. Even before Harry had banged his gong for the pre-dawn prayer session, locals were gathering in the street, excitedly recounting their frenzied awakening. Water pipes had broken throughout Munda and queues were already forming at the few rainwater tanks that held water, and at a well near the beach that became the focus of village life for weeks.

The radio reported that the epicentre of the quake had not been Kavachi as we suspected but between Gizo and Kolombangara. We had only left Gizo the previous day where we had been staying in a two-storey concrete resthouse perched on a steep hillside. Ironically Katherine had initially been apprehensive about leaving Gizo, but was now very relieved.

The previous week, after Katherine's maternal suspicions deepened, we booked a doctor's appointment in Gizo to seek confirmation and advice on her pregnancy. At 2 p.m. we dutifully slipped into the doctor's pokey waiting room, not wanting anyone else to suspect that Katherine might be pregnant. Perched on a row of dirty school chairs alongside patients with more obvious maladies, we could not help but listen into the doctor's consultation in an adjacent open cubicle. Every wheeze and cough was clearly audible. Katherine turned to me and whispered half-jokingly, 'I hope he doesn't want to do an internal examination.'

Eventually a slightly built, well-dressed man emerged and summoned Katherine. We both squeezed into the cramped cubicle that was obviously designed for only one sitting patient. Katherine was not overly keen to inform the coughing masses of Gizo that she might be pregnant and waited for an enquiry, or even an introduction from the dark skinned doctor. With no opening line forthcoming Katherine eventually leaned forward and whispered 'Um, I think I might be pregnant.'

Doctor Introvert nodded, blank faced. An uncomfortable silence ensued.

Katherine glanced at me in confusion then continued, 'but we're not sure . . .' tapering off expectantly.

Still no answer. Then the penny dropped – for us. In a country with one of the world's highest birth rates and where most pregnancies progress to full term without any medical intervention, women did not consult doctors to confirm their pregnancy. Changing tack, we asked the confused doctor if he had any dietary advice for pregnant women. The special breakfast cereals advertised by glowing expectant mothers in glossy magazines back home were not available over here. A few minutes later we were back out on the street again, with a jar of iron folate tablets but no answer to our most pressing question.

Walking back along a side lane we passed a little wooden building that we had never paid any attention to. A small 'Family Planning Office' sign was semi-concealed by faded mouldy cartoon posters demonstrating the use of condoms. 'Hang on' said Katherine 'they might be able to help'. I turned to follow her up the rickety steps before realising that the office was crammed with very maternal looking women. While Katherine disappeared quickly inside, I loitered outside, attempting to convince anyone who may have cared that my proximity to the Family Planning Office was merely coincidental.

Katherine emerged beaming. Her news, our news, had already been shared with the staff and five other local women who collectively inspected the test kit and welcomed Katherine into their sisterhood. After the initial euphoria of the news we started deliberating on how Katherine's official admission to the trimester sequence would affect our travels. A friend put everything into perspective 'You haven't got a disease, keep living'. So we had left the relative safety net of Gizo for the wilds of Tetepare, and in the process fortuitously avoided the epicentre of the earthquake.

Nervously we loaded our gear into the Tetepare canoe at the waterfront adjacent to Mary and Twomey's house, somewhat relieved that several fishermen were already on the water in Munda's sheltered lagoon. Tetepare's cultural sites, as much as its forest and wildlife, were a key to protecting the island from the loggers. We were really keen to check out Kaluvesu's stone canoe and other evidence of the once imposing civilisation on Tetepare.

The best guide to show us these sites was Matthias Daly, Tetepare's number-one pig hunter, who we collected from his home in Lokuru. A short, strong man in his forties with a dark triangular face, Matthias's unassuming presence belied his cavalier attitude and he bore more resemblance to Mick Dundee than Paul Hogan ever did. Like Mary, Matthias was initially suspicious of our intentions when we asked him questions about Tetepare but warmed when we assured him that the plans that we were helping to implement would not curtail his pig hunting.

After a couple of hours of listening to his crocodile wrestling and pig hunting exploits I broached the issue of snakes with Matthias. Surely anyone who caught three-metre crocs by hand and had spent so much time on Tetepare would be both familiar and comfortable with the island's snakes. To my amazement, Matthias conceded that he was terrified of snakes and he could only give me the briefest descriptions. Matthias, however, did mention a short stout snake called *bulisi* that can cut through branches, or arms, like a knife. Even if it did not dismember them, *bulisi* could kill people by knocking them from a tree.

Another vague snake story really aroused my interest. Matthias described a sluggish black snake that he had only ever seen near *tabu* sites on Tetepare. Initially I assumed they must have been dark specimens of the venomous *vasirai* snakes that I had caught on our first visit to Tetepare. However, Matthias assured me that the snakes at the *tabu* sites were slower and blacker than *vasirai*. I had ruled out any of the snakes recorded from the Solomons but was no closer to identifying this mysterious black snake.

My mind raced back to one of the most spectacular animals I had ever seen. Apparently restricted to remote mountains in Papua New Guinea, Boelen's python is a show stealer. So black are these snakes that their scales radiate a purple-red iridescence. Their striking appearance is enhanced by tongues of white, licking up from their bellies like flames painted on a hotrod. To top it off these pythons can grow enormous with diamond-shaped heads larger than my fist. Boelen's pythons are rare and breathtaking. Although unlikely, the Solomons archipelago may just harbour a relict population. If so, symbolic *tabu* sites on a remote, uninhabited and largely undisturbed island were worth investigation.

I arranged for Matthias to take us to the *tabu* site where he had seen the snake. At least I thought I had arranged the visit.

Unfortunately our boat driver, who had been informed of the plan and the location of our visit, omitted to take enough fuel to reach the area and return to Lokuru. We had to stop once we had used half of the fuel in our tank, just near the little white Sarumana Islet on the northern shore of Tetepare, the island where the young blokes used to test their mettle to reach their brides.

Matthias said that by camping near Sarumana we could still walk to *tabu* sites at the remains of Siokodi village, the village where Sifu lived before she finally left Tetepare. As an aside Matthias also said, 'Maybe we catch a pig.' Maybe catch a pig proved to be an understatement!

Heading inland, Matthias slipped into the forest behind his three dogs. Although he slowed his pace to accommodate Katherine, Mary and me, we still had to stride quickly along the rudimentary path to keep up. Matthias effortlessly swished at overhanging vines or penetrating saplings that blocked the path. His wristy bush knife flicks were the definition of deftness and a far cry from my aggressive and much less effective hacks.

Within minutes of leaving the coastal breeze my shirt was drenched with sweat but I was relieved to find the undergrowth remarkably free of thorny palms, lawyer cane or stinging plants. Matthias's track clearing permitted me to adopt the bird-watching gait of high stepping without looking at the ground. Above my head umbrella palms and tree ferns bedecked with brilliant jewel beetles and crab-like red spiders gave way to massive tree trunks that disappeared up into the faraway canopy. Katherine spotted a white-winged fantail among a flock of monarchs and flycatchers. It was the first of this species that we had recorded on Tetepare and we both trained our binoculars onto the active pied bird. As if knowing it was being admired, the fantail flitted lightly down to a branch illuminated by a spot of sunlight. Wagging its tail from side to side and shuffling its wings flirtingly, the show pony made sure we had all appreciated its display. Unsurprisingly, Matthias, who was patiently waiting for us to move on, called it a *pitikole*, the same name that they give to the similar looking willie wagtail.

Yelping dogs interrupted our bird watching and stopped Matthias in his tracks, like a hound sniffing the air. 'Big fala pig pig,' he smiled, before ambling off along the track again. I was confused. Surely the acclaimed pig hunter should be running after his dogs. For nearly five minutes Matthias traced the hunt in a broad arc through the forest in front of us, expertly translating the yelps of his dogs. 'They have got it now,' he announced, then slipped off into the forest.

I quickly lost him in the green maze but could also follow the yelp of the dogs and the pig's squeal. Occasionally I glimpsed a sapling or palm shake as Matthias brushed past. My boots were no match for his nimble bare feet so I was surprised to see Matthias only twenty metres ahead of me when the understory opened up near a small stream. He slashed at and collected a length of vine, then another, as he closed in on the fracas. The large black-brown pig had all three dogs hanging off it but had refused to concede, shaking and dragging them through the leaf litter. Matthias's trusty prime hunting dog had been disembowled by a boar about six months earlier, her life saved by the crude operation performed by her master, who stuffed her entrails back inside and stitched up the gaping wound with vines. The white bitch's sickle shaped scar across her flank was testament to the danger at this point so I expected Matthias to lunge into the fray with his eighteen inch bush knife and dispatch the pig before it could maul his dogs or himself.

Instead Matthias grabbed the back leg of the pig and shooed the dogs off, the old white one especially reluctant to oblige. In a judo move reminiscent of the way ringers or cowboys throw calves to brand them, Matthias twisted, pushed and lunged the pig onto the ground, at the same time pinning its chest with his knee. He expertly whipped one of the lengths of vine he carried around its back legs, then similarly trussed the front legs with the other piece. The big pig squealed in protest and the dogs danced around, willing it to escape. Somehow Matthias had managed to hold onto his bush knife, which he used to trim some excess *bushrope*, to bind up the pig's snout. 'Big one,' I offered and Matthias acknowledged my presence for the first time. His characteristic grin broadened into a beaming smile when he stooped over and swung the heaving trussed-up pig on to his back.

We rejoined Katherine and Mary at the trail, where I reminded Matthias that we were also looking for *tabu* sites. Uncurtailed by thirty kilograms of pig flesh on his back, Matthias then resumed the walk still deftly swishing at vines with his bush knife.

'Siokodi,' Matthias announced eventually, tapping a chest-high rock with his knife. Only once he had named the famous old village did I notice that the vine-smothered grey boulders formed lines that had once been a fortress. Like a miniature Stonehenge, these boulders were far too large for mere mortals to move. Mary and Matthias looked at each other knowingly before Mary answered my question, '*Haro Tetepare powers.*' Of course. No boulders were too large for their ancestors, to move after harnessing their spirits' powers.

Although Matthias informed me there were no shrines at Siokodi that may hide the mysterious black snake, he was able to show us a sacrifice altar. In *taem bifoa*, Mary's and Matthias's ancestors had circled this altar and thrown a live possum or piglet around in preparation for sacrifice. Should the terrified creature be dropped, it would be deemed unworthy for the spirits and allowed to escape. Mary pointed out several old Ngali nut trees that had been planted, like they are at modern villages.

My disappointment at not finding an awesome snake soon evaporated when Katherine glimpsed a tiny green bird, high in the canopy. We both craned our necks backward, kinking our oxygen supply in the process. Only a small window of tree trunk was visible yet after a minute or so, one, then two birds shuffled across our field of vision. We had seen pygmy parrots the previous year in Gizo but had not confirmed them for Tetepare until now. For ten minutes we watched intently as these brilliant pocket-sized birds shuffled around the trunk, nibbling at the multicoloured lichen that had enveloped the bark. Mary was surprised by our assertion that bird watchers would travel from around the world to glimpse these miniature parrots.

Walking back to camp, Matthias and his dogs collected two more large pigs that were dispatched by a knife in their hearts. Mary's teenage daughter Domu, who somehow tracked us through the forest, effortlessly carried one back to camp on her shoulders. Matthias then disembowelled all the pigs and fed their entrails to the reef sharks that patrolled the shallows. I teased the sharks into increasingly shallow water with discarded trotters, a violent thrashing and splashing resulting whenever they temporarily beached themselves. The trussed pig carcasses were then suspended over a roaring fire, filling the beachside forest with the sweet smell of burning hair and flesh. Once the flames died down, Matthias scraped off the singed hair with his bush knife, then butchered the carcasses into chunks. Most of these handfuls of pig flesh were wrapped in banana leaves and cooked in a *motu*, or stone oven, while some ribs were left out to grill on the fire.

While we gorged on barbecued pork ribs Matthias told us a more contemporary Tetepare story than those Harry and Suka had relayed in recent weeks. J.F. Kennedy visited Tetepare on a number of occasions during World War II as the Americans attempted to dislodge the Japanese from their base at Munda. Matthias's father was escorting Japanese prisoners of war back to the US base when one escaped and stabbed him with a sword. In retaliation, Matthias's father hit the aggressive prisoner and threw him overboard. Rather than being praised for preventing the escape, or receiving sympathy for his wound, Matthias's father incurred the wrath of the future American President. Apparently Kennedy wanted the Japanese alive not dead and ordered forty whip lashes to be added to the sword wound to stress his point.

Mary and Matthias continued recounting stories to Domu and me about Tetepare's great skull cave that still has not been rediscovered since the exodus. Katherine retreated to our tent, her morning sickness exacerbated by the overpowering aromas of ginger and singed pig hair. I was only half listening to the details. How could I ever enthuse my children with defining stories about their ancestry and their land? Could I borrow Tetepare stories for those future evenings when I hoped that my family too could sit around a fire eating the day's catch? Flickers of firelight illuminating her face showed Domu absorbing these stories intently. She had less worldly opportunities or material possessions than my children could expect, but at the same time she had far more. Tetepare gave Domu, like her mother and grandfather, a reference point, a sense of involvement with an evolving history. Tetepare also gave Domu a rich catalogue of stories that she one day would pass down to her children and grandchildren.

Every place that we visited on the island and every story we heard reinforced the uniqueness and value of the island. Tetepare's spirits, which were responsible for maintaining the island's near pristine state, had smiled on Katherine and me ever since Mary had explained that we were here to help. More than ever I felt compelled to repay the debt we owed them and our new-found friends who held custody of this special island. The best way for us to help now was not through more surveys of animals or tabu sites, or even securing more grants. Thousands of landowners were now echoing the simple challenge laid down by the Lokuru big men at the merger meeting a couple of years earlier. Conserving Tetepare depended upon TDA delivering income, education and the other improvements to living standards that the loggers promised.

3

Mary's Dream

The Black-and-White Pig

THE BEACH roared like a distant racetrack. As I slowly woke from my deep slumber I tried to remember where we were sleeping. For the past thirty mornings Katherine and I had woken in twenty different villages or campsites. The ripple and crack of transverse breaking waves reminded me that we were sleeping in a beachside hut at Baniata, on the weather coast of Rendova. Through the dumping waves I could also hear a rhythmic scritch, scritch, scritch like an overgrown chicken on its early morning rounds.

My curiosity lured me out from under our mosquito net to the sago palm window flap that was propped open with a stick. Bent over like a shearer, Rosella used a handful of dry sago palm leafstalks to sweep around her father's house where we were lodging. All around the village, women and girls were doubled over, rhythmically sweeping leaves and food scraps from the black sand. Their small piles of leaves and rubbish were scooped into leaf baskets and taken down to the beach to be swallowed by the pounding sea.

Washed clothes, or *calico,* were laid out to dry on the swept black sand. The white shirts and dresses would have embarrassed clothes detergent advertisers back home and definitely shamed our crude handwashing results. Next to the *calico*, green sago palm leaves cured in the sun before being stitched into panels to repair roofs or build new ones. Giant pomelo fruit hung pendulously from trees like oversized Christmas baubles. Floats and nets washed up from fishing boats draped from leaf houses as souvenirs. The village dogs, exhausted from a night of singing, snatched a few winks before they resumed beating up the lowest ranked dog in the village. As the sun lit the crest of the hills behind the village, spectacular birdwing butterflies lumbered around hibiscus and citrus flowers. I hoped this fantastic morning would prelude a memorable day; it was destined to be an important one.

I wandered over to a nearby leaf house to visit my sister and her family, who were the first tourists TDA had brought to Baniata. We were keen to demonstrate that if the locals supported conservation initiatives, tourists would pay for food, accommodation and handicrafts and, potentially, also help in schools and clinics. Providing benefits in landowners' villages was fundamental to convincing them to resist the logging of Tetepare.

'Baniata is my third-favourite place in the Solomons,' announced my niece. It was only the fourth place she had visited. Hannah loved her few days at Matikuri and Uepi resorts in Marovo but Baniata village was a challenging experience for a nine-year-old girl on her first overseas holiday. Fortunately for Baniata, Honiara had already been relegated to the bottom of her list. Hannah's first experience of betel nut stains in Honiara convinced her and her mother that they had narrowly avoided a massacre. Hannah now had to use a toilet that was flushed with a bucket and write up her daily journal in the light of a dim kerosene lamp. But worst of all she was served cold potatoes and slippery cabbage for breakfast.

Her seven-year-old brother Patrick made himself his second of thirteen cups of Milo for the day from the thermos and powdered milk. He quickly skulled it down, leaving a chocolate moustache as he ran outside to resume playing with the village boys before school. Within ten minutes of arriving in Baniata,

Patrick was kicking a soccer ball with the local kids and this morning he had pulled out his Aussie Rules football. The village boys, some of whom had never seen white children let alone an egg-shaped football, tried to emulate their new friend's mastery of the strange ball. Fortunately for the novices there were no windows in the entire village, so the ball bounced harmlessly off leaf roofs and walls.

Breakfast and football were the first of several big tests for the day. A week earlier we had visited Baniata and arranged for special meals and accommodation for these 'tourists' who wanted to see their special turtles. A year earlier the village elders had asked Katherine and me to help to generate income for the village in return for them agreeing to support the conservation plan for Tetepare. Through a series of community meetings the villagers had also tentatively agreed to protect their leatherback turtles and gather enough information to attract tourists to their isolated village.

Leatherbacks, or *oihare*, are as much a part of the life-blood of Baniata as gondolas are to Venice. Katherine and I had been keen to assist protecting *oihare* ever since our first visit to Baniata and Havilla on the eventful TDA-awareness trip with Mary. At that inaugural meeting we tried to determine how many turtles nested at Baniata. '*Staka tumas*,' meaning 'plenty', was the answer. More enlightening, Livingstone, the conch shell blowing village organiser, informed us '*In taem bifo, tracks blong oihare look olsem leg blong crabs.*' Turtle tracks approaching the densities of the ubiquitous sand crab tracks, which literally riddle the beach today, were a far cry from their current endangered status.

Back then an old woman named Domu used to look after *oihare* and make sure that most nesting females returned to the sea unharmed. It was probably no coincidence that Mary's oldest daughter was named after this protector of turtles. '*Who nao luk aotem dispela oihare dis taem?*' I asked, hoping that Domu's role had been continued. After considerable silence and sideways glances we were told what we wanted to hear but knew wasn't the truth, '*Everybody luk aotem oihare dis taem.*' Livingstone explained that the village ate 'Maybe two, maybe four' *oihare* each year. '*Hemi no staka tumas,*' he added. An intuitive skill of Livingstone, like most vocal Solomon Islanders we had met, was to assess the answer we were hoping for and modify his response accordingly. I doubted that only four leatherbacks were eaten annually and later learned that Livingstone had neglected to inform us that every turtle that was encountered on the beach was eaten. No-one was ensuring that any females, nor any eggs, survived.

Our questions stirred up considerable debate. The words '*oihare*' and '*azafe*' or 'to eat' cropped up frequently in the distinctive Touo language. Clearly the village people were undecided as to whether they wanted to continue eating the prized delicacy that they had dined on for generations or whether they preferred to attract tourism income by looking after turtles. Backwards and forwards the conversation bounced. Seemingly every senior man in the village felt compelled to have his say. Katherine and I were sitting on chairs next to Mary in front of the assembled throng. As much as we were dying to find out the opinions of the different players, we couldn't interrupt by asking what was going on. One old man stood up and made the shortest speech of the night. When he finished some of the locals giggled, others looked at their toes. His statement clearly struck a chord. I whispered to Mary, 'What did he say?' She smiled, clearly proud of the old man, and translated, 'After you eat all of the *oihare* will you start eating your children too?' The meeting was adjourned with a prayer.

The next day I asked Livingstone about what typically happened when a turtle was spotted on the beach. Upon being woken in the night by yells of '*Oihare, oihare*', men and boys would run along the beach to intercept the turtle before it escaped to the safety of the sea. I could understand the excitement in the village would equate to a side of beef arriving after six months of eating potatoes. Several men would grab one side of the turtle while others dug a hole in the sand on her other side. Carefully avoiding a swipe from her powerful flippers they rolled the turtle into the divot and over onto her back. The men then returned to their huts. Even if her soft back wasn't broken, the turtle was unable to right itself and, weighing up to a tonne, was in no danger of being stolen or eaten by scavengers.

The following day village elders and representatives of most families, along with a throng of inquisitive *piccaninnies*, would wander down to the flailing turtle. Even generations after Domu passed away no-one really liked killing *oihare*. Instead dead coconut fronds were dragged onto the beach and piled over the hapless creature. Once the turtle was completely obscured, the pile was ignited. Burning fronds would be swept aside by her massive flippers as she struggled in vain. She couldn't scream or squeal, an agitated heaving sigh being the *oihare*'s only means of expressing her pain. Occasionally someone would take pity on the poor beast and plug her nostrils with wedges of coconut husk to accelerate her demise. This was the only indication of remorse that Livingstone showed when relaying the story of how *oihare* were captured and killed. Otherwise his story contained as much emotion as we show when we place a polystyrene tray of meat into our shopping trolley.

Once the struggling ceased and the flames died down, her meat was soft enough to be carved into portions for distribution among the CFC families. *Oihare* and their eggs are off-limits to Seventh Day Adventists. Blood scooped from the concave shell was mixed with the cleaned entrails and stirred in pots over flames until it thickened to a mince-like consistency. This marine black pudding is a delicacy, as are the hundreds of undeveloped eggs. Even the fat from around the shell was layered between grated tapioca, like a greasy lasagne. Potatoes and cassava cooked in motu ovens with the meat dripped with turtle gravy, the meat being far greasier than pork. Islanders, who are unaccustomed to eating leatherbacks find the meat not only greasy but also overpoweringly rich. But for the Baniata locals, *oihare* is keenly sought after, a welcomed addition of greasy meat to augment their root-crop diet.

A nesting *oihare* faced a near impossible challenge. First she had to haul her massive body through the white water and up the steep soft beach, then she searched for suitable sand, avoiding rocks or debris. After excavating the nesting hole with her rear flippers, laying a hundred or so eggs and back-filling the hole she then disguised the location of her nest by bulldozing the sand around. This laborious work takes the female *oihare* over an hour. Time on the beach means danger. I cringed involuntarily as Livingstone raised his estimate to six or more *oihare* eaten in Baniata in the past year.

Six females, each of whom could lay up to eight clutches a year, is a serious loss for one of the world's most endangered turtles. From an estimated tally of 115,000 adult female leatherbacks worldwide in 1982, less than one-third remained in 1996. Thirty-four-and-a-half thousand sounds like a lot of adult females but when fifteen hundred female leatherbacks drown through fisheries mishaps every year, not including the intentional harvest, these populations can quickly crash. Large Mexican colonies declined from seventy thousand in 1982 to fewer than two hundred and fifty by the turn of the century.

The scenario for the western Pacific is even more perilous than the larger and better studied rookeries in Central America. Leatherbacks have already disappeared from India and Sri Lanka and have declined from thousands to a handful in Malaysia. The best guess of turtle researchers was that a mere eighteen hundred females nested in the western Pacific in 2000 and that such a population could only tolerate the harvesting of eighteen adult females each year. Crikey, a third of that number were being eaten at Baniata alone! It is no surprise that after swimming the world's oceans for seventy million years these living fossils are predicted to become extinct in the Pacific within a few years. Katherine and I were running out of time to see a live leatherback.

While my sister Meredith taught appreciative students at the single-teacher school, Mary and Livingstone convened another village meeting. After much discussion regarding the merits of attracting tourists and teachers as well as the drawback of not eating a traditional food, the village decided to protect *oihare* in return for a small cash incentive from the conservation donors. Rather than directly subsidising conservation, Katherine and I agreed to pay locals to monitor nesting events, ostensibly to assist in determining key locations and dates for potential tourism. Anyone who ensured a turtle nested safely received fifteen Solomon dollars, which is about what they would earn for a day of drying copra. To reduce their temptation to cheat, a turtle monitor was appointed by the village to verify the record with a photograph of the turtle or its tracks. George, a well presented ex-policeman in his fifties who exhibited confidence without being outspoken, was appointed to be the turtle monitor. If George's photos on the camera we presented him with matched the written records, we would also pay him ten dollars. To keep the rest of the community on side we agreed to place another fifteen dollars into a community fund to discourage others from killing the turtle. I hoped that for the first time since Domu had died the Baniata *oihare* would be safe.

A few months later we returned to Baniata, eager to learn whether the village had obeyed their new rules. While Baniata locals had apparently abstained and George had photographed several turtles, their neighbours at Havilla had eaten an *oihare* because we had not spoken to them directly. To solve this frustrating loophole I immediately walked the searingly hot two-kilometre beach between the two villages, accompanied by the loyal 'Chief' Billy, who supervised my every move. Although Billy was oblivious to the heat, the soles of my feet burnt on the dry black sand yet I sank ankle deep into the wet sand whenever I raced into the water to cool off. The shaded moist forest floor on the short path into Havilla, by contrast, soothed my feet like cucumber slices on sunburn.

At our hastily arranged village meeting I was assured that from now on the people of Havilla would look after *oihare* in return for the same cash incentive as we offered in Baniata. They appointed their own turtle monitor, Nico, who received another camera to provide evidence for each of his recorded nests. To reinforce these cash benefits Mary also felt we needed to reward the villagers by attracting tourists who would pay for accommodation, food and maybe even carvings when they came to experience the leatherbacks.

On young Hannah's expert recommendation, Katherine reckoned that cooking training was also needed before more tourists indirectly assisted the conservation of Tetepare by visiting Baniata and Havilla. Together with Andrea, an Aussie mate of ours who had learned many Western-style recipes using local produce while volunteering on Kolombangara for a year, she devised a cooking workshop for local women.

My expertise was biased towards cooking appreciation rather than training so I investigated other activities that could entertain tourists between night-time turtle patrols. Katherine and I had previously visited Lake Rano, one of the Solomon's largest freshwater lakes, about twenty kilometres south of Baniata. Peering through the undergrowth we had seen cormorants that were hitherto unknown in these parts and *staka* flying foxes roosting on islands in the centre of the lake. I had been keen to get back to Lake Rano to check out what other secrets were hidden away in this remote lake. Billy, the bloke who coined the 'eco-two-reason' expression, offered to paddle me across the lake in a canoe with his mate Anoi. Another friend, Katie, who was travelling with us, also opted for the lake paddle instead of the cooking training.

After dragging a two-and-a-half metre dugout canoe up the steep coastal ridge the boys slipped down the other side towards the lake as if they were holding onto a runaway toboggan. Anoi cleared the lakeside vegetation with his knife, creating a launching area for the canoe and a window for us to peer through the tangle of leaves and vines into the mirror-calm lake. Determined to create a good impression for the attractive *vaka* girl, Billy supervised Katie's every step.

The moment we had been anticipating yet secretly dreading had arrived. Knowing that crocodiles were likely to be lurking below the surface made us even more nervous about stepping into the canoe. Billy steadied the little dugout as Katie nervously stepped in and sat down, her legs stretching to half the canoe. To my surprise she insisted that I come too. There was no way she was going out into a crocodile-infested lake in a cramped unstable canoe while I stood safely on the bank. Anoi pulled rank and decided that he would be our guide while Billy waited loyally on the bank.

Sitting as lightly, low and still as possible, Anoi paddled us out from under the verandah of overhanging trees and into the lake. 'Look, there's a croc,' I said to Katie, who was staring straight ahead, concerned that rotation of her eyeballs would overbalance our canoe. 'Don't be stupid,' she snapped, becoming increasingly nervous as we left the sanctuary of the bank. Each time Anoi paddled on the left side, a splash of water accompanied the slight tilt of the canoe in that direction. After three or four paddles on the left Anoi paddled to the right, splashing my right leg with inflowing water.

'Oh my God. It is a croc!' Katie gasped as another croc surfaced in her line of vision.

'No *wori wori*,' reassured Anoi. I trusted airline pilots in dodgy situations and chose to believe Anoi that we had no worries. But I shouldn't have. I was soon to learn that our guide was absolutely crazy, with less regard for our longevity than he had previously displayed for nesting *oihare*.

In my naive reassured state I surveyed the lake. There did not appear to be any cormorants on the island but dozens of huge flying foxes unfolded their massive wings and dropped from the overloaded roost trees. Metres before hitting the water they started flapping and wheeled around in thickening clouds. Sensing their vulnerability, an enormous black Solomon eagle closed on an ungainly flapping bat in a controlled dive. With outstretched talons the eagle seized the flying fox from behind. Seemingly unfazed, the flying fox maintained a laboured but steady flapping until the eagle released it.

Anoi noticed my interest in the flying foxes. *'Iu likem me kasim disfala flying fox?'* he enquired, offering to catch one so we could have a better look. I was intrigued as to how Anoi would catch one and agreed. Our guide paddled to the lake shore approximately four hundred metres away from where we had departed.

'This is awesome,' Katie announced with new-found confidence as she watched three crocodiles patrolling underneath a particularly dense section of the flying fox colony. Anoi slashed his way through the dense forest while Katie and I waited in the canoe. My arse had developed acute pins and needles and my left leg was completely numb but I couldn't afford to move. Even though we were holding onto branches, the slightest movement could easily tip us into the murky lake. Through the gap in the branches we could still see two crocodiles.

After ten minutes of intense crocodile watching, Anoi crashed back through the undergrowth. Behind him he dragged what looked like a dozen shredded garbage bags. Katie summoned her spiritual leader for the second time since we boarded the canoe. Anoi had not set off to catch a flying fox to show us; he had gone hunting. Maimed flying foxes, hacked from their roosts with Anoi's long bush knife, were strung on a length of vine threaded through holes in their wings. A couple of lucky ones appeared dead, their fox-like heads flopping languidly. Others screeched and chewed at their broken wings spraying blood around as they flapped pathetically.

'Mi no meanim iu for hurtim disfala flying fox,' I barked angrily, feeling guilty that I had initiated this massacre by agreeing to Anoi catching us a flying fox.

'*Mi like kaikai flying fox,*' Anoi admitted, looking visibly chuffed that our guide fees had funded his hunting expedition.

'Those poor bats,' Katie pinioned, voicing my sentiments. 'Ask him to kill them.'

'*No gud flying fox garem staka pain,*' I explained to the hunter. '*Iu mas killim die pinis distime.*'

Anoi looked at me blankly. Simultaneously Anoi and I both thought to ourselves, 'Don't you understand, you stupid bastard.' Anoi had caught his meal and none of the flying foxes were in any state to break free from their tether. The longer they stayed alive, the longer their meat would remain fresh. There was no refrigeration in Baniata. These flying foxes were being treated just like a fish that had been hooked and left to die slowly in a canoe, or a turtle kept on its back until its captors were ready for a feast. There is little place for humane treatment of wildlife in subsistence lifestyles. I tried a different approach.

'*Disfala vaka meri hemi les for harem disfala flying fox karae,*' I explained, hoping that Katie's sympathy would strike a chord with the young hunter. Unlike Billy, pandering to Katie's emotions was not one of Anoi's priorities. Begrudgingly he swiped at the two most active captives with the back of his knife before slinging the string of bodies into the canoe at Katie's feet. The gory bundle of fur and wings heaved and wheezed through blood-filled lungs.

I couldn't stand it. Nearly tipping the canoe, I stepped out and sunk to my knees in the sulphurous mud. After extricating myself with the aid of an overhanging branch I urged Anoi to throw me his knife and the string of bats. Without lingering over their big sad eyes I brutally sliced at the heads of any of the bodies that were still moving. Adrenalin pounded inside my forehead as anger, guilt and horror filled my emotions.

In sharp contrast to the screeching, the ensuing silence was intense. I feared what would happen next. Worse even than the inhumane massacre of these doe-eyed creatures would be wasting them and jeopardising our relationship with the Baniata locals by leaving them behind. Yet if there was anything riskier than paddling an unstable canoe through a lake full of crocodiles, it was doing so with two dozen bleeding bats. Gingerly I got back into the canoe with the shell-shocked Katie and waited for Anoi's next move.

Nonchalantly the bundle of bats was tossed back on top of Katie's feet as Anoi expertly stepped off a branch into the back of the canoe. Blood from the maimed creatures mixed with water in the bottom of the canoe like strong raspberry cordial. This was not exactly the tourist-friendly excursion I had hoped for. As per our earlier plans, Anoi started paddling further out into the lake so that we could continue our flying fox count. But the equation had now changed. We were now paddling a smorgasbord past waiting crocs, our guide inadvertently splashing blood-tainted water out of the canoe like burley.

Then I saw a monster. Not fifteen metres away the eyes and then snout of a crocodile appeared. They were a metre apart. Oh my goodness! This beast was easily longer than our canoe. Right on cue one of the maimed flying foxes flapped a bloodstained wing over the bow. The dead bat's reflexes broke my nerve.

'*Iumi go straight back long Billy. No gud disfala crocodile hem like kaikaim olketa flying fox blong iumi,*' I instructed, pointing Anoi towards the lake shore and away from the monster crocodile. I loosely translated to Katie, 'This is one of the most stupid things I have ever done.'

'Oh my God,' she replied twice more, in response to both my statement and the big croc that had by now turned to face us.

Cooking training back at Baniata suddenly seemed like a better option. A crowded dugout canoe has the turning circle of a bus with flat tyres. Two smaller crocs emerged as the big monster sank to prevent us colliding with it. Visions of Moby Dick raced through my mind as I scanned nervously for any sign of the huge croc in the muddy water. For the next ten minutes Katie and I neither spoke nor twitched a muscle as Anoi inched our vulnerable craft towards the bank. The ever loyal and smiling Billy met us there, oblivious to our horrific adventure and delighted with Anoi's haul of flying foxes. Never before had dry land felt so good.

Meanwhile, back at cooking training, Katherine was battling issues of her own. Disgruntled women who had missed out on the training jostled for vantage points at the windows of the flimsy outdoor leaf kitchen. Eventually the wall gave way altogether, plunging the training into chaos and enraging the powerfully built kitchen owner, who chased the screaming interlopers away with an axe handle. A torrential downpour then flooded the stone ovens extinguishing the cooking fires, but the women toiled on with *staka* laughter, producing some remarkably good results.

After sampling the first fresh banana cake ever to emerge from a Baniata kitchen and visiting Anoi's kitchen for a roasted flying fox that tasted like a greasy rat, we asked Livingstone to call another village meeting. Katie and Andrea handed out incentive money to everyone who had found a turtle since our last visit. Mary, then Livingstone, confirmed the assembled throng's unanimous support for the turtle and tourism project. With cooks trained and Havilla joining the project, we departed Baniata the following morning confident that the *oihare* and their eggs would at last be reprieved.

Several months later we were disappointed to learn that more eggs had been eaten. This time the culprits were school children who had returned to Baniata and not heard our awareness talks. Our frustration and disappointment was boiling over. The community had decided to protect the turtles so why hadn't they informed their children of the new rules? The longer we stayed the more stories we heard. I was cornered down at the soccer ground in the afternoon; Katherine was enlightened around our host's table over dinner. It wasn't only school children who had transgressed. Some of our most 'trusted' informants apparently headed the list of egg thieves. We conceded that maybe no turtles had been eaten because none were actually found at night, rather than reflecting a conscious effort to protect them. I was forced to soul-search again. Why should they stop eating turtles just because a couple of *waetfalas* reckon it's a good idea? The rewards we offered were not as immediate as a basketful of eggs, let alone a hundred pots of turtle meat.

Despite our growing empathy and concern for the plight of the leatherbacks, preventing logging on Tetepare remained our main priority. The near unanimous and often emphatic support for TDA's objectives generated by Mary throughout our regional sorties mirrored the agreement that Baniata and Havilla residents made to save their *oihare*. But we now recognised that this support could evaporate overnight if a better offer appeared.

We were learning the appropriateness of WWF's black-and-white pig nickname in the Solomons. Pigs are the resource of choice here for weddings and other feasts. Loggers, conservation organisations and ourselves all represent a pig, a resource, an opportunity. Instead of hunting us with dogs and knives, we were being coerced with smiles and signatures. The panda, as a symbol of the exotic and endangered, relies upon empathy for other species and a belief that they represent more than simply a resource. Rich Westerners, with full stomachs and an understanding of extinction and ecological roles can afford to embrace conservation. But expecting subsistence gardeners, hunters and fishermen to embrace the panda is as unlikely as expecting a vegan to maintain their morals on a deserted island.

Simon Foale, our early mentor from WWF, suspects that the major conservation organisations had got it all wrong. They had marched into the Pacific believing Islanders would embrace conservation after raising their awareness of impending food or resource shortages. Had the Indonesians stopped cyanide fishing before it destroyed their reefs? Had the mariners stopped harvesting giant tortoises and dodos before they dwindled to extinction? Had Tasmanian farmers stopped slaughtering thylacines or the Americans stopped harvesting passenger pigeons before they too vanished? Human nature decrees that you look after your belly first and your future second, especially when you are hungry. When asked what he would tell his grandchildren if he ate the last turtle, a Solomon Island man replied, 'I would tell them that it tasted good.' He wasn't joking.

The descendants of Tetepare were all too aware of how rapidly the lives of many of their ancestors were terminated. Why leave turtles behind if you can feast now, given the likelihood you will not be around at the next opportunity? It is easy as a thirty-something-year-old Westerner to believe that I will be around for at least forty more years and that my children and grandchildren will rely upon the resources I leave behind. Our friends in Baniata had not historically shared that luxury and their grandparents certainly would not have instilled in them the importance of planning. 'Selling' the concept of conservation to a subsistence villager is no easier than marketing them life insurance.

I hoped that achieving real support for the *oihare* project would help us to solve the big issue of securing long-lasting maintenance of TDA's ideals for Tetepare. Perhaps, I had figured, experience with merging our conservation agenda with Baniata's desire for income generation, would provide a model that could be replicated in other villages. But it simply had not worked. Exasperated, I told some senior men how upset and confused we were that the harvesting ban that they themselves proposed had not been upheld. Before giving up on the turtle work altogether, I asked them, yet again, for their advice. After some *tok ples* discussion I was informed, 'The only way we will stop eating turtle eggs is if we are told not to.' I was flabbergasted. The village had been told, and asked, and coerced not to harvest leatherbacks for years. What game were they playing now? However, it transpired that they were not referring to an order by a fisheries officer, expatriate conservation volunteers or a chief. An edict from a far higher power was needed. The Spiritual Authority should be consulted.

One of the most significant legacies of John Goldie's pioneering Methodism in the western Solomons was his tutelage of an influential convert named Silas Eto. At seventeen years of age, Silas Eto tested the power of Christian prayer against traditional powers, which remained strongly held in the 1920s. A dead lizard that could not be revived by traditional techniques recovered following his prayer. As a result, this introverted teenager determined that his life charter was to become a 'man of prayer'.

Following Goldie's evacuation to Australia during World War II, Silas Eto assumed a leadership role with the Methodist church. He even wrote to President Roosevelt suggesting that the conquering Americans should take control of the Solomons from the British. Although unsuccessful in that quest, Eto's frustration with the traditional Methodist church yielded more tangible results. In September 1960 Silas Eto, who had by now assumed the title of 'Holy Mama', broke away from the Methodist church and established the Christian Fellowship Church, or CFC. The Holy Mama encouraged the hysterical powers of *taturu* and also challenged the Methodists' abhorrence of tobacco and betel nut. Far more important was that his flock followed his gospel of self-sufficiency and cooperation that existed in communities before *waetfalas* and capitalism eroded the local culture. John Kari, the paramount chief of western Rendova, embraced these ideals and decided that his villages, including Baniata, would follow the footsteps of his friend the Holy Mama.

Families were honoured if the Holy Mama adopted their adolescent girls as his constant companions or 'holy maidens'. Whole villages laboured to build schools or churches at his command. A prominent CFC leader, Samuel Porokuse, explained the power held by Silas Eto. 'Everything that the Holy Mama says must be obeyed. If we did not obey him death and *situ*, or ill fortune, would take place.' This reverence barely diminished following Holy Mama's death when his son, the Reverend Ikan Rove, better known as the 'Spiritual Authority', inherited the leadership of the CFC.

Like his father, the Spiritual Authority could demand financial support, food or volunteer labour from his flock. Strong community leaders obeyed his orders like rookie cadets. More conveniently than for their Catholic counterparts, the conduit for the CFC congregation to God lived nearby. And conveniently for me, the Spiritual Authority was currently holding his annual conference at Elelo in Roviana lagoon.

Mary summoned village elders from Baniata to accompany us on the two-hour expedition to seek support from the Spiritual Authority for the *oihare* project. Upon arrival at the Roviana lagoon village, Twomey, a Seventh Day Adventist, and I hung back as Mary and her CFC compatriots walked nervously towards the school grounds where the conference was being held.

Our delegation decided to leave the matter in the hands of the church elders. However, just as we were departing, Mary felt that something would happen if she stayed a little longer. It sounded like she expected an apparition, but I suspected that Mary intended making something happen if she could unshackle the protocol of the Baniata men who accompanied us. Therefore, while the rest of us slipped off as unobtrusively as possible, Mary stayed behind.

An hour or so later Mary returned to our canoe where we waited. Surprise, surprise, something had happened. Mary had spoken with the General Secretary, the Spiritual Adviser's right-hand man, who had advised her to write a letter, so that is what we did right then on a sheet of my notepad.

The General Secretary
The community of Baniata and Havilla have had many meetings and have agreed to protect leatherback turtles and ban harvesting of turtles and eggs because they are a rare species that will vanish if we continue. People have disobeyed these rules made by the elders with the help of a conservation team.

We have decided to protect leatherbacks because people like to see turtles and they will bring income to the community. We ask for the CFC Church's blessing to help to enforce these rules for the benefit of the people.

The elders signed the letter and Mary whisked it back to the General Secretary. Back at Baniata our successful mission was topped off by a lavish banquet of new recipes trialed during cooking training. Even Mary, who had previously been skeptical of the need for training, acknowledged that tourists would really like coming to Baniata now.

A few days later the edict from the Spiritual Authority arrived. I couldn't believe how easy and absolute this decision was. If only all TDA members were CFC followers and we could convince the Spiritual Authority to support our cause, Tetepare would be saved forever.

Development at Last

Crimson and Clover, over and over
Crimson and Clover, over Rendova

Whenever we canoed past Rendova to Tetepare this psychedelic love song rushed into my consciousness. As the lyrics suggested, I did 'wanna do everything' in our power to secure the conservation of Tetepare. For most of the Tetepare decision makers that meant immediate tangible benefits. Baniata now had a turtle project but the rest of the descendants were still waiting for cash and their patience was running out. Without 'development' the conservation agenda was doomed. 'When will the project start?' we were asked, more than a year after we considered that it had. Establishing the association, recruiting members and even securing funds meant nothing. Tetepare needed a focal point.

While we had been distracted by the leatherback project in Baniata and employing staff in preparation for the Tetepare development, the rug had been pulled out from beneath our feet. The plantation lease that we paid for at the conclusion of 'Operation Suicide' had been reneged. Although signed by the Commissioner of Lands, the receipt for TDA's lease payment was now worthless. The Commissioner had subsequently taken more cash for the lease from a politician with logging ties. This meant that the most appropriate location for the Tetepare development was 'officially' owned by a supporter of logging. Even more worrying, the new lessee was one of the few powerful descendants who had not joined TDA. We could not invest hundreds of thousands of Solomon dollars on building a base that was not even on TDA land. More so than letter writers or opportunistic loggers, this politician had snookered TDA's aspirations.

Again Mary came to the rescue. 'Don't worry about the lease or that stupid man,' she counselled. 'He can't stop what the people want. We have our own receipts and we will build where we want.' Despite our misgivings that is exactly what we did.

The plantation on the western end of the island seemed a logical place for TDA to construct a base for rangers, visiting scientists and ecotourists. It provided good access to Munda and Gizo and was close to Rendova, where most of the fishermen, hunters and potential cooks hailed from. Tavara, where the plantation headquarters were being consumed by the jungle, provided ready boat access and anchorage during the prevailing southerly winds. The site was within the plantation, hence we would not need to clear the virgin forest. Tavara also offered spectacular snorkelling, one of the prerequisites Katherine stressed was important in attracting tourists.

However, after camping there on a couple of occasions, we were acutely aware that Tavara was a long walk from the forest. Tetepare's forest, not its overgrown coconut plantation, was its primary drawcard. Tavara was also adjacent to the swampy margins of the warm crocodile lake, a haven for mosquitoes. Twomey, whose job it often was to collect drinking water, sensibly pointed out that there were no fresh streams nearby.

Ultimately Mary selected a low ridge at Nabo Point where the legendary eight-haired Kaluvesu had left his stone canoe. In the 1980s, Twomey had slept here in the two-storey number 5 copra drier, which had by now been reduced to rusted drums. This site offered a protected harbour where boats could anchor in any weather and afforded views of hunters and fishermen from Rendova. Nabo Point jutted into a shallow lagoon where dugongs and green turtles fed on seagrasses. Coral bombies in the deeper water provided surreal snorkelling and small streams on either side of the point were suitable for washing. A freshwater spring among the seagrass was called *buruvo bukaha*, or 'bringing up', a Tetepare language expression still used by Rendova people to indicate bringing *staka* food for feasts.

Arguably Nabo Point's best feature was Lelei Ridge, forested with untouched monster trees, and only a five-minute walk away. A close second was the regrowth that had not been cleared from the plantation since World War II. Spindly century-old coconut palms were suffocated by the encroaching canopy and eventually lost their crowns, then their trunks to the forest floor. A massive red strangler fig presided over a raised coral platform that gave, we imagined, commanding views of both sides of the lagoon. But views are at a premium in regrowth rainforest and we could only imagine what the site would offer once the coconuts and low scrub were removed.

Mary, Twomey, Katherine and I scrambled around the point, climbing rocks or low trees to find the ultimate site affording ocean views and also protection from big winds. A tree growing out of a big square black rock marked the site where Mary wanted to build a leaf house for visitors to stay, cooled by sea breezes from the south. Eventually we settled on a site for the field station. Mary strutted around, hacking trees with her knife. 'This one will go, that one will stay,' she decreed, signing the death warrant for coconuts and giving a reprieve to her favourite rainforest trees. The front verandah would look out over the sea; the back windows would provide an elevated vantage point into the strangler fig laden with pigeon-attracting fruits.

After securing funding and selecting the site we needed to organise the timber and hardware to build the station. Mary announced, 'Twomey will make a list.' She lied. Twomey had built several houses including the one that had survived the Munda earthquake, so we felt comfortable asking him to produce an inventory of necessary timber and hardware. The poor bloke had barely started before Mary was on his back. 'No, you must get extra iron for the overhangs.' 'You stupid man you don't need that many roofing nails', 'the windows must be bigger than that' in perfect derisive English rather than Touo language that she usually used when consulting his opinion. Mary raised henpecking to hornbill proportions, but when I quizzed her or asked Twomey to justify his plans, Mary always had the answer.

We did not need reminding who the boss was and who would ultimately make most of the decisions about the project. But Katherine and I had been charged with the responsibility of sharing jobs and opportunities fairly among descendants. At a subsequent TDA committee meeting I announced that the committee needed to select a construction supervisor from a family and region that had not yet benefited from the project. The selection criteria would have suited one hundred members but not Twomey, who wasn't a Tetepare descendant. Mary said nothing, but maybe the committee understood the rules. Twomey was unanimously voted the supervisor. At the same meeting Mary was appointed to recruit the millers, timber carriers, site clearers, chainsaw operators and construction team. The field station was to be Mary's baby.

Unfortunately, Mary had become flustered with the responsibility of acquitting funds. Despite our initial desire that she could be the local project manager who we could mentor to take over our role, it became clear that her strengths lay with motivating people and coordinating workers on Tetepare rather than administrative tasks. With our support, TDA appointed an agricultural scientist to be groomed for the management of the Tetepare project. Allan Tippet Bero, who answered to any or all of his names, was methodical, quietly spoken and cautious. This slight man in his thirties was a perfect foil for Mary's gung-ho bravado, and was universally trusted to handle funds. He lived in Munda but had many relatives in Lokuru. While Mary worked on Tetepare, Tippet performed administrative duties and attempted to resolve the Tetepare lease issue from his Munda base.

Tippet counselled that TDA would be unwise to challenge the blatant legal breach of the double-issued lease in the courts. Rather it should be sorted out 'in the Melanesian way'. I was concerned that bloodshed was implied but the ever mild-mannered Tippet said, 'No, we will encourage them to join TDA.' He arranged for the executive to visit the renegade politician's key supporters in Ughele immediately following TDA's second annual general meeting. Tippet decided that it would not be wise to take Mary, who had offended the big men by calling them stupid, but the rest of the executive were invited to demonstrate that TDA wasn't just a Lokuru association. To our dismay the TDA representatives vaporised as we prepared to depart. Even Jack Daniel, the Chairman, disappeared at the last minute. Later, when I confronted him, Jack explained his no-show at the Ughele meeting with another of his parables, 'Unhappiness is a sickness. Before we understand what medicine to take we need to understand their sickness.' The 'Melanesian way' continued to provide an education for Katherine and me.

We left the Solomons to dry out my fungusy feet and to complete the administrative tasks associated with managing the Tetepare project that could not be conducted from an overgrown coconut plantation. Once a month, for five months, I received a huge list of receipts and an equally daunting list of monetary requests for the next month. These had to be approved and emailed back to the EU office in Honiara within twenty-four hours so that funds could be issued for Mary to collect on her brief visit to Munda. Any delay would see Mary return to up to thirty construction workers with empty pockets.

Twomey's construction reports traced the progress and pitfalls of the construction. Anyone who has had a house built by professionals in a major western city with access to split-second communications, daily transport opportunities and hardware stores around the corner could sympathise with his challenges. The team needed to select, cut and mill the timber from scratch, cart hardware in small canoes and feed and accommodate a workforce of dozens of men and women in a remote location with no electricity or running water.

Five months later Katherine and I returned to Tetepare. As we approached the site in our canoe we could barely contain our suspense. Would the building be square and strong? Entering the lagoon we could not see any sign of the construction, which was surprising because we anticipated the two-storey structure with a shiny iron roof would stand out. I had approved payment for teams of chainsaw operators, brushers to clear the site, millers and carpenters but there was nothing to show for this expense. Had we been duped? Katherine noticed my concerned look and quipped, 'Lucky we brought our tent again.' But as soon as we started walking up a well-trodden muddy trail the huge brown structure on stilts was revealed. But something was wrong. The building frame was skewed ninety degrees from our planned alignment. The verandah looked into the forest, rather than onto the lagoon as had been decided. 'Where is the mighty *ambalolo*?' I asked, trying to get my bearings in the cleared area that looked like a cyclone had torn through it. Mary laughed nervously, 'Oh John and Kathy, I knew you would cry if I told you we had to cut down the *ambalolo* tree. But it was too dangerous.' The massive stump protruded like a sore tooth from the clearing next to the building. We were disappointed, but we didn't cry. To us the tree was a focal point of the site and its felling was an unnecessary and time-consuming waste. But compared with the other potential fates for the Tetepare rainforest its loss was trivial.

Local carpenters were working everywhere like spiders on a communal web. Some were hammering, others sawing, others hand-drilling holes into hardwood that would stall a power drill. A little radio was playing a Dolly Parton song. Twomey smiled, 'Very strong,' as I shoulder-bumped an immovable massive post. A single near-vertical log with nailed crossbeams served as the five metre ladder up to the floor bearers. Even though the floors and walls had not yet been installed, the framework did not vibrate as I edged along the bearers. From my initial disappointment at the strange alignment and the loss of the fig, I began to appreciate what Mary, Twomey and their band of workers had achieved with only hand tools.

The floorboards weren't yet laid so we followed the lead of the carpenters and dragged Masonite ceiling sheets from the stockpile to make a temporary elevated floor in the field station. For the first time on Tetepare we had a roof over our heads. The most anticipated luxury was that we were now elevated into a breeze that blew all night off the lagoon. At seven months pregnant, Katherine stoically slept on the Masonite but was not overly impressed about negotiating the steep makeshift ladder in the dark at the whim of her crowded bladder. Tetepare white-eye birds thrived in the clearing where the field station was being built. Like school kids on a camp, they whistled and talked all night. Listening to their distinctive Tetepare language, it was easy to imagine how the white-eyes were constant companions at Tetepare's villages, which may explain why they became a *kastom* bird of the island.

It was not only the *kastom* birds of Tetepare that visited the construction site. One night Mary instructed Twomey to find out what was wrong with the baby that had woken them both. But as soon as Twomey went outside the baby stopped crying and fled into the bush. We had heard the story of the crying baby that had been left behind during the great exodus of Tetepare before, but nevertheless it was spooky to have it recounted from the Field Station site.

Mary took me to check on fifteen 'carriers' from Baniata, who were ferrying flooring and walling timber from the forest to the field station in a small canoe. We stopped at a tree stump with bright yellow timber and tumeric-coloured sawdust. None of the timber at the field station was yellow so I asked Mary what it was and what it was used for. Three *zango edo* trees had been cut for flooring.

The wet planks were heavy and sharp on my shoulder as I joined the line of carriers. None of the carriers showed a skerrick of pain or effort with their loads, so I tried to look as casual as possible as I struggled past the boys returning for another load. Sweat poured off my face and back as I negotiated fallen logs. The sharp limestone of the shore-side cliffs hurt my feet through my sandshoes although the barefooted boys walked effortlessly. A large dugout with a seemingly inadequate fifteen horsepower motor waited just offshore, with one bloke holding onto a vine 'rope' tied to an overhanging branch and another at the shallow end holding the front of the canoe in waist-deep water. We manoeuvred the planks one by one down the rocky cliff, dunking them in sea water on the way into the canoe to ward off termites.

Along with ensuring that workers, food, tools and hardware arrived simultaneously on Tetepare, Mary assumed the role of quality control officer. She was ruthless. Many of the workers confided that Mary was bossy. Suero had thought that his friend would overlook a few wonky planks that he cut but Mary downgraded his entire work, paying him a reduced rate and setting the tone for the rest of the workers. At twelve o'clock one day Mary noticed that there had only been two loads to the field station. Roy, one of the carpenters, told me that she had stomped around in an increasing rage before grabbing a canoe and setting off for the milling area.

Some of the men were fishing and a couple of particularly unfortunate blokes were resting under a tree when she arrived. Mary cussed and ranted like the plantation managers of old, with a tenacity that would have chased a hungry dog off a wounded piglet. After dressing down the men on the shore she marched along the trails to where the trees were being milled and informed the lazy carriers that she was terminating their jobs the next day. That afternoon they carried a record five loads and Mary relented and allowed them to keep their jobs until their task was finished.

I asked Mary if she ever felt threatened. Although not admitting to being scared, she did say that some of the men had told her they were just going to take the pay they felt they were owed.

Mary told them, 'You can grab the money but you have a name and you can't hide.' The men became angrier but worked harder as Mary's Tetepare dream gradually came to fruition.

While we were carrying the flooring and walling for the carpenters to systematically nail into place, Twomey was busy making the tank stand. Eventually the day arrived that I had anticipated with relish as we helped carry the aluminium water tank from the small canoe that had ferried it across from Rendova. The tank filled within two days. Now we had sweet, cool water for drinking, cooking and even washing, which rendered unnecessary the twice-daily task of ferrying drums and buckets of water by canoe from the nearest stream. I was in the lap of luxury with a solid roof, an elevated breezy floor and fresh water on tap.

Katherine's own little piece of luxury was being built a hundred metres away. The wharf built from salvaged *hivilli* timber from the failed logging operation was braced by an iron strut salvaged from Mr Hodge's old Tavara copra drier. The timber decking overhung a deep pool where Sergeant Major Fish patrolled for food scraps thrown in after dinner. Large-eyed red fish hid nervously under the overhanging coral as blue-finned trevally sped past. Sunset views of rolling waves, splashing fish and turtles finally created the South Seas fantasy more appropriate for our honeymoon three years earlier.

Mary had been waiting for us to authorise the removal of more coconut palms. Both she and Tippet often asked us to decide on difficult questions for which they already knew the answers. We were their insurance in case their decision backfired. 'Cutting these coconuts will spoil some of the trees we have kept,' Mary acknowledged, understanding that the falling palms would break adjacent trees but then quickly added, 'Suppose we leave them and they fall during a storm they could damage the building.' We agreed that to protect the pride and joy of TDA, Twomey could cut the coconut palms with his mighty chainsaw.

Sure enough, the first ninety-year-old palm we felled smashed through the canopy of a small tree and became wedged in a forked branch ten metres above the ground. With the enormous chainsaw drowning out the sounds of the rainforest, Twomey effortlessly scaled the trunk with his bare feet. Within a couple of minutes he had trimmed branches, including those he was standing on, and sent the palm crashing to the forest floor. Using both hands I struggled to lift the massive saw with its metre-long blade and was embarrassed that Twomey had operated it with only one hand as he used the other for balancing on his wobbly elevated platform. I thought back to a story he had told me.

Twomey's great-grandfather was a giant named Faka. Had this tyrant lived in contemporary United States, Faka surely would have added a maternal prefix to his name. Faka was a legendary headhunter, immortalised as the head of the *Torotoro* dog dance of Lokuru and renowned for inviting women to crack Ngali nuts against his collarbone. Faka was also renowned for his short temper. He became annoyed at both his teenage daughter consistently arriving home late and his wife's persistent complaining about her tardiness. One evening Faka promised his wife that he would teach both her and his daughter a lesson. When the teenager stooped to enter the low doorway of their house, Faka chopped the top of her head clean off. Apparently no-one ever whinged to Faka again.

The shocking conclusion to this story concerned me as much as the matter-of-fact way that Twomey told it. Only three generations ago, big men presided over their villages with unbelievable terror. Life was cheap. Although possessing some of Faka's strength, Twomey is a gentle subservient man, usually smiling unless he had reason to be concerned about his wife or daughters. Mary told me that Twomey washed all of their daughters' cloth nappies when they were small, which says a lot about both Twomey and Mary.

Working at the construction site also gave Katherine and me a chance to understand Mary better. It intrigued us why Mary opposed the logging of Tetepare and spearheaded TDA, when nearly everyone else wanted to reap logging royalties from the island. Sitting down with Mary one night I asked her about the Timber Rights hearing, and how her Lokuru people had responded.

Mary had boarded the logging company's canoe from Lokuru to Munda with many of the logging proponents. On the way she had told the big men, including Jack Daniel and Henry Seda, that she opposed the logging of Tetepare. Her traitorous views stimulated serious argument for the rest of the canoe ride and the entire night before the hearing. Outside the meeting Mary found that Tetepare people from other islands had also gathered to support the logging. Many felt that supporting the logging would be their best way of being recognised as Tetepare landholders. Sharing in the spoils from the remote island was an added benefit.

With the exception of the son of the famed John Kari from Hopongo and Peter Siloko and his cousins whom she met at the hearing, Mary recognised that her stance was unpopular. Not only was she opposing logging but she was also challenging the authority of the big men who didn't accept that women should be decision makers.

I knew Mary revelled in a scrap, but this still did not explain why she fought so passionately for Tetepare. I probed further, 'Why have you, not your other sisters or cousins, spearheaded the push to save Tetepare?'

Mary explained that her father did not have a son when she was small, so instead he taught her to fish and walk in the bush. They often visited Tetepare and Harry relayed many stories about the island. Most importantly, Harry taught his daughter and protégé how to live 'in a man's world'. Mary had seen her father's Tetepare powers and had recognised from an early age that Tetepare was a special place that should be treasured. Harry's tutelage paid off in trumps.

I asked Mary again about the garden she had cleared on Tetepare, the one that she had told me was just 'a little something' several years ago when we first met. Mary acknowledged that her garden was a mark of ownership, a tangible claim made at a time when land disputes had escalated. Mary was not alone. Several other Tetepare descendants from Lokuru, including Jack Daniel and Lloyd Hodge, had also cleared gardens on Tetepare to stake their claims for the island. They had all intended resettling Tetepare when their resources on Rendova had been exhausted. It was no coincidence that many of the formative members of TDA and the fathers of many of the rangers or guides had staked their claim on Tetepare. Jack and Mary both recognised the value of prioritising opportunities for those families most likely to provide opposition to the conservation plans. The last person to clear a garden on Tetepare was Katie Soapi, who had obtained both a chemistry degree and a worldly perspective on the impacts of logging on her Lokuru community. Katie had been overseas when TDA was formed and quickly abandoned her plans to resettle on Tetepare once she witnessed first hand her *wantok*'s conservation agenda. She liked what she saw.

'Before logging,' Katie explained, 'the community looked after one another and the spoils of hunting and fishing were shared.' Small-scale money from the sale of trochus, bêche-de-mer or copra had been circulating in the community for generations, but the *bigfala* money, the easy money, introduced by logging companies had fostered inequality and jealousy in her community. What Katie described for Lokuru was exactly how New Zealand-based anthropologist Ross McDonald summed up the conflict between traditional Solomons cooperative spirit and individual greed promoted by capitalism in his eloquently titled book *Money Makes You Crazy*. The community-based agenda of TDA, which also aimed to protect 'her' special island, was a far better alternative for Katie than the logging or resettlement that loomed when she had left Lokuru.

Resettlement was the development that Mary and her *wantoks* favoured in the 1990s. However, with the broadening of her knowledge of potential conservation benefits, Mary now opposed resettlement. Although I was unaware the time we first met Mary, TDA and the conservation agenda arrived just in time.

Learning how close Tetepare had come to being resettled and then progressively hacked into gardens increased the pressure we felt to ensure the success of the ecotourism development and other benefits of sustainable custodianship of the island.

Meeting Vena

The Solomon Islands made world news again over Christmas 2002. On returning to Gizo from Tetepare, friends and family around the globe needed reassurance that we hadn't been wiped out by a cyclone. The island of Tikopia, hundreds of kilometres from Tetepare had been smashed by fifteen metre waves stirred up by Cyclone Zoe. Yet the first we heard about the cyclone was through worried emails. Concerns from home reinforced our inkling that Katherine should head back to Australia. Since entering the third trimester of her pregnancy, rough seas, perhaps stirred up by Zoe, were making canoe travel increasingly uncomfortable.

We both recognised the impending birth of our first baby placed an added urgency to train guides and rangers to staff Tetepare's new facilities. The frenzy of work and income from the building project had dried up. TDA now had to generate enthusiasm and income by catering for adventure tourists and scientists. A doctor friend offered to accompany Katherine back to Australia. Although worried about not returning with her, my concern also focused on how I would cope by myself. Apart from short 'suicide' missions, we had been inseparable in the Solomons, relying far more on each other than we did back home. As a team we had been able to bond and liaise with both the local men and women. Together we had dealt with a myriad of novel issues and provided mutual sounding-boards for frustrations. But now I was on my own.

While conducting the recruiting drive for TDA a year earlier, the interest of new members in any training or employment was gauged. Almost without exception the men aged under forty wanted to be rangers. Maybe the ever popular kung-fu movies or the quest for a uniform and a gun fired this universal ambition. Mary faced the unenviable task of recruiting a dozen would-be rangers from the list of over four hundred aspirants. Fearing her dilemma at selecting just one man from each local village, we decided to increase participants by combining the ranger and guide training with a second round of marine monitoring. Friends from WWF coordinated the marine monitoring and Mary and I trained the rangers and guides. Our new Tetepare field station, still without windows or lighting, was overflowing.

Training commenced by compiling a list of customary rules that should be followed by visitors to Tetepare. Protection of *sosi*, the goanna that represented the last men on Tetepare, and wild taro, which symbolised the spirit Olisoqo's ear, were essential. A trainee ranger, Kodo, explained that yelling is also *tabu* in the Tetepare forest. To illustrate, he told the story of a New Zealand soldier on a training exercise who had yelled out to his mates. Tetepare's spirits were offended and led him astray. When the young man was eventually found he was naked and very sick. Even a visit to the Munda hospital failed to identify his malady, which wasn't cured until an old Tetepare man learned of the problem and sought forgiveness from the spirits.

The powers of Tetepare's spirits have long been recognised, even by the white plantation managers. Sick workers would be taken across to Jonathan Suka at Lokuru, who could appease the spirits' wrath. Old Suka smirked when he once confided to me that several mischievous men sent to him from Tetepare had faked their illnesses to scam a free trip to Lokuru when their tobacco stocks ran out.

Trainee guides were then asked to describe how to minimise dangers to visitors. Most were surprised that Mary and I considered stinging plants, fire coral, stonefish and crocodiles to be dangerous. Having grown up with these threats, they considered centipedes and other small biters to be riskier. Their remedies for these bites were fascinating. The intense pain of wasp stings was alleviated by breaking a small stick over the bite, whereas yellow snake bites were treated by chewing the roots of lawyer cane. In some cases the treatment seemed worse than the bite. If the juice of the *pogala* tree did not reduce the pain of a centipede bite, they recommended cutting the skin around the bite and infusing crushed chilli.

Next on the training curriculum was a tour of the medicine plants of the forests, led by Mary. She explained that visitors would be interested in the *kastom* cures for all sorts of ailments, several of which she had already administered to me. One medicine plant new to me was *odo huqo huqo*, taken by people who intended committing suicide. I assumed that its leaves must be incredibly toxic and we should add it to our list of dangers, but Mary explained that it was not poisonous. Instead *odo huqo huqo* 'Just made people not worry about things,' including, presumably, their own mortality. Maybe it was a leafy green Prozac or tropical hemp? Because the guides were responsible for explaining the island's wonders to potential tourists, I taught them interesting facts about Tetepare's animals. The men were spellbound to learn that their lizards and snakes had two penises and that *barairi bukasi*, the little green tree skink, was one of only a handful of animals with green blood.

Once Mary and I had addressed the guides' main tasks we progressed to ranger training. Although several of the trainees had not even attended secondary school, most nodded confidently as we explained how to fill out the daily log sheets, recording rainfall, sea conditions and visitor details. More of a challenge was convincing the trainees of the importance of recording the resources harvested by their *wantoks*. Mary came to the rescue again. 'Last year,' she explained, '*mifala intervium tufala fisherman. Tufala kasim one thousand over mullet long net blong tufala.*' When Mary asked the fishermen what they had done with in excess of a thousand fish they had netted, they admitted that most were wasted. '*Stupid people*,' Mary cussed, shaking her head with exasperation, and the trainees nodded in agreement. Mary then relayed another story that generated more angst among the would-be rangers. A fish biologist from Queensland had recently used Tetepare as a research site for giant bump-headed parrotfish, or *topa*. He only needed to remove the oocyliths from the fish but according to Mary's informants the researcher took over a thousand kilograms of *topa* fillets for which he paid one Lokuru man a hundred Solomon dollars.

The parable of Mary's stories was that in order for Tetepare to continue to provide fish and *'Evri kaen samting long resosiss blong iumi'* it was important to make sure that fishermen and divers only took what they could use and what was sustainable. One of the trainees, Philip, expressed concern that Gilbertese fishermen were increasingly using 'hookah' compressed air or scuba tanks to strip the bêche-de-mer from local waters. Before long the field station was buzzing with stories of how the resources upon which these locals depended for food or income were being wasted or poached, convincing everyone of the need to record and manage what people were taking from Tetepare.

Peter Ramohia, the director of research for the Solomons' Department of Fisheries and Marine Resources, also helped with the training and explained how fish, trochus and bêche-de-mer had increased adjacent to a protected area in the Arnavon Islands, not far from Choiseul. Eggs and juveniles from this protected area repopulated harvested areas. The Arnavons, where important reefs and turtle nesting beaches had been protected for over a decade, provided a tangible model of regional conservation benefits. Rangers and marine monitoring boys unanimously agreed that TDA should stop harvests from some areas of Tetepare's coast to guarantee future catches.

Peter also explained that the Solomon Islands government had legislated that harvested crayfish, coconut crabs and trochus shells all had to exceed a minimum size. Most of the men scarcely believed Peter. None had any idea why the government would make such crazy rules. Peter explained that small crays or trochus were not able to breed and it was important that some grow into adults. He further shocked them by explaining that maximum size limits had also been placed on trochus shells in order to protect large females that could produce thousands of eggs.

The Fisheries Department was particularly keen for us to monitor coconut crabs. These massive land crabs were delicacies that few locals could resist. Weighing up to five kilograms and able to be kept alive for many days, these lobster-like crustaceans were taken from Tetepare to villages, towns, Honiara and beyond. In May 1989 alone, two-and-a-half thousand kilograms of coconut crabs were exported from the Solomon Islands. There was a risk that coconut crabs could be harvested to oblivion on Tetepare, like they have been on other islands within their former range.

Most of the trainee rangers had collected crabs all their lives and we modified their harvesting techniques to monitor them. Ripe coconuts were hacked in half with bush knives and then tied outside likely holes with lengths of vine. Coconut crabs typically hole up during the day inside rock crevasses, tangled tree roots or mud burrows but cannot resist the smell of coconuts in the evening.

An hour or so after dark we revisited each of our twenty coconut baits to count and measure the crabs attracted to them. Hobete taught me how to distinguish females by the feathery appendages under their tails. We were all surprised at how large a crab needed to be before it reached the minimum thorax length of forty-three millimetres. I had seen individuals less than half this size at the Honiara market selling for more than a ranger's daily wage! The larger individuals we measured were older than any of us, which made me, and only me, reluctant to snaffle one for the pot.

After a couple of days and nights of coconut crab surveys, we visited Qeuru beach to learn how to monitor turtle nests. Qeuru was the site of our ignominious landing a few years earlier and the seas were again rough so we couldn't land. Instead we swam from the canoe to a rocky ledge then scampered around the base of a cliff, like a reality TV challenge, except the reality of Tetepare was that there was no back-up crew ready if we got into trouble. In single file, we timed our runs over slippery rocks to miss the waves, at one stage stooping through a three-metre-long cave that was violently flushed to its roof every ten seconds. On the beach Peter taught us how to distinguish the parallel tracks of a green turtle from the alternate drags left by a hawksbill turtle, and of course the monster leatherback tracks.

In the evenings the rangers and guides discussed their day's experiences with the marine boys who had been monitoring the reefs. Their counts of trochus shells and bêche-de-mer were of particular interest to the rangers, who were keen to increase their stocks within the planned protected area. Dan Afzal, an American marine biologist working with the WWF, enthused about the largest table coral he had ever seen, despite having dived in many of the world's coral hotspots. His WWF mate Alec Hughes, also a marine biologist, was more impressed with the schools of huge barracuda, kingfish and trevally that he drooled at underwater, and then fished for each evening.

Although Mary had excelled at coordinating the cooks and food for such a busy program, the boys weren't happy. Within three days they had exhausted their entire tobacco stocks. Mary had no patience with smokers and told them bluntly that she supplied the food but tobacco was their issue. Not to be deterred, a couple of boys paddled a dugout canoe twenty kilometres back to Lokuru in the dark and returned with tobacco just before sunrise, too exhausted to do any work for the day.

A year after that first monitoring on Tetepare the marine boys and rangers repeated their surveys. This was the big test. We were comparing the number and size of coconut crabs, trochus shells and bêche-de-mer in the fourteen-kilometre-long protected area adjacent to the field station with the harvested areas, hoping that our new rangers would see the benefits of the conservation zone.

I had often watched the waves barrelling over the reef at the entrance to the Field Station passage and wondered if my mates could teach me to surf here. Now, rather than surfing, the boys decided this was a likely location to search for trochus shells. Although it looked dangerous, the four monitoring boys jumped in as our driver expertly nosed the canoe over the waves, just metres from where they crashed into the reef. I figured that I would also have a look.

When I bobbed to the surface the other divers had disappeared. I turned around and the canoe was gone too, hidden by the waves. Eventually I caught a glimpse of two of the boys in the surf zone and decided to swim over to see how they were going. Although we were a kilometre from the shore, the water was only a couple of metres deep. Immediately I saw a trochus shell on the wave-battered platform below me. After experiencing the tenacity with which much smaller periwinkles cling to rocks, I was surprised how easily the fist-sized trochus dislodged. With my prize in hand I continued swimming towards the divers.

Suddenly the rock platform fell away and I was floating over depthless inky water. Out of the darkness emerged a series of pale shapes, like a herd of buffalo appearing through the mist. They were *topa* and instinctively I counted them; seventeen. There were probably more in this 'herd' than in all the waters of Indonesia! Then behind the *topa* an apparition materialised. A massive pale tail beat at the water, either in hot pursuit of the *topa* or of me. *Topa* are huge fish but this thing dwarfed them. I gasped air through my snorkel, both in fright and astonishment. This creature did not possess the grace of a shark; instead it used an almost comical up-and-down tail thrusting. This was my first underwater *vena* experience. Several fishermen and divers had relayed stories of their encounters with dugongs in the waters of Tetepare, and I had been intrigued that they always said, 'We met *vena*' rather than 'We saw *vena*' but now I understood. The *vena* was definitely swimming rapidly towards this strange white-skinned creature that had entered its realm.

Amorous dugongs sometimes hug divers but luckily this *vena* had no such aspirations. Hurtling past the *topa*, it surfed a wave straight past me and disappeared into the bubbles. I screamed with excitement into my snorkel and was keen to share my amazing experience, but could not see any divers or the canoe when I surfaced. Rather than searching too intently I quickly dived back underwater. Would *vena* return? Would something more sinister appear out of the depths?

For the first time ever I was watching waves from the inside. Two-metre curved mirrors of water reflected an upside-down image of the distant rainforest. As if the *vena* had welcomed me into its world, the waves seemed to be protecting me. Just when it seemed I would be dashed on the rock platform, the waves sucked me up and pushed me along. I penetrated through the top of a wave and saw some divers collecting trochus inside the surf zone. Feeling indestructible, I decided to join them.

Just before the mirrored water shattered into effervescent bubbles, a young green turtle sped past underneath me. Why was the turtle, a seagrass eater like the dugong, surfing over a jagged coral reef? Maybe like me it was enjoying the thrill. The fish in the surf zone also demonstrated surprising energy and speed compared to the lethargic nature of lagoon and reef fish. Giant trevally sped towards me with menacing inquisitiveness, making me wish that I had a spear and was outside the protected area.

The best diver, Kennedy, got rolled by a big wave in only knee-deep water. I saw his bum, then his feet, then his bulging yellow rice bag firmly grasped in his left hand. His mask had been washed off his face and was only held on by the snorkel clenched between his teeth. Eventually he found his feet and stood up on the wave platform, spitting out his snorkel with laughter. With his bag of trochus intact and no damage done to his tough skin, Kennedy dived back into the shallow water, keen to top the trochus count. Back in the canoe, we recorded the size of all trochus shells before the boys reluctantly returned them to the sea floor.

After just a couple of dives in the protected area, Kennedy and his mates were astounded at the numbers of trochus and bêche-de-mer they found. I was confident that numbers of *topa* and coconut crabs had also increased after a year of protection. Although they made no secret of their own temptations, the divers encouraged their ranger friends to continue to keep poachers out of the protected area. Everyone now knew that these rich areas would help repopulate other nearby reefs. After chasing away the renegade loggers a couple of years earlier, TDA could now proudly boast these additional conservation outcomes. Now we had to attract the visitors who would provide the financial benefits that Katherine and I had promised nearly two years ago.

Tetepare's Big Five

Old Harry Bea had suggested that if Katherine had a boy he should be named 'Tetepare'. *Nangarita*, a *kastom* plant of Tetepare, was suggested as a suitable girl's name but we had other ideas. *Lelei* is another *kastom* plant of Tetepare, a little flower planted at ceremonial sites. Lelei was also the name of the forested ridge above the Tetepare field station. Mary had a smiling niece named Layla, which was coincidentally one of my favourite Eric Clapton songs. We compromised Harry's suggestions and our Layla was born, in Australia, two weeks late.

Doctors concerned about Katherine travelling to a malaria zone while pregnant were adamant that a newborn shouldn't visit the Solomons. Leaving Katherine at home was twice as hard now that Layla was around, but I needed to return to Tetepare to complete our donor reports and accompany the first researchers to the island. Instead of our usual three-month visit I went back for only a month. 'Only a month,' I said to myself, but it was the longest month of my life.

Sitting alone on the steps of the Tetepare field station, my thoughts of home were interrupted by an amazing performance. High on an exposed branch a brown-winged starling bowed its head like a subservient geisha. Suddenly it jerked its head backwards while emitting a sharp squeak, like the sound of a mouse being trodden on. This sequence, repeated at regular intervals, was reminiscent of a back-to-front sneeze. But unlike a sneeze, a different sound was emitted each time the starling repeated its elaborate bowing and head jerking. A hollow 'cluck' was followed by a perfect imitation of a microwave timer and then an amplified rain drop in a bowl. These bizarre noises were vocalised, apparently randomly, as the bird experimented with its repertoire.

As I pondered the magnitude of its musical talents the starling upped the ante and interspersed its clucks and beeps with a clarinet-like tone on the downward bob of its head, like the 'ahh' in a sneezed 'ahh choo'. The variety of these fluting calls was even more impressive than the first notes that had introduced the performance. Some represented a creaking door while others approximated the most haunting sound that I have ever experienced, the wail of Madagascar's Indri lemurs. I wondered how the Solomon bird book would describe this performance and was disappointed to read 'high-pitched whistles and squeaks'. Over the next few days I watched the maestro construct a basketball-sized stick nest not far from its stage.

Not to be outdone by the performing starling, a posse of myna birds duetted from a nearby tree. What they lacked in subtle variability in calls was easily made up for by their loud repertoire of shrill and strident buzzes. These were native yellow-faced mynas and not the Indian mynahs that had become Honiara's most abundant bird since being introduced during the war to feed on coconut plantation pests. Fortunately these feral birds had not reached the Western Province. Overhead, the whinny of a passing osprey sounded like a horse in pain. A harsh 'Now!' bark from a nearby tree briefly quickened my pulse until I remembered that it was one of the calls of the bumbling buff-headed coucal or *mozu*. These weird calls may explain why the people of Rendova and Tetepare consider these pheasant-like birds to be devils, and hence why they are more abundant here than in Guadalcanal and Malaita, where they are eaten. When I walked into the forest I detected the nervous, almost pained, three-note whistle of the white-winged fantail. A minute or so later I realised that, fused into the rhythmic background buzz of the cicadas, was the repetitive call of the aptly named cicadabird. The rainforest canopy's throbbing morning activity was so overwhelming that I was eventually distracted from my thoughts of Katherine and little Layla.

As well as being an inspiring rainforest and reef cathedral, Tetepare was home to several spectacular and threatened species that were sure to lure nature-loving tourists. Yet the Solomon Islands only attracted approximately the same number of visitors as Antarctica. If we were going to entice a piece of this scarce tourism trade we had to market 'our' island cleverly. Katherine and I had decided to compile a 'big five' to mimic the primary drawcards of the African plains. Instead of the rhino, lion, elephant, leopard and buffalo, Tetepare boasted less deadly but equally awesome candidates.

Bukasi, the prehensile-tailed skink, is both unique to the Solomons and the world's largest skink. Gigantean prehistoric leatherback turtles were also obvious contenders for the Tetepare 'big five'. As the largest land invertebrate and another herculean species declining throughout its range, coconut crabs were another easy selection. Saltwater crocodiles, the world's largest, which could be viewed in relative safety from Tetepare's Tavara Lake, quickly became the fourth.

Choosing the fifth member of the 'big five' proved more difficult. The Solomon eagle, like other great eagles of the world, was particularly vulnerable to habitat fragmentation and prey declines. If national logging continued at its current rate, Tetepare may soon become one of the last refuges for these eagles. We also considered the mighty *bakarao*, the huge frog that is reputedly the fourth-largest amphibian in the world. Even if it could jump further than any other frog, fourth-largest rarely qualifies for a medal so the big frog was dropped from the list. Blythe's Hornbills were also majestic creatures, guaranteed to thrill tourists, but they too were not the biggest of their kind. After my exiting encounter I reckoned that dugongs were a realistic contender, but we had not confirmed whether they were resident or even regular visitors to Tetepare. Maybe we should opt for the flip side of the size scale and settle on the pygmy parrot, one of the world's tiniest parrots and sure to entice keen birdos.

Two other creatures prevented me from settling on the last of the Tetepare 'big five'. One was the mysterious black snake that Matthias had seen at shrines and the other was *barogana*, the bird said to never land that squealed like a pig when someone had died. They did not resemble any birds in the field guide I showed to dozens of informants. Maybe *barogana* was a seabird, possibly even the potentially extinct Beck's petrel that had last been officially recorded near Rendova in 1929. Solving the *barogana* mystery became one of my focuses on Tetepare.

Each morning Twomey and I rose before dawn as the early morning clouds were turning orange. He had heard the elusive *barogana* from the field station a few days before I returned. We sat on the decking of the station that gave an uninterrupted view of the reddening sky. The sky gradually lightened and for the third consecutive morning I assumed our early start was in vain, except for the feast I was providing for mossies. Then out of the corner of my eye I saw a large gliding bird disappear behind the canopy. I raced down the stairs and out into the clearing around the building. Twomey raced down too, eager that we should solve the mystery.

'*Amaqi*,' Twomey sighed in a most unexcited tone. I agreed. The bird, which by now had been followed by a procession of others, was a frigatebird. With jet black sickle-shaped wings, frigatebirds resemble creatures from a fantasy story. A few months earlier in Lokuru I had counted over a thousand of these oceanic marauders departing from their roost on Boramane Island. Presumably the birds flying over the Tetepare field station were from the same colony. Although frigatebirds are too widespread to join Tetepare's 'big five', I decided to satisfy my ecological urges and count the birds. They streamed past in lines of five to thirty birds, usually in single file. Occasionally I became confused when a group circled on a thermal and passed over the field station twice, possibly mixing with new birds entering the 'kettle' of swirling birds.

As the light improved I could make out the distinctive white throats of immature birds and the white armpits that distinguished lesser from greater frigatebirds. For the next two hours, as the rangers and guides emerged from their sheet rolls and stoked their breakfast fire, I strained my neck backwards and moved around the clearing, following and counting the lines of *amaqi* as they passed over. 1,306 birds. Regular counts from Tetepare could reveal both the size of the colony and also the proportion of juveniles and moulting adults. These counts may help to establish when and where the birds nest. Although several roosting colonies are known, including one near Uepi Island, no-one I had spoken to knew where Solomon Island frigatebirds nested. Long-term counts may indirectly reveal changes in tuna or the baitfish that they chase. As the guides sipped their morning tea, my frigatebird counts were the first taste of the strange world of ornithologists they were to experience that day.

Within seconds of arriving at the field station Chris Filardi effervesced, 'You guys are right, have a look at that yellow elbow. Man that is so clear.' A tall man by Melanesian standards, Chris also had a big presence. His scraggly black beard, coiled fuzz of dark hair and expressive brand of Pijin, honed in the New Guinea highlands, defied his New York origins of Italian descent. We had described the white-eyes of Tetepare to Chris, noting in particular the prominent yellow patch on the bend of the wing that was not mentioned in texts on Solomons' birds. While his collaborator and recent bride Catherine struggled to supervise the unloading of the paraphernalia that accompanies travelling with a baby, Chris's binoculars were glued to a couple of 'our' small green birds in the tree by the new wharf.

Nearly half of the Solomons' birds are endemic. They are found nowhere else in the world. This alone is not a startling figure, particularly for remote islands. Seventy-one species or sub-species of Hawaiian birds were endemic before recent extinctions accounted for twenty-three of them. Most biology students, or connoisseurs of documentaries, know that Charles Darwin described a bewildering array of Galapagos Islands finches that had gradually evolved through natural selection to feed on different foods. Once these different offshoots could no longer interbreed, Darwin proclaimed that they were new species.

Perhaps the second-best example of bird speciation taught to biology students is the case of the Solomon Islands white-eyes. White-eyes are finch-sized fruit and insect eaters, related to the honeyeaters of Australia. Most of them have a characteristic white ring around their eye. Apart from the existence of the prehensile-tailed skink, the diversity of white-eyes was the only other biological fact I knew about the Solomon Islands before our first visit. The islands of Ghizo, Ranonnga, Vella la Vella and Kolombangara each hosted unique species; others were shared by several islands. I had assumed that these white-eyes had also evolved into different species through favouring particular fruits or insects found on different islands. Apparently I was wrong.

I had observed different white-eye species all feeding upon similar berries and small grubs. The most obvious difference between the white-eyes on different islands was their colouration, rather than the more functional attributes that Darwin had recorded in his finches. According to the original model of natural selection, speciation should be driven by differences in the environments or food types on the islands, but this didn't appear to be the case. Rather, social forces seemed to prevent interbreeding in white-eyes. The Tetepare white-eye, variously considered to be a different race or a completely distinct species from the white-eye on Rendova, was an important piece of the puzzle that Chris and Catherine hoped to solve.

Later we confirmed Chris's suspicion that the yellow 'elbow' arose from feathers typically lying under the wing that Tetepare white-eyes could choose to accentuate when seeking recognition. They allow a bird to hedge its bets, like a football supporter who wears the team's scarf with pride when it wins but removes it when they lose. It was easy to see how this 'movable badge' of recognition would not be apparent in dusty old museum skins that had not been prepared to accentuate this placement. The birds on Rendova did not show their underwing coverts to the same extent; neither did they have the white belly of the Tetepare birds. Chris's thesis was that white-eyes defend territories. In order to recognise members of their own population, they recognised subtle identification 'badges'. A bird from another 'team' without the correct badge would be ostracised from the flock. Such patriotism would thwart rare attempted colonisation events by adventurous or unfortunate white-eyes from adjacent islands.

Tetepare was the perfect place to test this theory. Less than three kilometres away from the birds that we were watching was Rava Point on Rendova. Nowhere else were two species of white-eyes separated by such a short distance. I had banded silvereyes, the white-eye's *wantok* from Australia, and some of our recaptures had flown hundreds of kilometres. Surely their Pacific cousins could fly over only three kilometres of sea? Furthermore, Tetepare was joined to Rendova only ten million years ago, before the Rava elders had ordered the shark to separate the islands to prevent the King from avenging their boys' fling with his lustful queen. If Chris and Catherine could prove that the white-eyes and several other birds on Tetepare were distinctly different from those on Rendova, they could then understand how long it took for selection of the team's badge to create new species.

Until now, Tetepare had been both difficult to reach and problematical to gain approval to study the birds but TDA's new research permit and field station presented Chris and Catherine a long-awaited opportunity. As soon as they were unpacked, we started catching white-eyes around the field station in fine mist nets. Unique combinations of coloured bands were placed on their legs to find out how far they moved, how long they lived and if they stayed in tight flocks. We also took blood for DNA analysis that would hopefully determine how dissimilar they are from the Rendova white-eyes. One by one the rangers rather nervously held these seemingly weightless green birds before they flew off, apparently none the worse for having a drop of blood removed from their wing.

Mist netting for white-eyes provided me with an opportunity to closely inspect several other birds, which were typically difficult to observe in the tall forest. Five species of kingfishers, including the finch-sized blue and white species known only as *Alcedo pusilla*, were trapped in my nets. Despite already spending several months on the island I had not previously seen these birds, and subsequently discovered that these shy kingfishers flew low and straight like darts, seldom perching in the open or advertising their presence with calls. Even Twomey and Suhero, who were familiar with every other bird I caught, looked puzzled at the little bundle of feathers that more closely resembled a baby's toy than any bird they were familiar with. One of my favourite birds was the inappropriately named yellow-vented myzomela, a small brown honeyeater with a brilliant red throat. On Tetepare, these elegant birds with a long curved beak and known by Twomey as *zeu zeu tarao*, showed no trace of yellow on their vent. The most striking aspect of these birds, and one that was surprisingly difficult to observe in the forest, was their dazzling crimson rump.

Soon after Chris and Catherine left, other researchers based at the field station recorded hitherto undescribed bats, butterflies and plants from Tetepare. Others studied the turtles and even the scorpions of the island. One of the most fortuitous visits was made by Guy Dutson, another Solomon Islands bird authority. The morning after he arrived he recognised the distinctive call of the nomadic channel-billed cuckoo, an uncommon winter visitor from Australia that I had never seen on Tetepare. Just as he was recording the species in his notebook, Twomey and the rangers rushed in yelling, '*Barogana, barogana*.' Finally the mystery had been solved as the bird flew off with its distinctive stiff-winged flight and long hooked beak resembling a flying walking-stick. Perhaps its eerie mournful call was uttered when it learned that Tetepare was not inhabited by crows in whose nest these monster cuckoos lay their eggs. Later Twomey joined elite company in his own right by becoming one of the handful of observers to ever see the yellow-legged pigeon. These unmistakable but very rare birds apparently favour primary rainforest, a habitat becoming increasingly scarce in the Solomons but protected on Tetepare.

The most spectacular survey was for freshwater fish coordinated by Aaron Jenkins, the principal fish biologist for Wetlands International in the Pacific. Aaron was no stranger to phenomenal discoveries. In the early 1980s his mother located the Hagahai tribe in remote Papua New Guinea, who hadn't made contact with the outside world. Aaron himself had discovered over twenty new species of fish from Melanesia. In his short Tetepare survey, Aaron had already sampled several undescribed fish and determined that Tetepare's rivers provided a benchmark for pristine tropical rivers. The water quality and numbers of big fish were second to none. Then came the show stopper.

The light was fading on the last day of their survey as Aaron's team were using the last dregs of their electrofisher battery at their final site. 'What the hell is that!' he screamed out in unison with his local student David Boseto. The TDA rangers and marine monitors, who were knee deep in the river spun around, alarmed that the biologists might have seen a monster crocodile. But Aaron and David were peering into the net, their faces buzzing with excitement rather than fear. A small red fish, more closely resembling a ruby noodle than any fish known to science, peered back at them through googly eyes. Aaron immediately suspected the 'noodle fish' was not only a new species, but a new family of fish, the first time such a unique discovery had been made anywhere in the world for many decades. The TDA rangers raced back into the river, trying without success to stun another noodle fish before their battery ran out.

Aaron and David, like several other researchers who have visited Tetepare, will be back, eagerly awaiting their next discovery. Each expedition employs guides, cooks and boat drivers, many of whom had previously worked in logging camps on Rendova. As well as providing much needed employment, each new discovery also reinforced the value of the last wild island of the Solomons.

Frequent snorkelling by tourists in the protected seagrass meadows adjacent to the Tetepare field station also revealed that dugongs were both resident and increasingly brazen. A few years later, Australian volunteers Michaela Farrington and Anthony Plummer filmed a herd of five *vena*, inquisitively swimming up to them. A mother brought her calf over to where I was snorkelling with young Layla and we proudly compared our progeny. That experience was sufficient to confirm the legitimate place of dugongs among Tetepare's key wildlife attractions.

Finally, we could cross *barogana* off the list of Tetepare's Big Five candidates and install the dugong. Ticking off prehensile-tailed skinks, leatherback turtles, saltwater crocodiles, coconut crabs and dugongs would not only be a thrill for visitors but should also ensure they spend long enough on Tetepare to enthuse the staff and local visitors.

Returning from the peace and excitement of Tetepare to the 'real world' of Gizo in June 2003 was depressing. Rumours abounded of Yugoslav mafia infiltrating the Solomon Islands with money laundering and illegal passports. Ill-founded media speculation touted incursions of Muslim extremists using the country as a stepping stone into the Pacific. For once it appeared that the coconut news was being heard abroad.

The *Solomon Star* printed daily excerpts of an Australian soul-searching position paper mounting a case for a Pacific intervention force to sort out the Solomon's problems. Provocatively titled 'Our failing neighbour', the first paragraph left the reader in no doubt that the Solomon Islands' casual regard for law and financial management had been noticed by the world.

> Solomon Islands, one of Australia's nearest neighbours, is a failing state. Over the past five years, a slow-burning political and security crisis has paralysed the country's capital, stifled its economy, disrupted its government, discouraged aid donors, and inflicted suffering and hardship on its people. The country has virtually ceased to function as a sovereign state, and on its present trajectory there is a high risk that its land and people will become effectively ungoverned.

Letters to the *Star* from a variety of individuals and community organisations unconditionally supported the arrival of a composite Pacific nation police and army contingent.

When I returned home to Australia, images of gun-toting 'militia' from the weather coast of Guadalcanal and Malaita were interspersed on the TV news with the high-stepping nuclear-intentioned army of North Korea and the continued quest for Saddam in the Middle East. *Time* magazine's banner headlines screamed, 'Can anything save the Solomon Islands.' *The Hapi Isles* were being compared with the world's worst trouble spots. It was becoming nearly impossible to attract any but the most adventurous researchers and tourists. The Big Five were of little value to Tetepare while the country was perceived to be in such a tailspin. The Earthwatch Institute, which we had courted to attract fee-paying international volunteers to assist with the monitoring and research at Tetepare wouldn't endorse visits until travel warnings had been lifted. Despite all the progress on Tetepare, the world wasn't yet ready to assist.

NEW LIFE

Katherine, Layla and I accompanied the third ecotourist visit to Baniata. Our Australian mates, Kelli-Jo and Dave Kovac, coincidentally also honeymooning in the Solomons, had decided to stay in the village for a week in the hope of witnessing a nesting leatherback. In response to the Spiritual Authority's edict, no turtles or eggs had been taken since our last visit and I was delighted to fork out $350 in incentive payments. Records from our main turtle recorder, George, confirmed Livingstone's story that female *oihare* returned every ten days to lay, usually on the same beach where they had nested previously. What Livingstone and George were not aware of was the epic lifelong battle for survival endured by the *oihare*.

Humans, goannas and occasionally even dogs, pigs and megapode birds eat any turtle eggs they find. Of the eggs that escape predation, some hatchlings are drowned by high tides or ensnared underground by vigorous roots. The little battlers that do emerge must avoid crabs, birds and then a multitude of fish as they make their way to the open ocean. Leatherbacks then swim and drift around on ocean currents while maturing, feeding on jellyfish and zooplankton in upwellings, maybe thousands of kilometres from Baniata. But the ocean is becoming smaller and more dangerous. Entanglements in fishing nets and long lines now kill more turtles than hungry villagers.

The few leatherbacks that survive to maturity return to nest at the same beach where they hatched. Weighed down by hundreds of eggs and accumulated fat reserves, the innately programmed females run the gauntlet of hungry villagers. If the beach is dark and quiet she hauls herself ashore and tests whether the temperature, moisture and grain size of the sand is suitable to incubate her clutch of eggs. She then endures another two-hour period of extreme risk. No wonder she appears to be crying; any maternity ward where the mother's survival is unlikely and her eggs are almost definitely going to be eaten within a couple of days cannot be a joyous place. For the next ten days the *oihare* swims around offshore, developing her next clutch of eggs. Few jellyfish live in these tropical waters so they depend upon fat supplies, both to build up energy for their next exhausting nesting effort and to sustain their developing eggs.

If fortunate enough to survive the nesting season and lay all their clutches, the female *oihare* heads back into the open water, thousands of kilometres from her nesting beach. Her fat supplies, that may have greased the *motu* ovens of Baniata, are now exhausted. For the next three or more years she slowly bulks up on jellyfish, which are not renowned for their high calorific content.

Livingstone and George were both surprised and proud that their *oihare* might be spotted by turtle watchers off the coast of Canada, Japan or Australia, but we were more interested in experiencing these awesome creatures right here in Baniata. While it was difficult to persuade village boys to check the beaches late at night, we had no such problems finding willing babysitters for Layla. Like a village-scale 'pass the parcel', our baby daughter was handed around from house to house, followed by an enraptured throng of onlookers.

All night Katherine and I, in tandem with Kelli-Jo and Kovac, patrolled the two-kilometre section of beach where George confidently predicted a turtle would re-nest. Moonlight reflecting off the frothy surf forging up the dark beach resembled a crisp white singlet on toned black skin. On our first patrol, I thought we had intersected the tracks of a nesting turtle until we realised we were following imitation turtle tracks made by little rascals from the village. Later we were nearly fooled by tantalising round boulders in the surf zone that were gradually exposed by the receding tide. On the second night, when I was walking the late shift, I counted dozens of flying foxes in the pre-dawn light heading back towards the crocodile lake where Anoi had terrified Katie and me six months before. On the third all-night vigil Kelli-Jo and Kovac encountered fresh *oihare* tracks as they walked back to the village at dawn. The turtle we had been searching for had nested a mere hundred metres past our patrolled section of beach and slipped back into the ocean without detection.

We now understood the Touo language names for the nights spent waiting for turtles. The eleventh night after a turtle nested is called *hiro varoa*, which translates to 'when the turtle watcher's fire is destroyed the turtle will come up'. So regular are the nesting turtles that the villagers blame their fires if *oihare* do not renest by the eleventh night. We had endured three nights of minimal sleep and despite all the willing babysitters, our six-month-old baby and the stifling humidity prohibited sleep during the day. Appropriately *roda*, the name for the twelfth night after nesting, means 'tired and fell asleep'.

Twelve months later, at the start of the main nesting season, Katherine and I returned to Baniata again, hoping to find ourselves an *oihare*, like Kelli-Jo and Kovac had raved about endlessly after we left. As before, Livingstone and George confidently predicted '*Oihare bae hem kam daon tonaet.*' '*Hiro varoa,*' Livingstone reminded us, 'Waiting for turtles on the eleventh day.'

We had just attended the inaugural conference on Melanesian Leatherback Conservation attended by scientists and community groups from Vanuatu, Solomon Islands and New Guinea. George's data indicate that Baniata was in the top ten, possibly the top six, nesting beaches for leatherbacks in the western Pacific. Accompanying us on our patrols was Colin Naru, a Papua New Guinean in charge of monitoring Lae's Kamiali beach, which was one of the top five leatherback beaches. With ten years experience of community turtle conservation initiatives, Colin accepted our invitation to tutor George and the growing band of TDA monitors to intensify their turtle monitoring and protection. Despite his small stature and moth-eaten dreadlocks, Colin was a big man in his village back home and was clearly respected by his Solomon cousins.

Also accompanying us were Dave Argument and Laurie Wein, who had recently embarked on their two-year volunteer stint on Tetepare. Dave had recently traded tagging bison in the Canadian Rockies with Parks Canada for tagging turtles. At over two metres tall, he towered over the four Tetepare rangers he was tutoring.

Laurie used her social science background to help Tippet and Mary with their new roles as managers of the Tetepare project and, like the rest of us, had became caught up in the excitement of finding a leatherback and joined the all-night beach patrols. Every thirty minutes we each walked designated sections of the beach, walkie-talkie radios in hand, staring at the black sand while searching for even blacker turtle tracks. At the same time we scanned the white water for an emerging dark hegemoth and felt with our feet for the telltale churned-up sand that would indicate a turtle had recently hauled its way up the beach. Before midnight, groups of locals occasionally sauntered past, only visible from the intermittent orange glow as they drew on a cigarette. In contrast, lying motionless up high on the beach, was a white apparition.

Scott Benson was in 'standby mode', a technique he used to counteract repeated nights of broken sleep when he travelled the globe searching for turtles. Scott worked for the leatherback conservation program of the US National Oceanic and Atmospheric Administration. Dressed in white pants and shoes that shone like beacons in the feeble moonlight, the balding, grey-bearded American was less concerned than the locals that turtles would not emerge if they could see the patrollers. 'They'll come up,' he drawled confidently, before reverting to standby mode again. Scott had brought unique tags and satellite trackers with fancy harnesses to attach to leatherbacks. Our mission was to reach the *oihare* as soon as she started laying so Scott could fit the transmitter before she returned to the sea. Like us, the American fishing industry was keen to learn about the nesting patterns and movements of the increasingly rare leatherbacks that migrated through the rich, yet hazardous, Hawaiian fishery to the western coasts of USA and Canada.

Despite a frustrating first night, we were thrilled when George informed us the following morning that a turtle nest he had relocated had started hatching. Katherine and I raced through the village to see five hatchlings swimming around in a bucket.

Aptly named, their leathery shells were jet-black and marked by seven ridges of pearly white beads.

Scott Benson urged George to release the hatchlings to make their own way to the sea. He even discouraged us from helping the poor little battlers out of our footprints or righting them when they were flipped by the surf. Something about that initial struggle to the sea may be vital in helping them relocate their nesting beach. George had thought by feeding them in a bucket for a few days then releasing them far out to sea he would improve their chance of survival, but Scott told him of turtles given a head start that attempted to clamber aboard canoes when they were ready to lay.

So exhaustive was their historic egg harvest that these hatchlings were the first many of the children at Baniata had ever seen. Although a few nests had been poached when the project was initiated, most nests at Baniata and Tetepare were now being eroded or inundated by high tides. Unfortunately peak nesting season coincided with the highest tides. The line of eroded coconut palms prostrate on the beach like fallen soldiers suggested that the high tides were getting higher, maybe as a result of climate change. Our need to relocate low-lying nests to safety became increasingly apparent.

Colin Naru, our Papua New Guinean leatherback authority, explained to George and the rangers that eggs needed to be moved soon after laying without rotating them, otherwise the developing embryo would die. Despite being such a risky operation, the hatchlings we were watching struggling into the surf confirmed that relocation could be successful. Scott shared another turtle secret. The temperature during incubation determines the sex of baby turtles, as it does with crocodiles. George's nest in the shade of the village trees would undoubtedly be cooler and more likely to produce males than one on the unprotected baking hot black sand of the beach. We urged George to relocate most nests to unshaded areas to ensure that females were born.

Colin shared another surprise with George. When their Papua New Guinea project commenced, turtle monitors had relocated nests into the protection of the village, just as George had done. They learned of their error a couple of decades later when adult turtles, presumably those that hatched from the relocated nests, bulldozed through the village searching for nesting sites that mimicked their own. One had even caused havoc by excavating the local cemetery! Like Scott's boat-boarding turtles, these cemetery raiders were innately replicating their first memories.

On the second night of turtle patrols an unusual glow illuminated much of the typically quiet, dark village. The village's only portable generator cranked away all night, powering a single fluorescent globe above an all-night *sing sing* vigil mourning the passing of Livingstone's ninety-six-year-old mother, Meseni. As I snuck back through the outskirts of the village with my head torch off to avoid disturbing the mourners, I heard the now familiar CFC chant of 'New Life' from the prayer vigil and wondered whether the CFC's policy on not harvesting turtles or eggs would eventually breathe new life into the local *oihare* population. Would Meseni's descendants ever again witness the thousands of turtles and hundreds of *oihare* feasts of the past?

The night after Scott and Colin had left I headed out alone for a beach patrol. An inquisitive village dog gave up following me and was swallowed up by the darkness. Again I was alone, on the world's blackest beach under the planet's darkest sky. Somewhere near Gizo, a bolt of lightening briefly revealed the distant horizon. I smirked. My confidence in the mantra '*Oihare* come up when there is lightening in the sea,' had been dashed by unsuccessful patrols on this very beach on half a dozen stormy nights. Perhaps it was the minimal sleep for nearly a week but I had started doubting whether we had been hoaxed by fake tracks and translocated hatchlings. If this was a prime turtle beach in prime turtle season I should have seen them by now. And there it was! Barely six strides in front of me, a shiny black mass lay motionless on the sand. Instinctively I dropped to my knees and held my breath while I struggled to focus on the apparition. I edged forwards. Had I been fooled by another exposed boulder?

'Whoaasshh'. As if from a deep sea dinosaur, the sigh bellowed from another world, another epoch. I shivered involuntarily. 'Scrrritch . . . Whack'. An enormous black flipper dragged forwards almost under my nose and cracked onto the sand. The bulk inched up the beach as I sidled forwards. No photographs or descriptions prepared me for the magnitude of the beast. I could now make out her eyes, golfball-sized expressionless disks on a head that was bigger than mine. She exhaled again, expelling the despair of a lifetime of tragedy. Transfixed by her suffering and the magnitude of her task ahead, I crouched motionless, sweating slightly in the still night air. Her plight was so unfair, so wrong. What evolutionary bungle had sentenced these hapless relics to such a torturous nesting process? I wanted to comfort her, to bury her eggs high on the beach for her while she escaped to the sanctuary of the waves. But I couldn't move. She inched higher and I was now behind her, out of sight.

At first sneaking, then sprinting, I raced back towards the village pandanas and coconut palms, silhouetted by the glow of kerosene lamps. Past George's house where I yelled '*Oihare, oihare*' and right through the village to where Katherine was drifting to sleep in our stilted leafhouse. George had emerged with his tags and measuring tape and joined a bevy of onlookers who seemed as interested in the two *waetfalas* sprinting down the beach as they were in the turtle. There she was, ten metres further up the beach and ignorant of her audience, despite the shrieks of kids and flashing of torches. And there, with half of our adopted community looking on, Katherine and I experienced one of the most anticipated and special moments of our lives.

George's records suggested that about twenty turtles each year dragged themselves up his beaches four or five times to nest. Remembering that until two years ago at least seven *oihare* had been eaten each year on Baniata, Havilla and Tetepare beaches, these relics from the age of dinosaurs were lucky to outlive Meseni.

With hatching success decimated by high tides and continued loss of adults to international fishing fleets, only a concerted effort for many decades would ensure that any *oihare* would survive until another generation walked the beaches of Baniata.

Those long dark nights of searching for turtles provided plenty of time for contemplation. While we were plodding the black sand, the president of the world was re-elected just months after John W. Howard was also handed another term on platforms of security and economic scare mongering. By failing to ratify the Kyoto Protocol, both re-elected 'leaders' failed to address global climate change that was extinguishing and threatening scores of species and now seemed to be replacing fishing as the principal threat to the leatherbacks. Ironically, the same *Solomon Star* newspaper that informed us of Bush's victory also ran an article claiming that Seventh Day Adventists embraced logging because they anticipated the Second Coming and hence were not concerned about long-term resource preservation.

As I trudged up and back along the beach in the wee small hours, my anger at the perceived stance of the SDA church turned to shame at my own society's failings. Two of the wealthiest bureaucracies on the planet had just opted for short-term economic growth at the expense of the environment. Although Australians would have been horrified at the prospect of villagers in the Solomons clear-felling their forests, my people feared that moderating their excessive energy use could diminish their perceived standard of living.

My remorse at Australia's ignominious response to global environmental issues came a year after feeling proud that we had spearheaded the rescue delegation for the Solomons. Army and police forces from around the Pacific formed the Regional Assistance Mission to Solomon Islands, or RAMSI, which arrived within weeks of the Solomon Islands' twenty-fifth anniversary of independence. On that day a squadron of six Australian choppers cut through the thick tropical air for the first time since World War II. Glass window shutters rattled precariously as the formation flew slowly down the main street to Honiara's trouble spots. Armed soldiers hung out of the low-flying choppers, taunting renegades and would-be gangsters to have a go, but not a single shot was fired. The balance of power in the city had suddenly changed.

RAMSI called their operation *'Helpem Fren'*, a South Seas version of 'Shock and Awe' that was being played out in Iraq. Despite its friendly name, the show of might had the desired effect. Criminals and rebels surrendered their guns even faster than the Gizo police had run away from armed thugs a couple of years earlier. Nearly four thousand guns were surrendered in the first two months. Within days of the commencement of *Helpem Fren*, two key adversaries in the ethnic tensions, Harold Keke and Jimmy Rasta, had been brought into custody without bloodshed. Aussie Army grunts on R'n'R leave jokingly dubbed their role 'Operation Overkill'.

Despite their intimidating choppers and redundant firepower, it was not the friendly armed forces that caused the most stir among the Honiara locals. *'Policeman blong Australia active tumas,'* my cabbie mate Ben admired, adding *'Police car blong Australia hem karae big.'* Until RAMSI arrived, Ben had never heard a police siren, a claim that cabbies in other capital cities would surely find unbelievable. *'Fastaem mifala lukim olketa arrestim man for overspeed or drive taem hem spaka,'* Ben also noted, seemingly amazed that a police force would act on trivial indiscretions like speeding or drink–driving.

It was the police, rather than the armies, that reined in the fearless youths that had taken the law into their own hands. Corrupt police and politicians were incarcerated. Ben, like most locals I questioned, was grateful for the transformation that RAMSI had overseen. A group of Kiwis I met in the Honiara Yacht Club bar were also proud that their country had finally come to the assistance of the Solomons.

But not everyone was so upbeat about the change of guard. I was amazed that shops and businesses that had survived the dark days of the 'tension' closed within months of the restoration of law and order. The partnering of RAMSI officials with local customs officials put an end to illegal duty-free rorts. In other cases, rents and lease fees, which had previously been absolved through bribery, intimidation or incompetence, forced corrupt enterprises to close. Airline passengers, too, had to comply with the new order. Six months earlier I had sat in the co-pilot's seat holding three bush knives with half-metre blades and nobody had raised an eyebrow. Now my hand luggage was searched for nail files and scissors by the Australian Federal Police.

Maybe it was the presence of the international police, or maybe the greater recognition and widespread acceptance that TDA had achieved, but for the first time I felt openly proud of our involvement with conserving Tetepare. Wearing a green TDA T-shirt I told anyone who asked, and several who didn't, what was happening on Tetepare. In the past I had been afraid of referring to Tetepare in Honiara for fear that mention of our involvement would stimulate jealousies or extortion threats that could jeopardise both TDA's agenda and our longevity. But now Tetepare was the talk of the town. Our ecolodge brochures adorned the walls of the Tourism and Solomon Airlines offices and the European Union touted our project as one of the most successful they had sponsored in the country.

Another year brought the third annual general meeting for TDA. This time over two thousand TDA members were asked to vote for seventy representatives who would nominate their committee. Unsurprisingly Jack Daniel was re-elected as Chairman. Predictably this charismatic larrikin with an uncanny knack of stifling discontent with humour or parables, closed the meeting with a classic quote that 'Leaders should be fearless in principles, firm in purpose and faithful in promises.' With one exception, the assembled members unanimously hummed in agreement.

While Jack was signing off, Mary was nodding off after her hectic few weeks of conducting regional elections and organising food, accommodation and transport for the assembled throng.

The constitution necessitated a minimum of three women in TDA's fourteen-strong committee and I assumed that Mary would fill one of those places. Yet she didn't stand for the committee, despite receiving more votes than any other representative. I was concerned that backroom deals by the big men had marginalised TDA's tireless champion but Mary wasn't concerned.

Like Tippet, who also boasted considerable community support but had not stood for the committee, she felt that she retained a major influence on TDA's direction. Their conclusion was supported when immediately following the meeting I suggested to Jack that he should convene a short committee meeting to establish ecotourism rules and visitor fees. 'Let Tippet and Mary sort that out,' Jack delegated. 'The committee must rest now.'

The Lonely Planet Guide for the South Pacific had been updated and provided a measurable benchmark of our progress since the original entry that referred to Tetepare as the battleground between the loggers and the environmentalists.

The 120-sq-km Tetepare is said to be the South Pacific's largest uninhabited island. It's one of the Solomons' conservation jewels – a large rainforested island untouched by logging companies. Tetepare is managed by the Tetepare Descendants' Association (www.tetepare.org). The island has important breeding grounds for leatherback and green turtles, dugongs and other rare wildlife. There is a research station, trained guides, canopy platforms for bird-watching and accommodation huts. The association is looking to have the island World Heritage listed.

Visits to Tetepare incur a one-off S$50 kastom fee, regardless of time spent. Accommodation is in a comfortable leafhouse (S$200 per person) and is arranged through the Tetepare Descendants' Association.

Walking and activities are offered, and oneway transfers cost S$400 per boatload from Baniata and S$1200 from Munda.

The Tetepare ecolodge was a demonstration of the dying art of *kastom* leaf house building that Matthew Suka, one of TDA's founders, had learned from his father, the storytelling Jonathan Suka. Nine workers had toiled for three weeks without spirit levels or power tools to erect the frame. The 'king' posts that reached the apex of the roof each took seven men to raise. Matthew's team dug wide holes then slotted the king posts into notches cut into the beams like a puzzle, and the expertly crafted joins were further stabilised to cyclone-proof standard by lashings of split lengths of lawyer cane, yet not a single bolt or nail.

While the builders sweated over their giant puzzle, thirty TDA members sewed sago palm leaves into roof panels with lengths of split lawyer cane. The roof crown was assembled on the ground by tightly binding leaf panels on both sides of the apex with more split lawyer cane. Next, a score of muscular men pushed and pulled and heaved the heavy crown up the roof frame using their shoulders and then poles from the ground. Once the roof was anchored by this heavy apex, successive panels were sewn underneath the upper ones, protecting the stitching under the shelter of higher panels. Sago palm was used not only for the roof, but the flooring as well. The hard trunk was split into up to thirty irregular slats which were sequentially numbered so they could be laid in the same pattern to form close-knit intricate flooring.

As Matthew's men completed the tying down of roof and flooring panels, rangers, guides and cooks all helped prepare the site for the arrival of our first official tourists. Suero impersonated a dog as he brushed rope shavings and leaf roof offcuts from under the low floor. It was important to remove these scraps that were both a fire hazard and termite bait. Suero never ceased to amaze me. At times he was the most frustrating bloke around, virtually impossible to shake from his comical trance, but now he was perspiring profusely, volunteering for an unpopular task. Likewise he could switch within seconds from being outrageously loud and mischievous, to full of heart-felt emotions. This morning he noticed that Layla had cut her first tooth, a development overlooked by her doting parents and the local women who fussed over her constantly.

Other rangers carried coral gravel for the paths that had been lined with *tutufa* clam shells from nearby middens. Tippet transplanted decorative palms to line these striking white paths and by the time the first tourists were being introduced to Tetepare by the nervous guides, Suero had installed a freshly polished carved wooden toilet seat. The comments in our new visitors' book four days later confirmed that everyone's efforts had been appreciated.

Katherine, Layla and I returned with the inaugural tourists to a reformed Gizo. The waterfront market was being renovated, buildings were being erected and new tourist operators cavorted on water-skis and windsurfers. Since RAMSI arrived, the Gizo jail had also been reinforced with razor wire but with one major oversight: I reckon I could have scaled the low iron grille gate within seconds! Instead of wandering in and out at their leisure, the inmates were supervised by a policemen lazing under a shady tree while they swam on the adjacent reef. Despite the fresh surge of aid money which was rebuilding the crumbling wharf, the houses near the prison gate remained precariously perched on memories of concrete posts.

RAMSI had made such huge inroads into improving security and governance of the country that we assumed that scandals, such as the government's backing of pyramid money making schemes, plans to sell passports or receive toxic waste from Taiwan would be relegated to the history books. Yet the Solomons were still the Solomons! The 'luxury' resthouse that we used in Gizo since Layla was born sported a private bathroom and an air-conditioner, but while we were away on Tetepare 'our' resthouse had been transformed into Kings University. Students from India who had enrolled for a medical degree via the internet, already occupied our room. The local doctors refused to allow the students of the phony university to train at nearby Gizo hospital and a couple of months later, when the last of the confused and annoyed students had departed, the doctors' suspicions were confirmed. Bart Ulufa'alu, the ousted prime minister and current opposition leader, claimed that in return for financial incentives, senior ministers had lobbied the World Health Organisation to recognise the university. Another article in the *Solomon Star* revealed that the retired Indian professor who was coerced to head up the scam university felt cheated when he arrived to learn that he did not even have a blackboard at his disposal!

Improvement in law and order in Honiara encouraged more tourists to venture to the Solomon Islands and visit Tetepare. Every visitor improved the confidence of the cooks and guides and left them with a more complete understanding of the value of the island. Equally as important, their Solomons experiences continued to reap benefits after they departed. On returning home, my young nephew Patrick wrote to major hardware and furniture stores asking them whether they used rainforest timber and questioning whether they were aware of the damage that logging caused in places like the Solomon Islands. Other visitors donated schoolbooks, wheelchairs and even paid school fees for TDA members to help convince them that their conservation agenda had merit. But some visitors brought rewards that Katherine and I could only dream of.

Three intrepid adventurers, Tim Jarvis, Ben Kozel and Taher Omari, storied about their conquests of the South and North Poles, Amazon River and other remote parts of the globe. Cooks and rangers were drawn into the light of the new pressure lamp to listen to and join in the storytelling. Increasingly the stories focused on Tetepare, reinforcing how special the island's forest and reefs were from a global perspective. The adventurers had camped on Qeuru beach where they filmed a nesting *oihare*. The locals listened intently to their awestruck descriptions of her Darth Vader-like sighs, massive head with huge teary eyes and intricate nesting process. Nesting turtles were being transformed from lambs to their slaughter to grandiose events that attracted tourists from around the globe.

Marga, one of the trainee cooks, was a dumpy woman with erratic teeth. We met Marga in the canoe-carving camp on Tetepare several years earlier when, without any guilt or apprehension she had explained how they had eaten all of the *tutufa* clams in the lagoon. Typical of rural women around the globe Marga was a jovial salt-of-the-earth type, perennially good natured and as honest as a brick. A couple of days earlier, after hearing me recounting stories about patrolling for and eventually finding an amazing leatherback turtle at Baniata, Marga told us that she too had waited for *oihare*. A year ago she had seen the tracks of one on a beach near Lokuru and then ten days later she and her friends had staked out the beach and eaten the turtle when it revisited. Even after learning about the plight of the leatherbacks and the efforts that her *wantoks* from Baniata were adopting to protect them, Marga showed absolutely no remorse. She was a gardener and an occasional cook at Tetepare who had embraced the opportunities but not the philosophy of TDA. I had no doubt whatsoever if another *oihare* emerged near her house at Lokuru she would be lining up to kill and eat it.

The boys finally finished recounting their nesting turtle story and everyone decided to retire to bed. Just as I was following the light of my lamp up the crushed coral path to our room in the leaf house, Marga summoned me into the leaf-walled kitchen. Orange flickers lit up her shiny black face as she poked a piece of firewood back into the embers. After burning her first attempt at a banana cake Mary had ordered her to bake another, a formidable challenge in an oven of hot rocks with firewood she had to chop herself. Marga knew that despite its charcoal margins and little pillows of sour baking powder, I would eat the burned cake. After thanking her I stood up to leave. Marga urgently pulled me back down. She whispered to me with seriousness I had never before experienced, '*John bae iumi no kaikaim disfala oihare eni taem moa.*'

Back in our room, Layla had crawled into bed with Katherine and baby Elke snored softly in her cot. While drifting off to sleep surrounded by my newly-enlarged family with neon-blue fireflies flashing through our peaceful room, I reflected on Marga's epiphany. It was one of the most profound I had heard in the Solomons. Marga's resolution never to eat leatherbacks again represented more than a politically shrewd comment from a *conman* attempting to secure incentive payments. The thrill and global significance of the nesting turtle expressed by our high-profile visitors had seeded a grassroots conversion beyond Katherine's and my expectations. Marga had just joined Mary, Tippet and a selection of the more astute rangers in believing the role and benefit of conservation. The future for the turtles and the last wild island of the South Pacific just got a little bit brighter.

THE ROLLER-COASTER CONTINUES

'*Mifala daddi moa*,' beamed Kennedy as he stepped out of the canoe to resume his shift on Tetepare. The local trochus monitor, who had been rolled by a crashing wave when I was surfing with *vena* a few years earlier, threw his head back in laughter.

A stocky man in his forties who loved a laugh, Kennedy was a dedicated family man. He was always eager to return to his village from Tetepare in time to lead church services on Sunday and catch up with his young family. Yet, paradoxically, I had no idea that his wife had been expecting another child.

'Really?' I stumbled, embarrassed.

'*Mi garem stakka picanniny . . . . Fifty over*,' Kennedy laughed, before resolving my confusion by explaining that every one of 'his' turtle eggs had hatched last week.

Still puzzled, since the rangers did not typically 'claim' turtle nests that they protected on Tetepare, I asked him which nest it was.

'*Nest stap long haus blong mifala*,' Kennedy explained. Two months earlier a green turtle nested on the beach at Lokuru. Like Marga, Kennedy and his *wantoks* had previously eaten any turtles and eggs they could get their hands on, but this one was lucky. Although off-duty from his ranger responsibilities, Kennedy had relocated the eggs to a safe location using the technique he had been taught on Tetepare and protected the nest until it hatched. He had not asked for or expected any inducements. The thrill of showing his family the first turtles to hatch among his community for many decades was the only reward Kennedy needed. Other rangers had also shown commitment to their new vocations by recording and releasing tagged turtles captured near Lokuru by hunters. One of these turtles had been tagged on Tetepare, another in Australia, which temporarily elevated both the intended meal and its hunter to cult status within the village.

Matthew Suka, a formative TDA member and the builder of the *kustom* ecolodge, had shown similar passion for the plight of leatherbacks on Tetepare. He had taken on the role of organising teams of rangers to camp on Qeuru and Tofa beaches throughout the *oihare* nesting season to relocate any nests that were laid below the high-tide mark. Matthew's role was particularly important after the massive 2006 earthquakes and tsunami, which caused considerable death and destruction throughout the Western Province.

Although buffeted by dozens of quakes, Tetepare was shielded from the devastating tsunami by Rendova Island. As soon as they felt comfortable enough to take to the seas, the rangers found that much of the Tetepare weather coast was barely recognisable. Dozens of landslides scarred the forest, some cleaving massive slices of hillside all the way to the sea. Two slides partially smothered the deep black sand of the main turtle nesting beach with sticky red mud. Even those beaches that were spared landslides were littered with massive logs that had drifted onshore from other landslides. Although Matthew's rangers burnt as many of these logs as possible to provide access to nesting *oihare*, precious little sand persisted above high tide mark, so virtually every nest needed to be relocated within hours of laying. Each successful nest was celebrated with jubilation at the field station, so important had the plight of the *oihare* become for the rangers. The dedication shown by Kennedy and Matthew was indicative of the growing pride and belief in their work shown by other TDA staff, who had been buoyed by repeated recognition from national and international observers that the Tetepare project had become a benchmark for conservation initiatives in the country.

But just as the status of leatherbacks and their tenuous chance of survival was increasing on Tetepare and Lokuru, nesting turtles at Baniata were enduring another frustrating chapter. By making them the focus of our conservation efforts and a source of income for the locals who protected them, we had inadvertently transformed the luckless *oihare* into a weapon. One jealous resident, annoyed that he had not benefited from TDA's employment and scholarship program, retaliated by encouraging his sons to exhume and eat turtle eggs. If that wasn't bad enough, the situation almost escalated to a civil war following another visit by the American turtle researcher Scott Benson.

Approaching the conclusion of his second visit to Baniata, Scott finally attached a satellite tracker to an *oihare* that nested on the nearby Havilla beach patrolled by our turtle monitor Nico. Scott vowed to provide regular updates on the travels of our special turtle, nicknamed Queen Havilla. Opinions in the surrounding communities were divided whether she would swim to Canada, where our CUSO volunteers hailed from, or to visit us in Australia. Unfortunately we never found out. When the same aggrieved villager who had been spoiling the nests came across Queen Havilla renesting twenty days later, he cut off and confiscated her harness. Blinded by jealousy, he didn't realise the difficulty in 'hiding' a transmitter that regularly beams its exact location via satellite. Nor did he appreciate the depth of his community's resentment towards his actions. Ostracised by his extended family, village elders summoned an unprecedented visit by RAMSI's policemen to confiscate the tracker and apprehend the offender. However, the damage had been done. We may now never know where our leatherbacks venture between nesting seasons and Baniata's opportunity to be recognised on the world conservation stage had been foiled.

Kennedy could not understand the short-sighted jealousies that were threatening to scuttle the very survival of *oihare*. He was now a 'man for conservation'. Yet soon after enthusing about his successful turtle hatching, Kennedy started preparing for work that appeared to hark back to his logging days. Although the other rangers ribbed him about his logging survey, Kennedy was proud that he was now spearheading an initiative on Tetepare that may have conservation outcomes exceeding even the persistence of Pacific leatherbacks.

Kennedy barked orders to his team as, compass in hand, he hacked paths through the Tetepare undergrowth. Behind him, dodging ants stirred up by his frenetic brushing, two assistants dragged a measuring tape. Once he had carved a boundary around a three hectare block of forest with his bush knife, Kennedy's real work began. With his team of forest monitors, he systematically scoured the block, identifying, measuring and mapping the trees. Special canoe trees and high-value timber trees were individually marked by a splash of paint left over from the construction of the field station. After a couple of days, Kennedy's team emerged with an inventory of the number 'of pieces' and size of key tree species.

Although ironically replicating pre-logging surveys that signalled the destruction of his forests on Rendova, Kennedy's monitoring could well be integral to the protection of Tetepare's forests from logging. The international market for carbon, a fanciful dream when I had exaggerated the potential for the intact Tetepare forest a few years earlier to Danny Philips and his pro-developers, was rapidly becoming a reality. The forest survey would estimate the amount of carbon stored by Tetepare's fertile lowland forests.

At 150 tonnes of carbon per hectare and US$5 per tonne, Tetepare's carbon is conservatively valued at US$9 million each year, a steal for an industrialised enterprise or nation attempting to offset their carbon dioxide emissions. When the forest's ecosystem services such as provision and regulation of food and water, nutrient cycling, pollution assimilation, biodiversity and genetic, cultural and recreational values are also considered, this value more than doubles. Although no landowners in the Solomons or elsewhere have yet been compensated for the full value of their forest, part payment for the carbon component is now a reality in several countries. We were optimistic that an intact forest may eventually be worth more to landowners than a logged one.

Our first circumnavigations of Tetepare in leaking canoes had been voyages of exploration, documenting the islands' wildlife and becoming acquainted with key landowners. Subsequent visits had concentrated on establishing protected areas and monitoring sites, then enforcing TDA's rules. However, our more recent challenge had become making these hypothetical forest values a reality. Tetepare had been nominated by the Solomon Islands government as their case study for securing international carbon payments. Tippet visited Copenhagen, along with the national Minister for Conservation, to make the pitch for TDA at the Global Greenhouse Conference. Along with calculating the amount of carbon, we also had to demonstrate to conservation donors and prospective carbon investors that Tetepare's forest remained intact. Zooming in on satellite images we identified several areas that could be mistaken for logging damage. Landslides, migrating river mouths and even some of the small gardens created by Mary and others over a decade earlier, invariably showed up as paler green patches in the sea of dark mature forest. Armed with a GPS and digital camera we documented each of these anomalies in Tetepare's wild coastline.

As resolute as I was to accurately document any blemish on the Tetepare coastline, I was frequently distracted. Grey imperial pigeons streamed into Tetepare from the low atolls of the Hele Islands, barely visible on the horizon. One exhausting day I had counted an extraordinary thirteen thousand of these birds, which nested on the Hele Islands, flying back to the rich feeding grounds of Tetepare. Interspersed among the imperial pigeons were occasional clumsy black Nicobar pigeons, locally known as *bakupa*. These comical short-tailed birds with long oily feathers were only known to nest on a single atoll in the entire Western Province. Their tenure on this island had been seriously threatened by local armed policemen during a pre-Christmas hunting frenzy prior to TDA awareness sessions and the gun amnesties that removed many firearms from police and civilians alike.

Layla and Elke could not comprehend their dad's fixation with landslides and pigeons. Far more interesting for them were the vivid blue starfish clearly visible through the crystal-clear water or the incredible flying fish that glided effortlessly away from the canoe in deeper water. But their real favourites, the ultimate enticement to spend a day in the searing tropical sun and big swells, was a chance to meet the Livutana dolphins, named after the river mouth near where we typically found them. Whenever we visited Tetepare's weather coast these gregarious show ponies converged on our canoe and rode the bow wave, or escorted us with a leaping guard of honour on both sides. Smaller than the bottlenose dolphins from Marineland, our spinner dolphins were distinctly two-toned, their dark grey backs contrasting markedly with their paler bellies. Sometimes they augmented their visit with a special performance, pirouetting clear of the water before landing with a triumphant splash, soaking everyone and leaving the girls gasping with awe.

Today the Livutana dolphins decided to up the ante. Five of the dolphins selected a watery stage some distance from where the rest of the pod were cavorting and slowly, in unison, raised their stiffened tails clear out of the water. After a brief and unconvincing tail wag, they slowly descended again. Seconds later their tails emerged again, bobbing up slowly like a half-full bottle. To the delight of the girls, our quintet of synchronised swimmers mastered a perfect tail wag before subsiding again beneath the turquoise waves.

Three years earlier this same dolphin pod had charmed the occupants of a US$40 million, five-storey luxury cruiser complete with a sexy red helicopter that briefly plied the waters of the Solomons. That night, the floating monolith moored unannounced outside the Tetepare Field Station. At first reluctant to approach the spectacular craft, I encouraged the rangers to paddle out to explain the rules of visiting Tetepare and collect the US$5 *kastom* fee, just as they did for any other visitors. The rangers and I stared aghast at the two metre wide built-in aquaria that hosted spectacular fish caught on recent dives. Before retreating to their air-conditioned cabin, the crew complemented the rangers on the friendly dolphins and spectacular numbers of large fish they witnessed on their dives in TDA's protected area. Kodo and Kennedy were visibly chuffed that the results of their endeavours had been endorsed by such rich and presumably influential appraisers.

I was willing with all my might for the crew, resplendent in crisp white shirts, to invite the owner out from his luxurious ensconcement to meet the rangers in person. I also longed to explain to the elusive owner that a trust fund, valued at a fraction of his boat's worth, could both employ and equip TDA staff in perpetuity. Furthermore, this fund would also provide sufficient financial benefits to other TDA members to assure the wealthy owner that whether he revisited in ten or fifty years time, the forest and reefs of Tetepare would remain protected.

Unfortunately, but not surprisingly, Tetepare was not kissed by a fairy godmother in a red helicopter. We were acutely aware of the tenuous nature of conservation initiatives in the face of ever increasing logging pressures. The WWF-sponsored Vanua Rapita guesthouse in Marovo lagoon, where we first stayed on our honeymoon a decade earlier, had long since rotted to the ground. In its place Michi village, led by its elders including Seri Hite, the former country manager of WWF, had embraced logging. '*Milo water*', brown sludge from eroded hillsides and riverbanks, spilled into the Marovo Lagoon, causing the very environmental impacts that Freeman and Seri had preached to their *wantoks* would eventuate from logging.

Vanua Rapita was by no means the only conservation-inspired failure in the Solomons. World Heritage listing did little to improve conservation outcomes on East Rennell. Two certified forestry enterprises, which were operated by well-intentioned international organisations, folded during the tension and were not reinvigorated. Landowners, who only receive 15 per cent royalty from logging companies, had been temporarily able to generate more income, with far less environmental impacts, by milling the timber themselves. Had Western consumers and the national government encouraged exports of Forest Stewardship Council certified timber, these schemes could have matched the booming western markets for free-range and organic products. Theoretically, the blight of large-scale unscrupulous logging could have been defeated.

Three more years of chasing the most likely global benefactors to protect Tetepare in perpetuity had led us tantalisingly close without eventually capturing the prize. Right from the shaky formation of the Tetepare Descendants' Association we had been aware that the last wild island would only remain unlogged and unsettled for as long as landowners had access to financial and other benefits. While we had been fortunate to secure three consecutive two-year grants from different donors to continue TDA's mission, eventually our success would wane. An unresourced TDA would be as lame as other failed conservation initiatives and Tetepare's forests too would fall to the ever circling loggers.

Chinese imports of round logs quadrupled between 1997 and 2006 and China is now the world's largest importer of timber products. Eighty per cent of Solomon Islands' production of round logs find their way to Chinese timber mills, where they are used for veneer, ply, furniture and construction. The thought of magnificent rainforest trees, stolen from their rightful owners, being used in the cheap Chinese construction industry was abhorrent. Maybe the worsening global economic crisis would slow down the relentless demand, but we couldn't count on that.

So great is the dependence upon logging that Solomon Islands' economic growth is forecast to drop from 10 per cent in 2007 to 1.5 per cent by 2014, when all the commercial forests will be logged out. Despite the inroads into law and order made by RAMSI and repeated pledges by Solomon Islands politicians, the logging scourge is not abating. Most logging concessions or timber rights are still granted illegally and Greenpeace has calculated that the aggregate losses from illegal tax remissions and logging exemptions have now exceeded SBD$1 billion.

The logging cancer had by now consumed nearly all of the accessible forests of the Western Province. The once magnificent lowland forests framing Marovo Lagoon were nearly gone. Tribes that had held out for a decade or more eventually succumbed to ever increasing pressure. The race to protect Tetepare in perpetuity was every much as real now as it had been a decade earlier. We were in no doubt that influential Tetepare landowners were still being approached by logging interests. The barometer of these pressures was TDA's annual general meeting, when Tetepare's descendants came together to determine their collective stance for their wild island.

Jack Daniel, his head slightly cocked, listened intently to the passionate statement delivered from the rear of the church hall. Wearing a black beret, reminiscent of Che Guevara, and a tailored grey linen lava-lava the one-time larrikin was in total control. This was potentially the riskiest part of the meeting, the 'Any Other Business' section that Jack usually abbreviated to avoid vexing questions or intending mutineers. But today the Chairman had the confidence to draw out the question time, to prolong his time in the spotlight. No longer was he flanked by his trusty sidekick Henry Seda or his politically astute ally Lloyd Hodge, who had both been instrumental in the formation of TDA six years earlier. Like several other founders they had moved on to other pursuits and been replaced by a more representative and democratically elected committee. No longer did Jack request Katherine to take the minutes or defer to me for the tricky questions. He no longer even insisted that we sat with him and Tippet out the front of the meeting. So assured was he in TDA's roles and progress that he had invited several prominent members of parliament to grace recent meetings.

Tippets' brow creased worryingly as he contemplated the question from the floor. TDA's devoted manager, who had stayed up all the previous night compiling Jack's address to the meeting, looked both tired and worried. Although no-one had yet advocated logging, this question about the treatment of poachers still affronted the ideology that Tippet had embraced and the protocols he had enforced. I studied his tension and Jack's contemplation and wondered and waited.

The rangers had reported that several men had repeatedly been caught poaching trochus shells within the Tetepare protected area. Since conservation was the measure of success that TDA used to attract funding, dissenting landowners employed poaching as a weapon. In the same way that aggrieved villagers set out to spoil the Baniata *oihare* project, some landowners had kicked TDA where it hurt, by poaching within the protected area if their families had not secured TDA work or scholarships the previous year.

'The poachers are desperate for food and money,' continued the loaded question, 'TDA should compensate them for lost opportunity because they cannot hunt or dive in the protected area. The only reason they poach is to put food on their table and maybe raise some school fees.' Tippet was seething and itching for the question to wrap up so he could fire it down. He had become increasingly frustrated with the flood of requests for TDA to pay, or compensate or reimburse members for a never ending array of personal and community requests. Just as Tippet was preparing to unleash his frustrations, Jack pulled rank. Slowly standing and grinning, he pushed his gold-rimmed glasses down his nose to eyeball his congregation and the distinguished guests in the front row.

'I'm going to tell you a story,' started Jack, stepping out from behind the table and strutting across the floor, pausing to ensure that the questioner had resumed his seat and that everyone had his attention.

'A story that I told the big men of East Rennel when TDA visited them last year to help them understand conservation. We need to remind ourselves about the benefits of conservation,' preached the one-time logging advocate, who was now revelling in his reincarnation as the figurehead for the most renowned conservation project in the nation.

'This is the story of two man-eating giants; a clever one... and a stupid one,' sniggered the Chairman.

'The giants lived in the mountains and looked down at the villages by the sea where there were plenty of people to eat. The stupid giant went down to Dunde and ate everyone in the whole village,' declared Jack pointing around him to his amused delegation in the Dunde Hall. 'Later, when he was hungry again, the stupid giant went to Kia,' explained Jack, motioning towards the next little village, 'and ate the whole village. He then went to Lambete and ate all of them and then there was no more food and the stupid giant starved.'

Tippet relaxed as he deciphered where the story was headed and proudly nodded as his Chairman won over the dissenter. Nestled among the women in the audience, Mary smiled a full-faced uninhibited smile. She watched her friends, who minutes earlier had nodded in agreement with the poacher sympathiser. Had Mary answered the question she could not have resisted adding more enemies to her expansive list by accusing both the questioner and the poachers of being stupid. But neither of TDA's dedicated stalwarts needed to say anything now, they kicked back and watched the master at work.

'The clever giant went down to Dunde and only ate the old men,' Jack continued, pointing out a selection of big men in front of him to the amusement of the whole meeting. Jack's sustainability parable drew heavily from his forefather's headhunting *modus operandi* of sparing the women and children. Eventually Jack's story concluded with the clever giant returning to Dunde village after selectively preying on adjacent villages. The Dunde boys had by now grown and he harvested another batch of men, but again left behind the women and children.

'TDA is a cannibal,' Jack sneered, before dissolving into laughter with 'a very clever cannibal,' to the appreciative roar of the membership.

Before the laughter subsided Jack slapped the table.

'Meeting adjourned. Meeting adjourned,' he declared with glee as he strode out of the hall, extracting a juicy beetle nut with his red-stained teeth to seal the moment.

Acknowledgements

WITHOUT THE dedication of Peter Siloko, Isaac Molia, Harry and Mary Bea, Petrie Sute, Kido Dalipada and John Aqarou to stand up against the original logging proposal, Tetepare would have joined the growing inventory of Pacific forests trashed by destructive logging. The founders of TDA are also acknowledged for their bravery, particularly those who admitted past failings in order to progress the conservation agenda. It is unlikely that Tetepare would now be managed for conservation under a harmonious partnership of landowners were it not for the roles played by Jack Daniel, Henry Seda, Lloyd Hodge, Allan Tippet Bero and Jonathan Suka to unite remote landowners with the Tetepare descendants from Rendova. Nathaniel Soto, TDA's early nemesis turned out to be a very enthusiastic supporter of both conserving Tetepare and the *oihare* that nested on his Baniata beaches and Danny Philips, the would-be instigator of logging, a casino or US base on Tetepare is admired for accepting, then embracing, TDA's conservation agenda. Likewise, Gordon Darcy, who was understandably initially suspicious of TDA objectives, supported the objectives and hopefully the future of Tetepare by endorsing TDA's objective to derive international REDD funds for carbon capture on behalf of the Solomons Islands Government in the Copenhagen COP15 conference.

Despite periodic management shambles, financial delays and frustration caused to staff, communities and associates like ourselves, Tetepare may not still be a wild island were it not for the black-and-white pig that is WWF Solomon Islands. Simon Foale introduced us to the vagaries of Melanesian conservation and project management. Vicki Kalgovas was an endless source of information on the Solomon's political and social scene and a welcomed stalwart of Phoebe's resthouse. Jackie Healy was a shining and hardworking knight who assisted immeasurably with the Tetepare project and keeping the communication lines open while we were back in Australia. Dan Afzal, Alec Hughes, Bruno Manele, Tingo Leve and Barassi Wale provided us with both friendship, a novice's guide to marine life and most importantly trained the local fishermen and women to monitor and manage their resources. While fitting uncomfortably in the same paragraph as these WWF staff, Sara Siloko's drive and commitment to Friends of Tetepare and TDA in its formative period was also integral to making Tetepare an icon conservation project. Lottie Vaisekavea, Nick Unsworth, Paul Barker and John Casey from the European Union, various staff of both NZAid and CUSO, and Dick Rice and Aaron Bruner from Conservation International are thanked for their belief in Tetepare and Katherine and I as managers. The Tetepare project would not have succeeded without core funding provided by European Union, NZAid, AusAid and VASS and project funds from WWF, NOAA, CUSO, AVI, Conservation International, South Pacific Regional Environment Program, Japanese Embassy, ADPLAN, MCIC and a host of other donors including many private scholarship sponsors. The recent announcement of seed funds donated by AusAID for a trust fund will be integral to the maintenance of ongoing protection of Tetepare. Dan Raymond and Ross Andrewartha from AusAID/ forestry provided advice on logging issues and provided the alarming map of the extent of logging in the Western Province. I am particularly indebted to Katherine Moseby, Vicki Kalgovas, Sara Siloko, Helen Kirkbride, Allan Tippet Bero, John Roughan, Jenny Read, Lindsay Moseby and Melanie Ostell for editing or proofreading this manuscript. Tricia Genat from PAGE for taking on the publication of a non-mainstream genre at a time when publishers are doing it tough.

Katherine and I welcomed the encouragement, advice and welcome breaks from the local diet provided by our friends in the Solomons, especially Ben and Jilly, Grant and Jill and Andrea. David Argument and Laurie Wein, then Mike and Jeanine D'Antonio, TDA's CUSO volunteers, followed by Anthony Plummer, Michaela Farrington, Gabe McGhee, Gillian Goby and Ingrid DeLacy from Australian Volunteers International are admired and thanked for their commitment and bravery in devoting two years of their lives and careers to the Tetepare cause. Keyvan Izadi and Emily Fitzsimmons from SICCP and Chris Filardi from the American Museum of Natural History also worked tirelessly for the Tetepare cause. Twomey was always there whenever we needed him and deserves a medal for supporting and putting up with Mary. Romis' boat driving skills in rough weather were much appreciated. All the cooks, rangers and guides on Tetepare and the many families we stayed with in villages around the Western Province are thanked for their friendship and hospitality. Many of the TDA staff have now demonstrated commitment to Tetepare beyond the expectations of their roles, a characteristic that bodes well for the island and their communities.

Allan Tippet Bero and Mary Bea, the stalwarts of TDA, are thanked for their determination, insatiable work ethic, guidance and friendship and for their invitation to share their journey towards conserving Tetepare for their *wantoks* and the whole world. Our families have supported and encouraged us throughout, despite fears and reservations, and both sets of parents volunteered as trial ecotourists before facilities were as well developed as today. Layla, Elke and baby Jarrah, I hope the 'staka fish at the wharf' and snorkelling lessons make up for the bumpy canoe rides and sandfly bites. My most sincere and grateful thanks are reserved for Katherine, who continues to ride every inch of the Tetepare roller-coaster with me and also had to sit through nights of me writing and editing our story through my eyes.

REFERENCES

Bennett, J.A. (1987). Wealth of the Solomons A history of a Pacific archipelago, 1800–1978. *Pacific Islands Monograph Series No. 3*, University of Hawaii press, Honolulu.

Bennett, J.A. (2000). *Pacific Forest. A history of resource control and contest in Solomon Islands, c. 1800–1997*. White Horse Press, Cambridge.

Cassells, R.M. (1992). *The valuation of subsistence use of tropical rainforest on the island of Choiseul, Solomon Islands: A comparison between subsistence values and logging royalties*. Masters Thesis (unpubl.), Massey University, New Zealand.

Coates, A. (1970). *Western Pacific Islands*. Her Majesty's Stationery Office. London.

COP (1996). *Solomon Islands Code of Practice for Timber Harvesting. August 1996 signed by Minister of Forests, Environment and Conservation and Commissioner of Forests*. Forestry Division. Ministry of Forests, Environment and Conservation, Honiara.

Costanza, R., D'Arge, R., DeGroot, R., Farber, S., Grasso, M., Hannon, B., Limburg, K., Naeem, S., O'Neill, R.V., Paruelo, J., Raskin, R.G., Sutton, P and Van den Belt, M. (1997). The value of the world's ecosystem services and natural capital. *Nature* 387: 253–260.

Dennis G.F. (1972). Nature notes on the Solomons. *The Journal of the Solomon Islands Museum Association* 1: 31–43.

Foale, S. (2008) Appraising the resilience of trochus and other nearshore artisanal fisheries in the Western Pacific. *SPC Trochus Information Bulletin* 14: 12–15.

Green A., Lokani P., Atu W., Ramohia P., Thomas P. and Almany J. (2006). Solomon Islands Marine Assessment: Technical report of survey conducted May 13 to June 17, 2004. TNC Pacific Island Countries Report No. 1/06. Brisbane, The Nature Conservancy.

Forest Trends & UBC (2007). Why China prefers logs. *China and East Asia Information Bulletin* 9. Forest Trends and University of British Columbia.

Gibbs, H.K., Brown, S., Niles, J.O. and Foley, J.A. (2007). Monitoring and measuring tropical carbon stocks: Making REDD a reality. *Environmental Research Letters* 2(4): 045023.

Greenpeace (2008). *Securing the future: An alternative plan for Solomon Islands forests and economy*. Greenpeace, Sydney.

Greenpeace Pacific and LaFranchi, C. (1999). *Islands Adrift: Comparing Industrial and Small-scale Economic Options for Marovo Lagoon Region of the Solomon Islands*. Greenpeace, Suva, Fiji.

REFERENCES

Hibberd, J.K. (1991). *Ecological resources and environmental implications.* Solomon Island Forest resource Inventory Working Paper #3, Honiara.

Horokou, J. (1996). *The biological and ecological impacts of oil pollution on Vacho River and its diverse aquatic life forms as caused by Eagon Forest Resource's logging operations in the north west Choiseul, Choiseul Province.* Environment and Conservation Division, Ministry of Forests, Environment and Conservation, Honiara.

Hviding, E. (1995). *Of Reef and Rainforest: A Dictionary of Environment and Resources in Marovo Lagoon.* Centre for Development Studies, University of Bergen, Norway.

Hviding, E. (1996). *Guardians of Marovo Lagoon* Pacific Islands Monograph Series 14. University of Hawai'i Press.

Hviding, E. and Bayliss-Smith, T. (2000). *Agroforestry, logging and ecotourism in Solomon Islands.* Ashgate Publishing Company, Burlington, Vermont

Kereseka, E., Varina, F. and Carter, G. (1977). A leader who cared for his people: Kevu of Lokuru. *The Journal of the Solomon Islands Museum Association* 5: 20-22.

Laracy, H. and White, G. (1988). Taem blong faet: World War II in Melanesia. *'O'O A Journal of Solomon Islands studies Volume 4.*

Lewison, R. L., Freeman S.A. and Larry B (2004). Quantifying the effects of fisheries on threatened species: the impact of pelagic longlines on loggerhead and leatherback sea turtles. *Ecology Letters* 7: 221-231.

MacNeill, I. (2000). *Sweet Horizons. A history of the Solomon Islands.* Acland Press, St Kilda West.

McCallum, R. and Sekhran, N. (1997). *Race for the Rainforest: Evaluating lessons from an Integrated Conservation and Development 'Experiment' in New Ireland, Papua New Guinea.* PNG Biodiversity Conservation and Resource Management Programme, Waigani.

McDonagh, S. (1990). *The greening of the Church.* Orbis Books, Maryknoll, New York.

McDonald, R. (2003). *Money makes you crazy. Custom and change in the Solomon Islands.* University of Otago Press, Dunedin.

Olsen, M. and Turnbull, M. (1993). *Assessment of growth rates of logged and unlogged forest in the Solomon Islands.* Final Report Solomon Islands National Forest Resources Inventory.

Read, J.L, Argument, D. and Moseby, K.E. (2010) Initial conservation outcomes of the Tetepare Island Protected Area *Pacific Conservation Biology* 16: 173-80.

Read, J.L. and Moseby, K.E. (2005). Vertebrates of Tetepare Island, Solomon Islands. *Pacific Science* 60: 69-79.

Reina, R.D., Mayor, P.A., Spotila, J.R., Piedra, R. and Paladino (2002). Nesting ecology of the Leatherback Turtle, *Dermochelys coriacea*, at Parque Nacional Marino Las Baulas, Costa Rica: 1988-1989 to 1999-2000. *Copeia 2002*: 653-664.

Solfrip (1992). *Interim report on the forests of region three: Choiseul.* Solomon Islands National Forest Resources Inventory. (unpubl.) Forestry Division, Ministry of Natural Resources, Honiara, Solomon Islands.

Spielman, A. and D'Antonio, M. (2002). *Mosquito: The story of man's deadliest foe.* Faber & Faber, London

Spotila, J.R., Reina, R.D., Steyermark, A.C., Plotkin, P.T. and Paladino, F.V. (2000). Pacific Leatherback turtles face extinction. *Nature* 405: 529-530.

Woodford, C.M. (1890). *A Naturalist amongst the Head-hunters.* George Philip and Son.

Paragraphs about Tetepare were reproduced with permission from *Solomon Island* © 1997 Lonely Planet and *South Pacific & Micronesia* © 2000 Lonely Planet. Ian Cleverly granted permission to quote lyrics from 'The River'.

Part proceeds of the sale of *The Last Wild Island: Saving Tetepare* contribute to maintaining the functioning of the Tetepare Descendants' Association, and the conservation of Tetepare Island. TDA can also be assisted through sponsorship of education scholarships or projects, donations of medical, educational, civic or scientific equipment or contributions to the Tetepare endowment fund. The future of Tetepare as one of the world's iconic wilderness islands and a resource for future generations remains uncertain until a sustainable financing mechanism becomes a reality.

Details on Tetepare developments, research and monitoring updates, Tetepare Ecolodge bookings and sponsorship/donation opportunities are provided at www.tetepare.org. Feedback to TDA members through visiting the Tetepare Ecolodge and member's communities or contacting via the website is invaluable in maintaining the morale and environmental commitment of Tetepare descendants and the Solomon Island Government.

Ecological Horizons Pty Ltd is an ecological organisation with a passion for pragmatic and innovative solutions to environmental challenges and a strong belief that individuals, corporations and governments should strive to create a better environment than what they inherited.

To contact the author or learn more about other projects that Ecological Horizons is involved with, visit www.ecologicalhorizons.com